THE MAGIC OF THEATER

The MAGIC

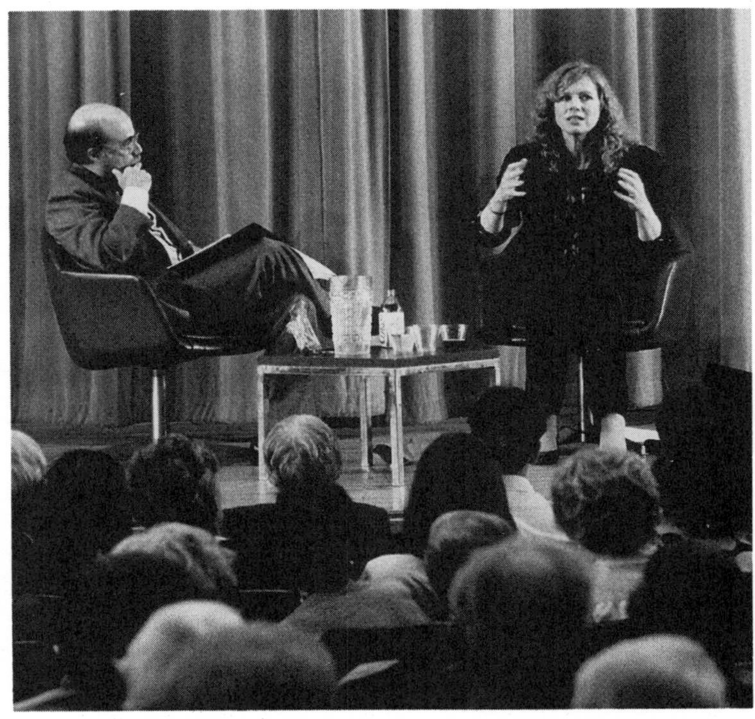

David Black in conversation with Liv Ullmann on stage at the New School

# of THEATER

BEHIND THE SCENES WITH TODAY'S LEADING ACTORS

DAVID BLACK

COLLIER BOOKS
MACMILLAN PUBLISHING COMPANY
NEW YORK

Maxwell Macmillan Canada
Toronto

Maxwell Macmillan International
New York Oxford Singapore Sydney

Collier Books
Macmillan Publishing Company
866 Third Avenue
New York, NY 10022

Maxwell Macmillan Canada, Inc.
1200 Eglinton Avenue East
Suite 200
Don Mills, Ontario M3C 3N1

Macmillan Publishing Company is part of the Maxwell Communication Group of Companies.

Library of Congress Cataloging-in-Publication Data
Black, David, 1931–
The Magic of theater : behind the scenes with today's leading actors / David Black.—1st Collier Books ed.
p. cm.
Includes bibliographical references and index.
ISBN 0-02-030651-2
1. Actors—United States—Interviews. 2. Acting. 3. Theater.
I. Title.
[PN2285.B57 1994] 93-36468 CIP
792'.028'092273—dc20

Book design by Maura Fadden Rosenthal

First Collier Books Edition 1994

10 9 8 7 6 5 4 3 2 1

Printed in the United States of America

For Anne,
who added to the magic

CONTENTS

ACKNOWLEDGMENTS

This book would not have happened without the actors who gave of their time to appear in the "Magic of Theater" series at the New School. Space did not permit including all the sessions in this book, and I am grateful to all the actors who shared their insights and their time with me.

Lewis Falb, associate dean and chairman of the theater program at the New School, originally encouraged me to undertake the series and he supplied the support needed to carry it out. He was a producer who was there when I needed him. Brian Kase at the New School provided the technical know-how about lighting, acoustics, and stage management. Jennifer and Ursula Burton did valuable research and offered gracious assistance to my guests.

David Meese supplied early ideas and encouragement, and Larry Green was a devil's advocate for theoretical arguments that became the basis for many of my questions. Michael and Marlene Fine, Elinor Schnurr, Abby Notterman, and Frank Siciliano were a loyal support group. Joseph Notterman, professor of psychology at Princeton, contributed ideas and support, and David Grossberg gave valuable counsel. Gene's Restaurant provided the corner table for my guests and friends before and after the sessions.

The manuscript for this book was begun on Barbara Niner's typewriter at the Spear-O-Wigwam Ranch in the Big Horn mountains of Wyoming, and it was finished on a laptop computer given to me by my son Jeremy. Maylene D'Oliveira displayed infinite patience as she helped me learn the intricacies of that wondrous invention.

My agent, Diane Cleaver, found my publisher. My editor, Mark Chimsky, was all I could have asked for. He is an informed and zealous theater buff, and he provided inspiration as well as talent. His capable assistant, Rob Henderson, worked hard and was an inventive problem-solver. Thanks also to Martha Swope for the beautiful photographs. As always, my wife, Anne Rivers, was an invaluable helper, supporting my work and making use of her expertise to suggest ways of improving it.

Finally, I would like to express my gratitude to the audiences who attended all of the sessions at the New School over a period of two years. They were a loyal and enthusiastic group. Their love of theater communicated itself to my guests and helped make the series a success.

THE MAGIC OF THEATER

"I have tricks in my pocket, I have things up my sleeve. But I am the opposite of a stage magician. He gives you illusion that has the appearance of truth. I give you truth in the pleasant disguise of illusion."

TOM
THE GLASS MENAGERIE

PROLOGUE

I have been working in the theater for most of my life, but I have never fully understood its basic mystery: What makes us believe the actor is somebody else? A few years ago, I decided to try and find out. I invited a group of our best-known stage actors to join me in conversation in front of a live audience at the New School in New York City.

To learn how actors convince us they are other people, I realized it would be necessary to understand the nature and purpose of theater itself, and what sets it apart from film and television. My questions pursued these themes as they related to the careers of my guests, and I left myself room to improvise new questions, following the candid and often unpredictable flow of the conversation.

Usually I talked with two actors in each session. Some of them I knew and had worked with before and others I met for the first time. Many of them were appearing in shows and gave up their free Monday evening to be in the series. My guests contributed their time without pay, with the opportunity to explore theater's mysteries as their only compensation.

I would pick them up with the car and driver supplied by the New School and take them for tea or a drink in a little restaurant behind the New School's auditorium. The relaxed atmosphere of the almost empty, dimly lit restaurant had the womblike quality of a dressing room. As a producer and director, I am accustomed to visiting actors in their dressing rooms before a performance. Now I was to appear onstage with them. The restaurant gave us a chance to collect ourselves before facing the audience.

When I prepared for these conversations I reviewed the history of theater from its beginnings in ancient Greece when Thespis first stepped out of the chorus. I discovered that in 1888 an Englishman named William Archer sent out a questionnaire to the premier actors of his day. Archer was the translator of Ibsen, whose naturalistic dramas were being performed for the first time. At the top of his questionnaire he wrote, TO FEEL OR NOT TO FEEL? THAT IS THE QUESTION. Archer wanted to settle the debate over who had the greater effect on the audience: the actor who actually feels an emotion or the actor who successfully imitates it. He published the results in a book called *Masks or Faces? A Study in the Psychology of Acting.* In the end Archer concluded that there should be a compromise between the two positions, but he also wrote, "Someday, perhaps, a better psychologist may tread the maze to its inmost recesses."

It had been one hundred years since Archer's book. Instead of filling out a questionnaire, my guests agreed to answer my questions in front of several hundred aspiring actors and students, teachers and theatergoers.

What happened on each of those evenings was unique and, like an evening at a play, will never occur in quite the same way again. This book is an account of what took place. It's a record of our search, our journey, if you will, and the discoveries we made along the way about the magic of theater.

D.B.

CHAPTER ONE

JULIE HARRIS AND JOEL GREY

"Where did Julie go?"

© MARTHA SWOPE

Julie Harris in "Lettice and Lovage"

Joel Grey in "Cabaret"

BILLY ROSE THEATER COLLECTION/THE NEW YORK PUBLIC LIBRARY FOR THE PERFORMING ARTS; ASTOR, LENOX AND TILDEN FOUNDATIONS

Julie Harris is the only performer to ever win five Tony awards (for *I Am a Camera, The Lark, Forty Carats, The Last of Mrs. Lincoln,* and *The Belle of Amherst*). Julie was born in Grosse Pointe Park, Michigan, a suburb of Detroit. Her mother adored the theater and her father acted in school plays. She attended Miss Hewitt's classes, a New York City preparatory school that offered a course in drama, and she remembers telling her teacher, "Acting is my life." Julie enrolled in the Yale University School of Drama and became a member of the Actors Studio in New York. At twenty-four she was cast as Frankie Addams, a lonely, motherless twelve-year-old tomboy in Carson McCullers's *The Member of the Wedding.* In an interview Julie said, "That play was really the beginning of everything big for me." A year later she left to play Sally Bowles in John Van Druten's *I Am a Camera.* Brooks Atkinson said of her opening night performance, "Julie Harris has the quicksilver and genius we all long to discover on the stage." Julie recreated her stage roles in film versions of *The Member of the Wedding, I Am a Camera,* and *East of Eden* opposite James Dean. A two-time Emmy Award–winner, she has starred in two of her own TV series and appeared as Lilimae Clements in "Knots Landing." In 1976, Mount Holyoke College made Julie an honorary doctor of fine arts.

Joel Grey was born in Cleveland, Ohio, the son of Mickey Katz, a clarinetist with the Cleveland Orchestra who later became a popular comic musician with his own musical revue, *Borscht Capades.* Joel made his debut at the age of ten, as Pud in *On Borrowed Time* at the Cleveland Playhouse. At sixteen Joel began doing featured acts in his father's show, and in 1951, he was "discovered" by Eddie Cantor, who booked him for his television show. The exposure led Joel to a nightclub career. "It was lonely, going out there by myself," he said. "And then the clubs didn't know what to do with me. I always knew what I wanted to do—theater." Joel's first Broadway role was as a replacement for Warren Berlinger in Neil Simon's *Come Blow Your Horn.* He also replaced Anthony Newley in *Stop the World—I Want to Get Off* and took over Tommy Steele's role in *Half a Sixpence.* Producer-director Harold Prince saw Joel and hired him to play the M.C. in *Cabaret.* Joel won the Tony for his performance, and went on to star in the musicals *George M!, Goodtime Charley,* and *The Grand Tour,* and plays such as *Harry, Noon and Night,* and *The Normal Heart.* Joel's films include the film version of *Cabaret* opposite Liza Minnelli, for which he won the Oscar.

Riding to the New School with Julie Harris and Joel Grey, I couldn't believe that twenty years had gone by. In the 1960s, Julie had starred in a play I produced called *Ready When You Are, C.B.!*, and Joel had played George M. Cohan in my production of the musical *George M!* Something happens during rehearsals and out-of-town tryouts for a Broadway show. The people you work with become part of an extended family, different from relatives, but a closely knit group nevertheless. After the trauma and birth of the show are over, the feeling remains that you have lived through something momentous together. As a producer, however, I was never totally relaxed with members of my cast. It was basically an employer-employee relationship. But now with Joel and Julie it was different. I could enjoy their company on a different basis. Just before I walked onstage to introduce them, Joel patted me on the back and asked if I was nervous. It was the kindest thing he ever said to me.

When Julie and Joel made their entrance, it seemed as if they "belonged" there. Looking at Julie's fine-boned face with its childlike innocence, I suddenly felt I was in the presence of the many women she's played. Quite a few of them have been historical figures. I asked her if it is easier to get into the skins of real people.

"You have a great help and a great springboard with real people," said Julie, "because those ladies—Florence Nightingale, Mary Todd Lincoln, Emily Dickinson, Charlotte Brontë, and Nora Carrington—have all left letters and journals, so you can read what they wrote. It's like going into a trunk in your attic and finding your grandmother's letters, somebody in the family you never knew. Suddenly you are reading their words and the way they put the words together, and you have a feeling just from that. When I did Carson McCullers's *The Member of the Wedding,* I felt it was very autobiographical, so I read Carson's books and that was a great insight into the kind of woman she was.

"When we did a movie called *The Hiding Place,* set in the Ravensbrück concentration camp, there were many of us together in the hut. Many of the actresses didn't have any words to speak, but James Collier, who directed the film, made them all write their own life stories so that *they knew* why they were there, which made a great difference. They weren't just extras sitting there on a bunk, they knew their own life stories. You have to manufacture that or use something of your own life. Every moment in the theater has to be accounted for in your mind so that you're centered in some kind of reality."

In the musical *Skyscraper,* Julie played a woman who refused to sell her brownstone to a developer, in *A Shot in the Dark* she was up against the police, in *Requiem for a Heavyweight* she opposed the boxing profession, and as Joan of Arc in *The Lark* she was up against the church of France. Is it more rewarding for an actor to play underdogs?

"Squalor is very appealing to me," Julie said in her reedy, schoolgirlish voice. "I do like the underside of things. I find that very interesting. There's so much pain in the world and there's so much darkness. I love to be like Joan of Arc, of course. She carried the light of life because she was a very creative girl.

"The original transcripts of [Joan's] trial have been preserved. They were first written in Latin and then translated into French. It's fascinating to read her answers to their questions and the way she conducted herself. There's a line that she spoke when the churchmen asked her, 'Do you believe that you are in a state of grace?' They held off asking her this question, and I'm not quite sure I know why, but they were afraid to ask it for a long, long time. Finally it was asked in the court, 'Do you believe you are in a state of grace?' And her answer was, 'If I'm not, may God bring me to it. If I am, may God keep me in it.' " Julie paused, her eyes shimmering. "And everybody sighed because they thought, well, that's perfect. That was the perfect answer. In Shaw's play and in Anouilh's they kept that because you can't improve on that. That was perfect. The light of the world coming through the darkness, and she was that medium for that truth."

Reading the transcripts of the trial of Joan of Arc must have come in handy when it came to playing her in *The Lark.*

"And many biographies," added Julie. "Mark Twain's biography [of Joan] and many, many more that were fascinating. Shakespeare's Joan is very different. She's sort of a real witch. It's fun to do all that reading. It gives you so many different facets, and [you can] look at your role from many different points of view.

"I get great help from seeing where people lived . . . seeing the trees that they saw, and walking on the ground they walked on. All of that feeds you. It's actually food that the actor takes in. I got a strange feeling looking out Mary Todd Lincoln's window.

"Even if the character is fictional, research is important. Every play has a base, a home, and a story. You need to involve yourself with that."

Joel agreed. "Even though the M.C. in *Cabaret* was a fictional character, there was real stuff to expose myself to, like all the George Grosz and expressionist art of the period. I listened to all the early Kurt Weill music. I spoke to Lotte Lenya. I think that that was probably a very important lifeline, because I had her hand on a daily basis. It was almost like having her hand took me there. Her having been there, and watching and observing and not saying no somehow meant yes to me." Joel has one of the most animated faces in the business. His smile is infectious, exactly the opposite of the menacing grin he wore as the M.C. "Lotte would say to me, 'How do you know that? How do you know to do that?' I'd say, 'I don't, but there's a kind of a life that begins when it's the right part for you and you've done the work.' I feel the same way as Julie—I adore the research. I can't read enough, I can't meet enough people, I can't get enough various opinions so that I can then make my choices. Very often those choices, because of all the research, can alter things if you're in a long run. They can refresh, and also *new* things come into play.

"I played a Korean in a film and I wanted very much to go to Korea for even a week or a couple of days. I felt that was really important. It was one of the hardest, most far-fetched things that I could ever have taken on. But it wasn't possible for me to go. I spoke to greengrocers who troublingly did not want to speak. They were afraid, because of the way in which they've been treated in this country, that they were going to be the butt of something negative. Knowing that immediately gave me the core of something that was part of the Korean nature. All of a sudden everything else that I read connected to that, and I finally did meet someone who would tell me something. I also went to a concert at the Met of Korean music that had an enormous impact on me."

When Joel did the Jerry Herman musical, *The Grand Tour,* which was based on *Jacobowsky and the Colonel,* he made up a story for himself about his character's earlier life during the pogroms.

"I always thought of Jacobowsky as the opposite, the complete mirror of the M.C.," said Joel. "To have had the Nazi experience and then to become the hunted, from the hunter to the hunted. It was very powerful because I reverted back to my early experiences as a grandson of immigrant grandparents. That whole experience was wildly alive in me again. *We're so lucky to do what we do!* The making-believe makes us so aware of all the stuff people are not often forced to know about themselves. It's very healing. At least it is for me."

Is it necessary for an actor to like the characters she plays?

"Like or admire, yes," said Julie. "I think you have to have some kind of empathy for them. But that wasn't hard. All of those women were extraordinary in some way."

Was there something to like about the M.C.?

"Yes," said Joel. "There was also a great deal to abhor, which made it all the more interesting to find why he was doing what he could and what he must, no matter what it led to and no matter how many people were affected by it. He was doing the best he could, and I had to approach it from that standpoint. I don't think you can play any villain without believing or finding some rationale for his behavior."

How did the M.C. evolve into more than just a song-and-dance man?

"It was difficult," said Joel, "because there was no script. There were no lines. It was five songs when it was handed to me and they were all supposed to be in the second act to represent Berlin's nightlife. Just before rehearsals began, the creative team decided that these numbers should be spaced during the show to keep that life of the cabaret going. I was terrified because I started out at age nine as a classical actor. Legitimate acting was my life and my dream and my passion. I came a long way to create a part of my own on Broadway after taking a number of other people's roles and being an understudy, and here I was opening as a song-and-dance man without a word to say.

"My focus was on finding a full character, and making a very extensive and complex biography for myself about what happened and what my life was like *after* those numbers. I would go back to my dressing room and continue to live that life. I made an enormous scenario with all the girls in the Kit Kat Club. The problem in *Cabaret* was that you did a number and then the book happened and then all that energy would stop. I had a full night backstage, keeping that terror and that energy that has to do with not knowing if you're going to be there tomorrow. I could only do it with the kind of focus that had to do with 'Will we be here tomorrow or an hour from now?'

"I went to Paris right after they had the bombings a couple of years ago and nobody was going to Paris because they were afraid. I went anyway and when I arrived somebody said, 'There's a screening of a movie tonight. Would you like to come?' I did and afterwards they said, 'There is this reception at this nightclub. Would you like to come?' The jet lag hadn't hit yet, so I said sure, and I walked into this place and it was wild! People were standing on tables, pouring champagne into shoes. It was like the end of the world, because life was so precious and so scary. People were in major denial and that was the core for me of the M.C. He was denying everything that he was, and everything that the world was for a couple of hours."

When I saw Joel as the M.C. back in the 1960s, I was so impressed I offered him the leading role of George M. Cohan in the musical *George M!,* which I was about to produce on Broadway. Joel's compact agility was perfect for the part. But Cohan had a reputation for being difficult, and this was reflected in the script. How was it possible to make him into a likable guy?

"The problems of George M. Cohan were different because he wasn't George M. Cohan to our audiences," said Joel. "He was James Cagney. And I loved Jimmy Cagney. It was very scary to think of following Cagney, but luckily I didn't have to do any makeup or try to impersonate him. I found out a lot about Cohan that made it difficult to play him. He was not the kind of guy I would have hung out with. I admired his talent enormously. It was important to see a different kind of character from the sugar-coated Yankee Doodle Dandy. The truth of Cohan was starker.

"We found out in Detroit that audiences didn't like that very much. They wanted it to be much happier. We didn't sugar-coat it, but we softened it a bit. We didn't soften his deeds or his character, but we restored more of the joy of him . . . We reworked the show. We rehearsed an all-new production number, with new songs, for two weeks at enormous cost, with all new costumes and glitz and flags. And that's what turned the show around. They wanted the story but they also wanted those songs."

Julie is known as a dramatic actress. I asked her if she had done any musicals during her career in addition to *Skyscraper.*

"Just *Skyscraper,*" she said. "They took Elmer Rice's *Dream Girl* and wanted that to be part of the story, so I was Georgina Allerton, a sort of female Walter Mitty. She was a very appealing girl who had a little antique shop in a section of a block that was being taken over by a great building that was going up. And she refused to sell.

"I don't know how I did it. I wasn't a trained singer and Cy Feuer had seen me in plays and I guess something about me appealed to him, that I could be this girl. I said, 'But I can't sing.' So every day at rehearsal I was saying, 'Well, what about so and so?' I'd say, 'Tammy Grimes would be great in this part!' I hung on and everybody would say, 'Wait till you hear that first rehearsal, when you first hear the orchestra!' We opened in Detroit and I thought, 'My heart will stop and I'll fall dead on the stage.' But I didn't. I got through it somehow. I took vocal lessons every day that we did the show. It was a strain for a non-singer to sing eight performances. By the time Saturday night was there I was really hoarse."

"Did you ever get to like the singing part?" Joel asked.

"I never felt secure," said Julie.

"Never?" asked Joel.

"Never," said Julie.

"That's amazing," Joel said. "I had a similar thing happen to me in *George M!* I wasn't a tap dancer and George M. Cohan was one of *the* greatest tap dancers ever. Our choreographer Joe Layton is a terrific choreographer, but he was not about to allow the fact that I didn't know how to tap-dance change the choreography. It was difficult." Joel sat on the edge of his chair. "I have to go out there and be this 'best tap dancer' and I never, ever did a performance without going downstairs into the basement and running through this very complicated routine before the show every single night."

I asked if an actor takes a different approach to a role when it's a musical as opposed to a play.

"I found that it was a different technique," said Julie. "In *Skyscraper* every scene had a button. Charles Nelson Reilly, who was with me in the musical, would always say, 'Now what's the button?' The button was da *da* da. The ending of a scene in a musical has to have a da *da* da. You don't have that in a play. It's like condensed acting."

"In musicals we walk into vague spaces between scenes," added Joel, "whereas in plays you really go from scene to scene. The use of music somehow lets us all go into another kind of acceptance of reality. I had a way of dealing with this recently. I was asked to redirect Anthony Quinn in *Zorba* when he went back out on tour. I had just directed some things that I had been in off-Broadway and touring, but I always liked the idea of helping actors. Quinn thought that in a musical the acting is different. Nobody told him [otherwise], and he had a director who didn't understand that in a musical the music gives us another reality. It doesn't mean you have to necessarily play bigger, which is the idea he had, but that a scene can be played as intimately and as truthfully in a musical. Truth and reality are as necessary to good work in a musical as they are in a play. He was so grateful. He was so happy because it freed him to say, 'I'm Zorba,' instead of" (Joel yelled) " 'I'M ZORBA!'—which is what he thought he had to do. People will listen and they'll adjust. We as actors, we don't change. The truth is the truth is the truth."

When an actor performs a role in a drama, he is "in character" throughout. In a musical, what happens when he comes to the song? Does he stop feeling like the character in order to prepare to sing?

"There's no difference," said Joel. "The character is singing. *I'm* not even there."

How does an actor begin to approach a role?

"It's an exploration," Julie said. "We are explorers, aren't we?"

"Archaeologists," said Joel.

Julie continued, "The old French word for 'to rehearse,' means to turn over the earth. I am a slow learner, and I spent many years as an actor full of self-doubt, thinking I'll never understand this, I'll never be able to do what I want to do . . . It took a long time for me. I find that the last fifteen years of my life as an actor, I finally got out into the deep water and was able to stay afloat.

"I used to say to Ethel Waters, when we were in *The Member of the Wedding,* 'Oh, I was so terrible tonight, what can I do?' She said, 'You just have to have faith, baby.' I said, 'I know, but when do I get that? Where do I go to get some?' I gradually began to understand what she meant.

"In the beginning, when we are children, we have this impulse to throw ourselves into it, to show off; in *Chorus Line,* one of the dancers that the choreographer put in the back row keeps getting into the front row. That's what we want to do. We want to get out there in the front row. That impulse is a very good impulse to use. We want to be understood. We want to be noticed. We want to be seen. Gradually, you learn to develop that so it's not a hindrance to you, it's a help. In the beginning is the story. We want to tell the story. We want you to understand it. We want you to listen. We want you to feel. We have to be completely absorbed by it so that we are sort of evangelists. We want to thrill you with it."

"We want to thrill you with it," Joel repeated, "and we have this need to commit ourselves to it, whether it's good or not. That's the strange part, to work in a play that doesn't work. Or to do any work. I go to see actors in something that is utterly dreadful and they're saying, 'If it's better tonight . . .' You must believe. Otherwise, you can't go out there."

Actors need passion and commitment, but they also need technique. Both Joel and Julie received training at well-known acting schools: Julie at the Actors Studio with Lee Strasberg and Elia Kazan, and Joel with Sandy Meisner at the Neighborhood Playhouse. The great Russian actor Constantin Stanislavski is considered the father of the Method, and today many different people teach his technique. Is there one Method or are there many different versions of it?

"I think there are many different versions all over the world," said Julie. "I would love to be able to go to Russia and see the actors being trained there, because just as in music you have to learn the scales of the instrument, we actors have to learn the scales of *our* instrument. That's really what Stanislavski was interested in. He said, 'I don't want to leave it to chance. I want you to be able to understand your own psyche and be able to use it. There are times when the actor will not be one hundred percent and those times your technique will help you so that you can give a good performance.' Certainly there has to be a way to learn that for acting. Stanislavski changed his own view about acting several times during his life. The Actors Studio and the Neighborhood Playhouse were concerned that it not be representative acting. They believe actors should feel what they are supposed to feel, they shouldn't just pretend."

The debate on whether actors need to feel the emotions they are supposed to be expressing goes back two thousand years. There was a famous Greek actor named Polus, whose son had died tragically. Polus was playing Sophocles' *Electra,* and in the scene where Electra is mourning her dead brother, Polus brought onstage the urn which contained his real son's ashes. He had taken it from the tomb so that he could use it to trigger his grief. Maybe he was the first Method actor! The Method uses emotional memory, in which the actor recalls a powerful event from his past in order to stir the specific emotion he's supposed to be feeling in the play. Is that also part of the Meisner technique?

"Yes," said Joel. "It's about using your own life and bringing what's appropriate and applicable and correct for the character. To find that, that's the trick. To find the fullest place, where you can bring the truth of your character and the truth of yourself so that there are no seams."

"I remember Lee Strasberg used to talk about Eleonora Duse, the great Italian actress, when she did Ibsen's *A Lady from the Sea,*" said Julie. "In her character's past, she had been in love with a man, and now she was in a loveless marriage. Somebody came and said, 'You know so and so? I saw so and so,' who was the man Duse's character was in love with. In the play, Duse had a parasol and she was sitting on a bench by the sea, and when they spoke about this man from her past, she got very pale, and she began to slowly grind the tip of her parasol into the ground. It was like everybody knew something; it was all internal and she got pale. That's the ultimate example. That's how deeply you want to be involved."

"I don't see that often enough on the stage," Joel added. "I'm not interested in a technical performance. When I see the wheels working and covering the interior life, it's always less interesting to me."

Eva Le Gallienne wrote that "Duse succeeded in making of her body an instrument capable of responding effortlessly to the slightest shade of thought and feeling . . . once she had gained complete control of all the externals of her art, she was free to forget them and could concentrate on bringing about in herself the actual thoughts and passions of the women she gave life to on the stage." Can an actor reach this inner life of the character *without* the use of emotional memory?

"You have to listen to the play," said Julie. "The play is the most important thing. In *Saint Joan,* Shaw has given Joan a beautiful speech after they make her sign the paper and then tell her they'll never let her out of prison. 'Perpetual imprisonment' is the phrase she hears. She gets up and tears the paper." All of a sudden Julie became the headstrong young Joan of Arc facing her inquisitors, her eyes blazing with defiance. " 'And you want me to give up the life that I had? You want me never to hear the lambs crying through the healthy frost, never to be free, never to feel the grass under my feet?' . . . Shaw's words create the feeling. You don't have to think about anything except what she is going through."

"There's nothing the actor loves more than great words," said Joel.

When an actor works in film or television, is there a different road to the inner life of the character?

"I find it very different," Julie said. "In the first place, you don't have the three weeks' rehearsal we have for a play. In film, you sometimes have no rehearsal, so it's all work you've done on your own, by yourself, not with the other actors."

"And sometimes there is no time to even do *that* work," said Joel. "They call you yesterday and you start tomorrow."

"It's a different technique, but it has to be *true,*" added Julie.

When Julie played Sally Bowles in *I Am a Camera,* John Van Druten, the playwright, said, "Julie, you are like a glass of water. You put in pink lemonade and you become pink. You put in green lemonade and you become green." He meant it as a compliment. Does this mean an actor must empty herself of her own characteristics in order to take on another's personality?

"When I was rehearsing *Driving Miss Daisy,*" Julie recalled, "Alfred Uhry, who wrote the play about his grandmother, told me some things about her. I had never played a woman like this, and I had one very difficult scene. She is having a slight stroke and she doesn't know where she is. She thinks, in fact, she has got to go to school, and she is looking for her school papers. When I did the scene, I started to hit myself. Alfred saw what I was doing, and he said, 'Why did you do that?' I said, 'I don't know. It just came upon me.' He said, 'Well, Grandma used to do that!' "

"*We* don't do this work," Joel said. "*It* does us."

"Something takes over," Julie continued. "It's the alchemy of what the playwright has written. If you get that into your pores, something happens. That's our job, to find that, to absorb that, to chew it, to make it happen. It's agony."

"And ecstasy," said Joel.

"It's like an operation," said Julie. "You have got to put that psyche *inside* yourself. It's very shocking and very scary, but you have to go for it every second."

"When I was trying to find the character of the M.C. in *Cabaret,*" Joel recalled, "there were no lines and there were no real clues for me. One day in rehearsals, I said to Hal Prince that I had an idea for the character. I had seen a lot of really second-rate people performing in variety and I always thought they were bad. I had made enormous value judgments about these people and how bad their work was, how unprofessional and broad.

"I went offstage, and I decided to be all of those bad guys. I came out and did it, but I was so embarrassed. It was like I was standing there *being* them, which was the last thing I ever wanted to be. I finished doing it and I went into a corner and I started to cry. I was so ashamed. Hal came over and put his arm around me and said, 'That's it!' That was the beginning of finding the terror of that man."

In film the actor performs without a live audience. When the movie is finished, it can be shown without anyone being there to see it. Theater is different. Both actor and audience are present when it happens. How much does the audience response affect the actor's performance?

"We're doing it for you and we want you to respond," said Julie. "We're only half-alive until the audience gets there. I keep going back in my mind to the child's desire to show you. In bullfighting the bull has never fought before so he doesn't know any of the things that are going to happen. The matador has to set the stage for him. We have to do that, too. With words and language and emotion we take you on this journey. When I was doing *The Belle of Amherst* there was a passage toward the end of the play that was particularly beautiful and I always felt like I was the matador standing up there and that the audience would say, '*Olé! Olé!*' We were both on this journey together, the audience and the actors, and that's the ultimate. It's a voyage that we take together. So after three or four weeks of rehearsal we say, 'Where's the audience? I need the audience to complete this.' "

Since Joel had asked me if I was nervous before our session, I asked him if *he* had been nervous before coming onstage.

"I had," Joel paused, grasping for the right word, "an excitement. There's an excitement that's appropriate."

"I was looking forward to it," Julie said with enthusiastic vigor.

Some nervousness gives energy, but what about the more serious kind that produces fear? How does an actor deal with that?

"I hate to be nervous," Julie said, "so I fought against that. Nothing happens to me when I'm really nervous. I can fool you to a certain degree but I'm not doing what I should be doing because of fear, and I hate to feel that. So I really try to talk to myself and do away with that, like I'm going to make a cake or a batch of cookies and dream. Ralph Richardson once said, 'Behind everything an actor says should be a dream.' I love to come to the theater and dream for you. That's important, being free. If I'm nervous I'm not dreaming."

Before the actor starts to dream he has to dream of becoming an actor. For many actors it seems that it all begins in childhood. Joel's father was Mickey Katz, a popular comic musician in the American Yiddish musical theater. Was he an important influence?

"My father was essentially a musician when I was a small child," Joel said, "so there was no theater in my life at home. When I was nine my mom took me to a production of children's theater and I saw it and I said, 'I want to be there.' I didn't know why, when, or where or what, but the next thing I knew I was there and the next thing I knew I was hired to play a brilliant, complex, extraordinary role in a play called *On Borrowed Time.* So I was given the gift of a lifetime. I was taught. I was inspired. I was respected. They called me Mister! I had the time of my life and I knew that it was so rich and so wonderful that it was going to be my life.

"A lot of people said, 'You didn't have much of a childhood.' Actually, I had my childhood, which had to do with being an actor, and that was in Cleveland, Ohio. I'll never forget those times. I think that what I learned from nine to twelve, as an actor then, was probably the very stuff I'm made of today. The working with Sanford Meisner was just honing whatever that was. I'm really grateful. It was the richest time for me to have all of this excitement and to know the possibility of great beauty coming from something that I might be a small part of at that young an age."

Did Jennifer Grey, star of *Dirty Dancing* (and Joel's daughter), also begin her acting career at an early age?

"Jennifer did not act as a small child because of me," said Joel. "There were a lot of negatives to being a child actor, but in retrospect, now that I look at my life with a little more distance, they don't in any way imbalance the love of theater. The joy of what I get to do was worth all the pain. But when my child began, I didn't think that I wanted her to do that as a kid. She wanted to do it, and she finally prevailed, and I'm all for it now and very proud of her."

I asked Julie if there was a moment when she knew she wanted to act.

"It was in a school play at Christmastime," she said. "We were doing the story of the juggler of Notre Dame and I was chosen to be the juggler. I don't remember how much rehearsal time we had, but it wasn't very much and I wasn't very well prepared. So the actual performance in the school auditorium was sort of improvised. I found it thrilling. People came up to me and said, 'Oh, it was so moving!' I thought, 'How wonderful. I've got to be in this, I've got to be part of this. How wonderful!' I think I was about nine or ten."

When we watch a good actor on the stage, there's a magic click that goes on in our brain. It's the moment we start to believe the actor is someone else. It's also the moment when we start to *care* what happens to the character. Do actors have this experience when they're members of an audience, or does their knowledge of the craft get in the way?

"I'll forever be an audience," Julie said. "The excitement of going to see a play or a movie, or television, is always there. Whenever I'm in the audience, I'm full of excitement for the thing I'm watching. It happens very soon that I propel myself into it."

"I'm also willing to forget," agreed Joel. "I don't have to do anything. When I go to the theater, my anticipation is so great, it is so full of positive expectation, that it has nothing to do with when I'm excited or preparing for a play backstage. Sitting in front, waiting for that curtain to go up, is such a magical moment—even to this minute."

What happens if the actor is watching someone she knows and has worked with?

"It doesn't matter," said Julie. "I once was doing a solo play about Charlotte Brontë by William Luce, a play that he called *Brontë*. I had an unusual experience while I was in the process of memorizing the play. I live near Shirley Booth, and Shirley asked me to do the first act for her, so I hopped up and did the first act for her in her living room. Then, several years passed, and she said, 'You know, you never did the second act for me.' So I said, 'Fine.' We were on her back porch. I was sitting here, she was sitting there, and I leaned forward and said the whole second act to her. Now this was a great experience for me in acting, because at the end of the play Shirley didn't move. So I said, 'That's it, that's the end.' Then Shirley said, 'Where did Julie go? Where did Julie go?' "

C H A P T E R T W O

CHRISTOPHER REEVE

AND

ELIZABETH FRANZ

"Theater is life with the boring parts cut out."

Christopher Reeve in "The Fifth of July"

Elizabeth Franz in "Broadway Bound"

Christopher Reeve grew up in Princeton, New Jersey, and discovered theater at the age of eleven when he volunteered to sing in the McCarter Theater's production of Gilbert and Sullivan's *The Yeoman of the Guard.* By fifteen he was a member of Actors' Equity Association and had worked as an apprentice at the Williamstown Theatre Festival in Massachusetts. Christopher majored in English and music theory at Cornell University and studied acting with John Houseman at the Juilliard School for Drama in New York City. He paid the rent for two years by appearing as the heartless bigamist, Ben Harper, in the TV soap opera "Love of Life," and received his first big break when Katharine Hepburn picked him to play her grandson in the Broadway play *A Matter of Gravity.* Christopher was signed for the lead in the movie *Superman* after the producers acquired Marlon Brando and Gene Hackman for supporting roles, and felt they no longer needed a "bankable" star. After its success he turned down lucrative film offers and headed for Broadway to play a gay paraplegic Vietnam War vet in Lanford Wilson's *The Fifth of July.* At the time Christopher said, "You need the challenge of going in front of real people to extend your ability as an actor." He has appeared on stage in *The Aspern Papers* (with Vanessa Redgrave) and *Summer and Smoke.* His film roles include *Deathtrap* and *The Bostonians.*

Elizabeth Franz was born in Akron, Ohio, and wanted to be an actor starting at the age of five. "I always knew there were a lot of women inside me, and I think acting was just the right way of finding and expressing them," she once said. Elizabeth graduated from the American Academy of Dramatic Arts and earned her reputation as a serious actor in regional and repertory theaters. Her roles ranged from Gertrude in *Hamlet* and Mary Tyrone in *Long Day's Journey into Night* to Dr. Martha Livingston in *Agnes of God* and Julie in *The Royal Family.* She appeared at the Ahmanson, the Yale Repertory Theater, the Berkshire Festival Theater, and the Arena Stage. Elizabeth created the title role in Christopher Durang's hit play *Sister Mary Ignatius Explains It All for You,* and won the Obie Award for her portrayal. On Broadway, she originated the role of Kate Jerome in Neil Simon's *Brighton Beach Memoirs,* for which she received both Tony and Drama Desk nominations. She then went on to play an older Kate Jerome in Neil Simon's *Broadway Bound.* Elizabeth has guest-starred on television in "Spenser for Hire" and "The Equalizer," and played the infamous Alma Rudder on "Another World."

When Christopher Reeve and Elizabeth Franz joined me on the stage of the New School's auditorium there were oohs and ahs from the audience. Christopher had an imposing presence; tall and square-jawed, with his head bent rather shyly, he looked like Clark Kent with Superman's figure. Elizabeth and I exchanged smiles. I had directed her in an off-Broadway play, and had watched her hold an audience in the palm of her hand as Kate Jerome in Neil Simon's *Broadway Bound.*

I asked Christopher why he works in the theater since film is so much more lucrative.

"Theater gives you a chance to really plug into what you have to offer as an actor," said Christopher. "It gives you a chance to dig for a deeper truth, and it gives you control over the audience. The actor in film is a gardener in someone else's landscape."

When we sit in a theater, we watch human beings like ourselves, pretending to be other people in a different time and place. We believe the actor, when *the actor* believes in what he is doing. How does an actor come to believe in his character?

"There are certain things we do to do our work as actors," said Elizabeth. "I have found a method, which is writing novels about the characters I play. This helps me live with the character and feel what she is feeling, and express what she is expressing.

"It was an extraordinary feeling to write the first novel about Kate Jerome when I did *Brighton Beach* and then to write a new novel about what happened to her in the ten years leading up to *Broadway Bound.* In the first play, the most important thing in Kate's life was to get her family through the Depression, and to do what she does best, which is being a mother. Ten years later, Kate is deserted by her sons as well as her husband. In *Broadway Bound,* she has the remembrance of the happiest moment in her life, when she danced with George Raft. Neil Simon gives her that, so she can become a child again, the girl that no one ever knew she had ever been, especially her son. Writing the second novel gave me the ability to express the softer side of Kate."

As she spoke, Elizabeth's voice began to tremble and her eyes became moist. Her method of writing full-length novels, of plumbing the depths of her character, works so well that as she described Kate she started to *become her* right before our eyes.

Linda Lavin had played Kate in *Broadway Bound* before Elizabeth took over and brought an entirely new conception to the role. How does an actor arrive at her own interpretation of a part when someone else has created the character?

"I went to see Linda's Kate Jerome," said Elizabeth. "She was wonderful. [Her Kate] just wasn't the woman inside of me. I didn't know where she found her. I had to drop [her interpretation] because I was getting into trouble. That soul was not mine. I had to just totally drop it and go for *my* reality and my sense of getting into that soul."

"The actor's job in theater is to find as intense a personal connection with the part as he possibly can," said Christopher "Whatever it takes to do that, that's fine.

"What I have worked on is a process of unlocking, which has to do with a very basic belief. This is something Katharine Hepburn told me the first day I showed up for rehearsal with her for *A Matter of Gravity.* I was fresh out of drama school, and very nervous to be around somebody as impressive as she is. She said to me, 'You must remember you are already a real person, and a real person is always more interesting than any fiction, because you exist and the piece of fiction doesn't. So don't deny your own reality. Don't think, "Oh my God, here I am over here and there is this part over there, how am I ever going to get to it?" Assume there is a good reason you were cast in the part. Assume you have the power within you to play it. Allow yourself to say,"All right, this is me." '

"I look at every script in a kind of backwards way. I assume this part was given to me, whatever part it is, because of the lessons I am to learn about myself. It's like the fates have given you a homework assignment. Your job is to go and play part X and take in what those lessons are. Now you are already starting from the point of view that *'This is me.'* So now all I have to do is learn more details to fit in with this basic belief of who I am. Usually this is a technical adjustment.

"For example, in *The Fifth of July,* I had to learn what it is like to have no legs. This man is a bilateral amputee and I don't know what that feels like. What do I do to find out? I call up the VA hospital, get to know somebody, and go to work with a coach. That's a technical adjustment, because the basic core in the middle is, I *am* this part. This part is me. An actor who believes that onstage is going to communicate that belief when you pay money to go and see him."

In theater, actor and audience participate in an illusion. Why do we need this illusion? Why didn't the playwright write the story as a novel, which we could read in the peace and quiet of our home? If we get tired or bored with a book, we can put it down. In the theater, if we are not happy with what we are watching and want to leave, we face the problem of getting up and stepping over other people. Or maybe the person we are with wants to stay, which creates another problem. And what of the time and expense it took to get there? What does theater do for us that makes it worth all the effort?

"What we go to the theater for," said Christopher, "is to celebrate the connections between us; the connectedness, the universality [among] all of us. The differences between human beings are much less than we think. Underneath all the flak that we send out—the social conditioning, the education, the regionalisms, whatever it is that makes us behave on the surface in certain ways—underneath that, the core humanity is so universal, that when you plug into it, that's where the power of theater comes from."

I asked Christopher and Elizabeth how they applied the idea of a universal core humanity to Ken Talley in *The Fifth of July* and Sister Mary Ignatius in *Sister Mary Ignatius Explains It All for You,* two of their recent roles.

"I happen to be a heterosexual," said Christopher, "but why should I have a problem playing a homosexual, since the only difference is that the object of my affection is different? Whether you are in love with a car or your stamp collection, the feeling is the same. You don't put a value judgment on it. You don't say, 'Gee, I'm straight . . .'

"Three actors from the Gay Activists Alliance showed up backstage, before they saw the show, to object to the fact that a straight actor was playing Ken Talley. I asked them to see the play and then come back and tell me if I had done anything to offend gay pride. They came back after the show and said they had been absolutely devastated by it. The part had worked. The show had worked. Once you have the willingness and the imagination to find that core humanity as an actor, the only other limitations are purely technical, and you can get over those."

"Once again, I found it useful to write a novel about my character," said Elizabeth. "This made it possible to get at the core humanity of Sister Mary. In this case, I wrote about her childhood. This made Sister Mary real for me, even though she might appear bizarre to someone else.

"There was a woman who was a nun who lived inside of me. Finding her beliefs, before the church had changed on her, was important. She was losing her identity because everything was changing; the habit had changed and the pope had changed. She was teaching eight-year-olds. When the older children came back and challenged these things in front of the eight-year-old, she had to defend him. So, to me it was very precious. It was very important that that eight-year-old *believe* what I was saying.

"People wanted to know, 'Why did this nun carry a gun? How can you make such a bizarre character real?' My answer was, 'If you were a nun and you had to listen to the news every night with an eight-year-old sitting beside you, how could you justify *not* carrying a gun?' If I am protecting eight-year-olds and listening to the news every night, I *have* to carry a gun. That was very clear to me."

"One of the most exciting things about the job of acting," said Christopher, "is that in a lot of modern plays we don't get unassailable logic the way you do in the classics. If you tackle Shaw or Shakespeare or Molière, there is a richness, not only of language, but of logic and development, so a lot of your work is done for you. You just follow the road signs and do your best. In a lot of modern plays there may be amazing effects, but it's not always clear how we get there and why this is happening.

"Our job as actors is to fill in those blanks so that all those moments make sense. If you ever see an actor out there without a complete justification for all the things his character has to do, you're not going to believe what he's doing."

What happens when an actor takes on a role where he cannot find a way to justify his character's actions?

"It's our duty to connect with the role," explained Elizabeth. "If you don't connect with it, you shouldn't take the job."

"Your question," said Christopher, "leads to the very basic decision an actor has to make if he wants to get into the profession: What do I want to do with it? What is the purpose of acting? Either you are going to be an actor who actually changes and transforms, without placing a value judgment on any of the parts he plays, or you are going to try to be somebody the public recognizes, who deliberately *doesn't* change. This is a more old-fashioned way of doing things.

"The old star system meant you really wanted to see the dependable reappearance of somebody. You wanted to know all about him, you wanted that familiarity. In that case, the actor's job was to be the most convincing version of himself that he could be. A lot of actors went that way.

"I love that famous Peter O'Toole line in *My Favorite Year*, when he finds out he is about to go on live television. He says, 'I'm not an actor, I'm a movie star!' That's what he had become. You have to make that choice. If you are a star, you just occupy a special corner of the market and you try to be the best product of yourself that you can be, and you stay there. But if you want to act, you have to keep saying, 'All right, I don't know where it's going to take me or what I'm going to do. I'm not going to worry about image.'

"Let's take two greats, Katharine Hepburn and Meryl Streep. They are two completely different kinds of actors coming from two different eras. I don't think Meryl Streep would have become a star in the twenties or thirties. She would have been considered too offbeat. Katharine Hepburn was offbeat but she had patrician looks. She could compete in a man's world in a way that hadn't been done before, and there was an originality about her that really took Hollywood by storm. That is the trademark of the great stars.

"Have you ever noticed that all great stars have a truly unique voice? And there is something absolutely unique about their appearance, no cookie cutters. None of the greats look like anybody else, nor do they sound like anybody else. They also have a sheer weight of personality so that you couldn't mistake them for anybody else, and they know that. So they know they are not going to really transform into somebody else. What they do is come out with the sheer weight of their personality, and kind of browbeat you into believing they are somebody else. If you watch Katharine Hepburn, you know she is not really that character, but you *want* to believe. You go into a contract with her as you watch her. You say, 'I'm willing to go with this, because this woman is so fascinating and I like her so much that I want to watch whatever she does.' That's what a great star does.

"On the other side, let's take a great actress. I think Meryl Streep has more talent than any other five actors or actresses put together. I think she's *genius* level. I know her just slightly. She's the one person in this business who makes me come all to pieces when I'm around her. I just can't handle it. At one point Gene Shalit, who lives near me in the country, was having a summer party, and I know that Meryl Streep lives not too far away. I wrote Gene a letter saying, 'Please invite Meryl Streep and may I sit near her so I can try to get over this problem I have and see if I can get through a meal and have a conversation?' Well, we managed. We had children to talk about, and I'm over that stage in my life.

"But to come back to my point, what Meryl Streep really does is genuinely transform. You know she's Meryl Streep. You know she's got a wig on. For example, in *Cry in the Dark:* You know it's another wig and she's got an Australian accent, and yet after the first thirty seconds of adjustments are over, you are willing to believe that she is that woman. This is because she has gone with the 'I-don't-give-a-damn, I'm-going-to-transform' route. She has become a star just because of the sheer weight of respect for her transformational talent. Meryl is a completely different kind of movie star. She got there by acting talent, rather than by force of personality. I think, personally, that that's the kind of star to be. To really transform so successfully that people want to see what you are going to do next."

Do actors who "transform" have to work at not allowing their personalities to appear in their performance?

"What the audience responds to is truth as opposed to acting," said Christopher. "When you catch an actor acting, there's a phrase we have for it in the trade, which is 'commenting.' This means you're not just doing the action, you're commenting on it. Like commenting on drinking a glass of water." Christopher exaggerated the gesture of picking up his water glass from the table, drinking it, and then making a very audible sigh. "See?" he said. "It's too much. Acting is not *how* you drink a glass of water. If you want a glass of water, you just pick up the glass of water and drink! Commenting is a lie because that's not what you do in real life. If you just drink the water, the audience will get it. That's hard for a lot of actors, particularly when they're young and enthusiastic and they want to show the director they're doing their job. The director gives a note and says, 'Cross to the table and get the water,' Boy, are you going to make sure that you're doing your job! And you do too much. I have certainly been guilty of that."

How does an actor know when he's doing too much?

"It's like the vibes when you're not telling the truth," said Christopher, "and you know the other person isn't believing you. They just wander. You haven't got 'em. And when we're not telling the truth onstage, we haven't got you. And when we *are* telling the truth, it gets you. Meryl Streep, and people like that, they do have extraordinary personalities, but the main thing about them is that they are receptive rather than aggressive.

"Meryl Streep once said that [the reason] she's so good is that she's an 'ape.' She's able to mimic. To be able to mimic means that you've got to be open enough to see what's happening. If you're out there selling your own personality, which is what star acting is—'You're going to like me, damn it, no matter what'—then you're not in a position to receive what other people are doing and to be able to re-create it.

"As an actor, you use as much of your personality as you can, and where it's not appropriate, you have to get rid of it. Certain things that you do, you just know are not right for the character. You're generally not going to be given something that is hideously wrong. Donny Osmond is not going to play *Othello*. He just knows it's not a smart thing to do. You've got to have a realistic sense of who you are and what you can do. You can't be too bold about it or too cowardly. You have to keep taking risks but not go off and do things which are totally inappropriate."

Among the best places for an actor to take risks are this country's regional and repertory theaters.

"The popularity of regional and repertory companies bodes well for the theater," said Christopher, "because if you have a group of actors coming up in this generation or the next who don't want to sell out and just make money and look like themselves all the time, that means they will return to legitimate classical theater. Then we won't keep losing all these actors to Hollywood.

"There was a real drain. A lot of the best people would come up and make a little money. They would have one or two good shows on Broadway, and then disappear to Hollywood. Now, a lot more of them are willing to stay in the theater. Kevin Kline, for example, is always going back to the theater. Bill Hurt is always in the theater. Dustin Hoffman just did Willy Loman in *Death of a Salesman,* and now he's going to do Shylock in *The Merchant of Venice.* The more [that] terrific actors stay in the theater, the better it's going to be for audiences, and for keeping theater alive.

"One of the things that's happening now is that it's getting too expensive for producers to take *any* kind of a chance on Broadway. Broadway has become a place to take people on expense accounts. It's become a sightseeing attraction for New York. It's not really live theater in the traditional sense, the way live theater exists in London, where there are fifty things running in the West End at any given moment.

"I just came from London today. The top ticket price is the equivalent of twenty-one dollars. In the West End right now are Derek Jacobi in *Richard II,* Vanessa Redgrave in *Orpheus Descending,* and Maggie Smith in *Lettice and Lovage.* There's a big column of what's going on at the Royal Shakespeare Company. Classical plays mix with *Sugar Babies* with Mickey Rooney, and with Alan Ayckbourn. They don't mix here because of the economic factors and because of the fifty-dollar ticket.

"I'm on the council at Actors' Equity and one of the things we're working on is how to get companies to subsidize the theater. You know the way Mobil brings you 'Masterpiece Theater' on television. Why doesn't Mobil bring us the fifteen-dollar ticket? Then we'd get more coming out of Arthur Miller's pen. Basically we've got David Mamet and Lanford Wilson. They are really the only two modern playwrights who *automatically* can get to Broadway.

"People are still going to the theater. But the average person who comes in from out-of-town knows that between Fifty-second Street and Forty-third Street there are twenty-five theaters. They don't know how to *find* Second Stage or Playwrights Horizons or Circle Rep when they come in from Kansas. And they're afraid to go. We need to create an awareness of what theater's available and we have to underwrite the cost of a reasonable ticket."

Elizabeth's *Sister Mary Ignatius Explains It All for You* was an example of what Christopher had been saying. It came from the Ensemble Studio Theatre *and* Playwrights Horizons.

"Yes," said Elizabeth. "It was first at Ensemble, and because of the nature of the piece, it was only a one-act play at that time. [Christopher Durang] had to write a curtain raiser for it. They tried to get it on commercially for two years and finally Playwrights Horizons picked it up and put it on. Then when it was successful they moved it, but there again was a conflict. I could not have stayed in it for a year if I hadn't done a soap opera at the same time. I was being paid one hundred and fifty dollars a week for doing the play, as were all the other actors. I was going to have to leave a role like that, but a soap opera came along and that made it possible for me to stay in the role."

When times get tough, do actors ever think about giving it up and trying something else?

"Today," said Elizabeth. "And I'm not joking. I didn't know how I was going to come here. We go through a lot of rejection. We go through a lot of tough times in this business because you constantly have to prove yourself if you are going to be an actor who loses yourself in the role.

"I have not worked for the director [of] *Sister Mary Ignatius Explains It All for You* since [that play], and I adore him as a director. I never experienced working with anyone like him before or since. But he is so used to me being Sister Mary. He asked me to come and read for his new play, and I did. I opened myself up to it and I got rejected. And I did very well! Reading is very tough. You have to go through all the preparation to read for a play because you have to get lost in it to try to win the role. When people are used to you being a nun or a Jewish mother, they don't know if you can do anything else. And to do something else in ten minutes in a reading is very hard."

Christopher said, "I think a hundred out of a hundred actors in a room would admit that at some point in their lives they say, 'They're going to catch me. They're going to find me out. The art police are going to come in the middle of the night and they're going to exile me.' As actors we're dealing in drama and comedy with high stakes, where people are living the essential, trying crises of their lives, the life and death matters.

"I sometimes look back and I think, *'I'm from New Jersey. What do I know?'* You know that sense that we all feel sometimes? You don't sense that you're special. You don't feel, 'I've got all this richness and incredible stuff going on in me.' You ask the question, 'What is in me that anyone would want to see?' Every actor feels that at some point. [There are] actors who are brilliant largely because they are so disturbed (and we could name a few), who are just really unhinged. They use acting as therapy. They're either onstage or locked up somewhere. It's a very generous, courageous thing to do. They are people who really have trouble with reality and theater is therapy for them. What happens is really interesting to watch. I often say to myself, 'If I could be brilliant, would I want to be that disturbed? Would I want to pay that price and be that neurotic?' I almost always cop out.

"I go back again to Katharine Hepburn. I drop her name too many times but I adore this woman. My first big job out of drama school was the play with Hepburn. She really gave a seminar on life for that year we were on the road and on Broadway. I look at her and say, 'Now here's a woman who can cope with reality. She can laugh. She can have fun. She can live. She has enthusiasm. She has outside interests. She does other things. She's a human being with capital letters and she's an actress, too.' So I would opt on the side of health finally."

Both Christopher and Elizabeth are devoted to theater and to the challenge of new and interesting roles. I asked Christopher if he was able to avoid being typecast in the minds of prospective employers after his success as Superman.

"Typecasting is something that is done by other people and

it happens to them, not to me," said Christopher. "I hope that doesn't sound egotistical. *Superman* was a wonderful time in my life. I really enjoyed it. It was a great privilege to work with Marlon Brando and Gene Hackman and Trevor Howard and Susannah York and Terence Stamp and with a screenplay by Mario Puzo. Who at twenty-four wouldn't want to do that?

"Bill Hurt, who's one of the best actors of this generation, was sharing a dressing room with me when I got that part, and he just about fell on the floor with jealousy. Any actor would have done that role because we all grew up with the idea that an actor changes. You do one part and then you play another one. You finish with that one and you play another one. It's like life is a big Whitman Sampler and after you've had the peppermint cream, then you're going to have the one with the nuts. That's perhaps naïve, but that's what I thought when I went into it. I probably underestimated the hype that [would be] attached to it.

"In my mind, I've never been typecast because Superman, even though it was an important job, has no more or less value than the next job. And whether you're playing Superman or Henry James or Pete Gurney, the actor's work is always the same. We're not putting value judgments on the character. We're not saying a comic book is worse than Chekhov. It's all the same process to get inside it and believe it. If other people don't want to move on and imagine that I can be somebody else, I really have to say I think it's *their* problem. It's not my problem. I just have to keep doing my work."

Why would an actor who has been successful in film want to return to the theater?

"One of the exciting things about working in the theater," said Christopher, "is you get cast in the part, you show up for the first day of rehearsal, and you are into an experience which grows out of a group of people who are there to do the job and commit to it for the same length of time.

"In a movie, you've got the money problem, you've got the producer problem, you've got the studio, and the fact that they only keep you there for the minimum time they possibly can because they don't want to pay the money. You do a scene and the girl who plays your wife, you met her yesterday. It's very hard to bring out any depth. But in theater, what comes out is the collective, the group.

"In film, the best movies have the most lucky moments:

when the light was right, the camera was right, the makeup was right, and the horses went by at the right time. Theater, on the other hand, is a place where, through doing it again, you find out how to get past what satisfied you yesterday, and you see if maybe there is something more there. It's that process of digging for a deeper truth that ultimately is much more rewarding.

"There's no tremendous mystery to [acting]. Another Katharine Hepburn quote: She was watching *Captains Courageous* with Spencer Tracy and Freddie Bartholomew. Freddie gave that performance when he was nine years old, and Hepburn said, 'If a nine-year-old can do that, then there's no great mystery to it.' "

The playwright, unlike the novelist, cannot always explain what his or her characters are thinking or feeling when they speak their lines. And so different interpretations are often possible. How can actors be sure that their interpretation is the one the playwright intended?

"If you're lucky, the playwright is standing right there," Christopher said, "and he says, 'No, that really wasn't what I had in mind.' That's one of the advantages of doing a modern play. But even if he's not there, meeting characters is like meeting people, and it's not that great a mystery what people want or what they are doing.

"When people talk, they very quickly reveal themselves, particularly if they are put in any kind of stress. Plays are *about* emergencies and dire situations. Theater is life with the boring parts cut out. Even *Waiting for Godot* is high drama, because they really believe that *today* Godot is going to come; and that makes today worthwhile. There are high stakes. If there are no high stakes, then there is no drama. If there *are* high stakes, people are going to react, and their true natures are going to come out."

"During rehearsals for *Brighton Beach,*" added Elizabeth, "Neil Simon was there for the whole time, and we were playing his family. Matthew Broderick was playing Neil Simon, and I was playing his mother. To get at being able to say an 'I love you' that means 'I hate you,' you have to live through certain experiences as an actor.

"We were having trouble with Neil being there. We were being restricted. We were saying what we thought he wanted us to say. I had to speak up and say, 'Neil, give us five hours without you. Come in three hours a day.' Neil said, 'Oh, is that what you want? Sure, sure!' In those five hours it was amazing what we could do. This was the actor's process. We learned how to do it every way, so we could do it the way it was supposed to be. Then it had other meanings, so you as an audience can see it and say, 'She does love him, but there is some reservation there. This is very interesting. I wonder if I'd feel the same way about *my* husband.' The actor has to go through that process, and we had to do that with the director. The playwright couldn't do it for us because he knew how he wanted it to end up."

The director is at the heart of the collaboration in theater. A good director can get the actor on his side by asking for his help, to make the actor feel free to find new things and make his unique contribution.

"That's true," said Christopher. "Actors always have to feel that they are doing it themselves. They don't want to feel like, 'Now you go over here and do this.' They get very resentful."

How do actors prepare for important moments in a play without diminishing their spontaneity?

"I can remember a moment that happened in the end of *The Fifth of July*," said Christopher. "Ken Talley has no legs and walks around on leg braces and there's a moment when he's suddenly brushed by somebody going by and he falls over backwards. To someone with no legs that is the most terrifying thing that can happen because it can lead to spinal injury and paralysis. So to fall backwards is a big, big trauma and it's the key moment five pages from the end of the play. I learned how to do the stunt so that literally when I fell backwards it would get a gasp from the audience because they had believed the illusion all evening.

"Ken Talley's whole problem in the play is that he refuses to accept that he has a problem. He's *denying* everything. He keeps saying, 'I'm going to go to Spain next year. I'm going to do this, I'm going to do that.' He's not dealing with his past and his reality and his relationships. He falls, and that physical fall is a metaphor for his fall in the play. He's got to finally accept people. His journey in the play is that he finally reaches out and embraces people. The way that that would happen every night, I never knew what would happen to me after the fall. After that event, I never knew on any given evening what I would actually feel like, but because the eight of us had played together so long and trusted each other so much, we never preprogrammed how it would happen.

"What I'm saying is that the rolling effect, the momentum of that group working together and the trust that's engendered, allows you to get to the big moments of a play and not have to figure out ahead of time, 'Oh, here comes my big moment,' which is the worst thing that can happen to an actor onstage. There was one critic in this town who has retired. He was respected but he was very damaging to actors: Walter Kerr. Every Sunday [he] would write about actors' great moments. That is what his reviews usually were. 'That moment where he goes to the lamp and turns it on is the funniest thing . . .' and of course the actor couldn't do it again for the next three weeks because he'd read [the review]. Kerr was famous for doing that.

"*Innocence.* Innocence is the key. Innocence means I'm going to go onstage not knowing any more than I need to know at this moment and I'm going to trust that as we roll along and we get to those big moments, all the homework that I've done, all that life that I've lived, all my trust in the other actors is going to allow something real to happen, where just like in life I don't know how I'm going to respond.

"It's like you see a car crash. How do you know what you're going to do? You might stand there. You might call the police. You might go and help. If you allow yourself to respond to a crisis in an innocent way by just being attuned to other people, something truthful is going to happen that's going to be worth watching."

During rehearsals, the actors and the director collaborate to find a truth they can believe in. Once the play is in performance, the audience becomes involved. How does the audience reaction affect what is happening on the stage?

"The audience is a barometer of truth," said Christopher. "You have a little meter there. Every time there is a true moment, the meter goes off. If it's a comedy, it's in laughter. If it's a drama, the participation of the audience is very palpable. You know how it is when you go to the theater and you've got your program, and maybe a bag and your coat . . . that comfortable feeling . . . you're a little bit detached from the play. You're moving a little bit in your seat . . . and then something stunning happens onstage. A truly great moment happens, and there is suddenly a moment of danger. You are so drawn in, you forget yourself. It's almost like what happens when an actor forgets his lines. You think, 'Oh my God, we are now out of charted waters. I'm not safe sitting here anymore. I don't know what's going to happen. Is the curtain going to come down?' When those moments happen, they are always caused by emergencies, like an actor going up on lines or some tragedy happening onstage. But they're also caused by great performers fully concentrating. You can hold those moments in your hand.

"This, in my opinion, is what always happens when Vanessa Redgrave works. I had the pleasure of working with her in a play in London. I was absolutely amazed by the depth of her concentration and how she would still an audience.

"And then there are moments when things *don't* work and the audience gets restless, which means we are not concentrating. When there is a real communication happening, both sides are interested. Any human being who is telling a compelling story truthfully is watchable. It's up to us to make sure we are telling the truth."

When I saw Elizabeth as Kate Jerome in *Broadway Bound*, I experienced one of those great moments Christopher was talking about. It happened when she danced with the actor who played her son. I could feel myself being transported along with the rest of the audience. How did that moment come about?

"It's that concentration," said Elizabeth, "and the relationship with the actor, and knowing the soul of the woman so totally. It's the combination of the actors and the stillness there, and the belief in that moment, and the need to live through that moment. It comes from the need for me to lose myself in Kate Jerome, and Kate's need to express to her son a story. The story transports her back because she *needs* to be transported. It takes concentration to make that happen night after night, and then the audience relates to it as well."

What is happening at that moment in the play?

"The boy is asking his mother to tell him about the night she danced with George Raft," said Elizabeth, "so she begins to tell the story and it begins to evolve. He delights in it, and he starts asking her more and more questions, and then he says, 'Wait a minute, wait a minute,' and he turns on the radio and he says, 'Dance with me. I'm George Raft.' And she has to do that at that time. It's the moment of transporting herself from that moment of reality, back in time. She's afraid of being hurt, and having this not be magical and being laughed at, but the need to dance is more important.

"So she does it, and in the moment of dancing she becomes young again, and she becomes embarrassed afterwards, and joy-filled for that experience. All of those things happen. Now, who can't relate to that, male or female, old or young? That is the magical moment which combines what was written by the playwright with the work of the actors. I've never experienced as much magic in the theater as that moment. I've never seen an audience transported like that. They become very important, because they become very still. They become involved in the music and the dance. Afterwards, they break out in laughter and applause, and then they cheer. It's a magical moment."

"I'm really glad to be an actor in the twentieth century and not the nineteenth," said Christopher. "In theater history class we learned about the days of the actor/managers. The great guys like Macready and Kean. They would go on tour but they planned all their effects ahead of time by themselves. They would learn the great classical roles like an opera singer does and they would arrive at East Podunk and plug into the local company who'd been rehearsing under a stage manager for two weeks. On the day of the performance they would say, 'I do that speech there. I do the sleepwalking thing there. I do that over there,' and then it was 'Places please, everyone.' Everybody else in the company had to stay out of the way of the star, who in his own little world would do a preprogrammed performance for the audience. That was considered good acting in 1885. I'm really glad we live in an age when the audience wants the truth. They *demand* the truth. They don't want stars. They want a truthful experience in the theater and we have to give it to them. That puts more of a demand on us but I'm glad that we have it."

Shakespeare said the actor holds a mirror up to nature, but the meaning of nature changes. The truth of our existence today is different from what it was in the nineteenth century, or in Elizabethan or Greek or Roman times. The way theater is practiced also changes. What is the future for theater?

"I just hope that there still is a theater," Christopher said. "I hope that we will not be so homogenized that we get used to staying home in our space stations or colonies on the moon or wherever we live, where we punch up a video and sit there with our microwave ovens. I think because people have wanted to communicate face to face since time began, that even technology won't kill that impulse. As long as people allow that impulse to survive, we're going to have live theater."

"Regional theater trains audiences," said Elizabeth. "People are going to theaters at a very early age. They can't afford to [go] in New York but they are doing it outside of New York."

"It's great to see young people discover classical plays," added Christopher. "I went on tour with the Juilliard Acting Company in a play by Molière called *The Love Cure.* We toured some very, very heavy high schools and junior high schools in the Bronx and Staten Island and in Queens and Bedford Stuyvesant. We went places with our little laces and shoes and swords and funny hats, and we'd walk in there and there were some people there who would sit in the audience and would want to cause trouble and not show that they were going to be interested." Christopher's voice became hushed. "Within ten minutes they were hooked. That transformation we were talking about before *happened.* They stopped moving. They got into it. They started to respond and they were taken in by Molière, who they probably never even heard of before. If that can happen, there's always going to be theater."

CHAPTER THREE

TONY RANDALL

"To act is to do."

Tony Randall in "The Crucible"

Tony Randall was born in Tulsa, Oklahoma, and received his primary and secondary education in Tulsa schools. One of his teachers used to send home notes: "Please stop him from making faces." At ten Tony was the school comedian. "I don't know why. I wasn't good at sports, and I guess that's it," Tony said. "The kid who's good at sports has an acceptable way of showing off." Tony saw his first play—a school production—at the age of twelve and was hooked. He majored in speech and drama at Northwestern University and then moved on to the Neighborhood Playhouse in New York, where he studied acting with Sanford Meisner and "movement" with Martha Graham. Tony earned a living as a radio announcer and soap opera actor, and he made his New York stage debut in *A Circle of Chalk* at the Dramatic Workshop of the New School for Social Research. His first big Broadway role was the cynical newspaperman opposite Paul Muni in *Inherit the Wind* and his other stage credits include *Candida, The Corn Is Green* with Ethel Barrymore, *Antony and Cleopatra* with Katharine Cornell, *Caesar and Cleopatra* with Lilli Palmer and Sir Cedric Hardwicke, *M. Butterfly,* and the musicals *Oh Captain!* and *The Music Man.* Tony's films include *No Down Payment* with Joanne Woodward, *Let's Make Love* with Marilyn Monroe, *The Mating Game* with Debbie Reynolds, *The Seven Faces of Dr. Lao, Will Success Spoil Rock Hunter?,* and the trilogy of Doris Day/Rock Hudson movies: *Pillow Talk, Send Me No Flowers,* and *Lover Come Back.* Among his many television credits are his starring roles in "Mr. Peepers," "Love, Sidney," "The Tony Randall Show," and "The Odd Couple."

When I invited Tony Randall to be a guest in our series, he was in the middle of realizing his lifelong dream of creating a national repertory company. He had raised all the money required, and was preparing for the first season of his National Actors Theatre. Nevertheless, he agreed to join us. I was especially careful in researching the questions I planned to ask, because I knew Tony's reputation for accuracy. He had even corrected my grammar over the telephone, which served as a warning that I'd better do my homework if I planned to have a successful conversation with him.

Several of my guests had studied acting at the New School early in their careers, including Tony. After he sat down, he turned to me and asked, "Is *this* the auditorium where I made my New York debut? It looks different to me but it's not."

Although our series was about theater, each of my guests had also had successful careers in film or television. Tony had had success in all three: stage, screen, and television. I asked him how he accounted for that.

"I'm not so sure I've had that much success," he answered in his authoritatively clipped voice. "I've never been as big as Arnold Schwarzenegger. 'The Odd Couple,' which you would *think* was the biggest success I have been in, was not a success. No. We were always in the bottom ten. We were canceled every thirteen weeks. We never had a rating. But when it came back in reruns, then it went right over the top. I have never been in a success on television. None of the shows I have been in lasted. Isn't that amazing?

"One show—I can't remember the name of it—'The Tony Randall Show' was the name of it! It lasted two years, forty-four shows. 'Love, Sidney' lasted two years. 'Mr. Peepers' lasted three years. 'The Odd Couple' lasted five years, but only because there was a guy at the network who happened to like us. His name was Marty Starger. This one guy kept us on the air. With the others, there was no one to keep us on even though we had good shows and we knew we had good shows. We were proud of them. But the ratings weren't there and off you go. It's a ratings game."

Tony studied acting with Sanford Meisner. Part of the Meisner technique involves stripping away certain habits before getting down to the actual business of acting.

"When you're in acting school, you have problems," said Tony. "Inhibitions are part of your problems. The actor must free himself. You do have to free yourself. There are exercises to free you—relaxation exercises. If you remember Stanislavski's book, the first chapter is on relaxation, the total relaxation of all the muscles. Once you're totally relaxed, you're stripped away. It's hard to relax. It's especially hard to relax with a lot of people looking at you. It's something you must learn to do. That is a technique. You *learn* to relax. Everyone has to learn that, because everyone gets tense in front of an audience."

In Tony's book, *Which Reminds Me,* he says Sanford Meisner taught him that all acting is the same. There is no less, no more, whether it's for television, film, or theater. Acting is acting. You don't have to make it bigger for the stage, or pull it down for the camera. I asked him if that was one of the reasons for his success in all three media.

"No," he said, "and many people would argue about that. Olivier, who was more successful than I, and also knew more about acting than I, fully believed that you acted one way on the stage, and another way entirely on camera. It doesn't become me to say it, but I think he was wrong. I think if you only know Olivier from his movies, you might be inclined to wonder what was so great.

"Why was he called the greatest actor of the twentieth century? If you saw him onstage, there was no doubt about it. In movies, he believed that you have to act very small for the camera. Onstage, he believed that you had to blast it out so it could be heard in the last row of the balcony. The fact is, you don't have to blast it out to be heard, if you have a good voice. Actors with weak voices have to yell. He didn't have a weak voice. He had a very strong one, and he didn't have to yell on the stage. But when he was onstage, he was a wild animal. He went all the way. He was a possessed creature. He was demonically possessed onstage. It was almost frightening to watch him sometimes. He didn't act like that on film. He was very reserved and, I found, mostly uninteresting. He was not *Olivier* on camera.

"I think he was wrong in his approach. I think he should have acted the same way in front of the camera as he did onstage, and he did once. He did *The Dance of Death* by Strindberg. There's a film record of it. It's not a real movie. It's just a television record of the production. But he really is Olivier in it, with that almost unbearable intensity and emotion. He goes all the way. He goes beyond what you think a human being could take. He just tore himself to pieces, as he did in *Othello,* and as he did in *Long Day's Journey.*"

If acting is acting, and you don't have to make it bigger for the stage or pull it down for the camera, does that mean that a film actor can automatically transfer his skills to the stage?

"It's been done," Tony said. "People who have never acted on the stage in their lives and have acted only in film come out onstage and have been very good. Generally speaking, though, they don't have much projection. It's a matter of training."

Much has been made of Robert De Niro's preparation for his role in the film *Awakenings.* It was so extreme that the director was fearful that he was taking on the neurological symptoms of the character.

"You've got to do that," Tony insisted. "He was playing an extreme case. Supposing you're playing a man who's dead drunk. You can't just turn it on and off. You've just got to get into it and once you get into it you tend to stay in it all day long on a movie set, because you're in and out all day long. You shoot and then you don't shoot for an hour. If you get out of it you lose your concentration. In the theater it's not the same thing. You just do it when you do the play. You're on the movie set eight or twelve hours a day. A difficult physical condition [is created by] what we call sense memory, not emotion memory. A really difficult sense memory is being freezing cold or having a blinding headache, something like that. It's hard to get it and once you get it, you hold onto it."

Marilyn Monroe studied sense memory as part of her training in the Method.

"I worked with her towards the end of her career," said Tony. "Whether she ever could've acted, I don't know. She had so many other problems that everything interfered with [her] doing good work. She wouldn't show up till four-thirty in the afternoon. That just drives you up the wall. You very soon lose sympathy with people like that. After about the tenth day of sitting around all day in makeup and you can't work . . . you begin to get fed up."

In comparing acting in theater to acting in films, is there a greater demand on an actor because of the need to sustain a role over a period of two hours?

"That's not hard," Tony said. "It's harder to break it up and do little bits. I've always found that harder than to do the whole thing from beginning to end, which seems natural. But to pick it up in the climactic scene and do one minute of it, that's hard."

In his book, Tony uses Marlon Brando as an example of an actor who understands there is no difference between acting on the stage and in film. He mentions the scene in *Last Tango in Paris,* where Brando is alone with his wife's corpse and he praises Brando's intensity and discusses how it isn't "pulled down" for the camera. Tony played a role that required a similar emotional intensity when he took over the part of René Gallimard for six months in *M. Butterfly* on Broadway. Very few successful film and television actors are willing to take a chance on Broadway anymore.

"I needed the job," said Tony, pleadingly. "Almost anyone would have taken that part. It's a marvelous part. In acting, it doesn't matter where you act. The medium doesn't matter. The theatrical form doesn't matter, whether it's opera or ballet. It's all the same. You must be human. You must live out the part. If you ever saw Margot Fonteyn dance, you saw someone *become* something. She didn't just do steps. There were people in the corps who could do the steps better than she could. She was not a great technician at all. She didn't have a good jump. She didn't have a great turn, but whatever it was, she *became.* She *became* a swan. She *became* Giselle. She became it before your eyes. She lived it. That's acting! You have to do that. You have to become something fully and unselfconsciously. It's easy to say, it's hard to do."

An actor is in the business of imitating human behavior. How does an actor take this into account when he prepares for a role?

"You've got to find out what the man wants," Tony stated, like an instructor going over the day's lesson. "That's what you have to do. What does he want? To act is to do. In life, we say so-and-so is a man of action. Character is not how you look or how you walk or how you wear your hair or your clothes. That's not character. Character is what a man *does.* In life and on the stage, it's the same thing. If a man smiles and he's warm and friendly, but tells nothing but lies, then he's a liar. That's his character. No matter how nice he seems. You have to find out what the man *wants.* That's not enough. What he wants *to do.* That's it! Then you have to take it one step more. What he wants to do *to whom.* Your action needs an object."

An actor puts himself into the shoes of the character, by substituting imaginary circumstances that make it possible for him to experience the kinds of feelings the character might have. Does this change the actor?

"No," said Tony. "Acting is my job. While you are doing it, it can be a very draining emotional experience. Mostly it's fun for me. That's not true for a lot of actors. It's not necessarily true to say you put yourself in the character's shoes. When we were students we argued about that every night. Do you become the character? Do you change and become that man or do you make that man you? There is no man. It's just typing on a page. It's an imaginary life. It's better to say, 'What would I do *if* I were he?' "

Does the actor's experience of getting inside the skin of other characters enrich the actor's life?

Tony shook his head. "I wish I could say yes. It would be a good plug for the profession. It's a wonderful feeling to feel good in a part, to feel you got there, but you never really get there. One of the good things about the theater is that you do it again and again. You get to restudy it and try it different ways. The best way to explain the experience is to say your life is going on all the time. From the moment you are born until you die, that's your life. It can be thought of as a river, but it's always your life. You can't lead another life. That's impossible. You can divert your life for an hour or two, but it's still your life going on."

Tony's first acting job on Broadway was in *Antony and Cleopatra,* which starred Katharine Cornell. Tony played a messenger who had to describe the battle of Actium in six lines, and he didn't go on until ten o'clock. To work himself into a state of rage before going on, he used to bang his fists against the wall and shake the fire ladder. One night, Katharine Cornell suggested he try *not* preparing. The next night Tony went on without preparing and gave exactly the same performance. Does this mean it's not necessary for an actor to feel the emotion he's supposed to be expressing?

"Acting without emotion is dull," Tony said drily, "but emotion is not acting. That's the big problem for people training to be actors. Stanislavski described emotion as the salt and pepper on the meat, but the meat is the important thing.

"You should prepare for what you have to *do* in the scene. Olivier's book *On Acting* is full of some good common sense. He says you should not be ashamed to prepare in the wings. A lot of actors are. You should also not be ashamed to vocalize in your dressing room; good, plain, decent common sense. When your character comes through the door, he has come from someplace. You must prepare that. Where has he been? What did he do today? If he just came from outside, was it raining? Was he late for his appointment? Did he have to climb steps? Does he have a bad heart? You prepare that so that when you come in, you are already living. You must! Otherwise, you are just an actor who comes in through the door. That's the basis of good acting, that you are already in it before you come on."

Another well-known actor used to shake a ladder backstage. William Charles Macready was known for his Shylock in nineteenth-century England. William Archer mentions him in one of the questions he sent around to the leading actors of the day in 1888. "Macready as Shylock used to shake a ladder violently before going on for the scene with Tubal in *The Merchant of Venice,* in order to get up the proper state of white heat."

"I was a very young actor when I did *Antony and Cleopatra,*" Tony said. "It was necessary to prepare. The man comes on in white heat. It's an impossible scene. He's just observed the Battle of Actium, which was the most important point in history up to that time. If it had gone the other way, it would have been the end of Rome and the rise of Egypt in world affairs. Instead, Rome won. It's what we call a 'messenger part,' where the action can't be shown onstage, so someone comes out tearing his hair and saying, 'What have I seen?' and describes it for the audience. It's never terribly convincing. The first one you will think of is in *Oedipus,* where Oedipus goes offstage and puts his eyes out. The messenger comes on and says, 'What have I seen! I saw him take the pin and stick it in his eyes.' It's a playwright's device and it's always terribly difficult to play. It almost always goes to a young, inexperienced actor."

When an actor is in a play and doesn't go on until quite late, how does he prepare for his entrance?

"Thanks God, it's been many years since I played a part that small," Tony said emphatically. "In *Antony and Cleopatra,* I'd come to work at seven and I went on at ten. I prepared for three hours! It was terrible. I'm not like other people. Others can relax, read a book, play cards, they do this and that. I have to be in it all the time. Once I come to the theater I'm there to work. I vocalize. I do calisthenics. I begin to go over the character's previous life. I reread my notes on it. I then play a five or six minute improvisational scene backstage before my first entrance."

The purpose of William Archer's questionnaire was to settle once and for all the controversy over the use of emotion in acting: *Does the actor have to feel the emotion he portrays?* The controversy began in Roman times when Horace told the actors of the day, "If you would have me weep, you must first of all feel grief yourself." In Archer's day, the French actor Constant Coquelin disdained the use of real emotion and the English actor Sir Henry Irving was in favor of it. Among the other major actors Archer sent his questionnaire to were Tommaso Salvini, Ellen Terry, and Sarah Bernhardt.

Tony guessed at their responses. "Bernhardt probably said no and all the others said yes. Bernhardt was very emotional . . . The point is *how much* emotion do you need?"

When we see an actor we like, we say, "He's so believable!" What makes us believe the actor?

"It's a very subjective thing," said Tony. "Unsophisticated audiences believe anything. In the early nineteenth century, the old barnstormers *literally* played in barns. In the nineteenth century, when we were a frontier country, we had a very small population, probably only twenty million for the whole continent. Almost everybody lived on the farm and most people could barely read and write. They could read their Bibles. At that time, we had a whole race of Shakespearean giants: Edwin Booth, of course, and his brothers, and his father and Edwin Forrest, and John McCullough and E. L. Davenport and James O'Neill. Mighty Shakespeareans, recognized as such all over the world." Tony's voice fell. "Today, we don't have any. When Junius Brutus Booth, Edwin's father, would tour around in barns and play *Richard III,* and he would come in with a horse, the audiences would think that since the horse is real, he's real. They were very unsophisticated people. Today audiences are very well-educated. It's harder to fool them."

Is good acting a matter of opinion, like a good painting or a good piece of music?

"Yes, it is," said Tony. "That has a great deal to do with it. The audience believes the play for the most part. They are following the play. If a barely competent actor comes on, and says, 'The baby's dead,' half the audience will begin to cry anyway. You can't do that in comedy. In comedy you have got to be good. You don't have that kind of automatic pull working for you. You have to be true, and you have to be funny as well. That's why comedy is more difficult. The main thing is that the actor has to believe it himself. If he believes it, the audience will believe it."

Can anyone learn to act?

"Yes," said Tony matter-of-factly. "Anyone can learn to act. Anyone can learn any of the arts. You can learn to play the piano. You can learn to play the violin. You can go to painting school and learn how to paint. You can learn these techniques. Anybody can learn them. They are not difficult. If you want to put in the time and practice you can go to ballet class. To be a professional is something else again, but you can learn the techniques."

Tony has compared charm in acting to musicality. He has said, "You either have it or you don't. It's nothing a director can ask of an actor."

"Again I'll quote Stanislavski," Tony said. "Stanislavski wrote two books. They are the bible on acting. The first is called *An Actor Prepares* and the second is called *Building a Character*. Every conceivable element in acting is discussed at great length in these books. There is nothing you can't find about acting, until the last sentence, when he says, 'But what can I say about charm?' You can act without charm but you will never be a star. Charm is what makes a star. Audiences *like* certain people. They just like them. And they don't like others, and it doesn't have too much to do with acting skill. Olivier was a star. When he came out onstage you could not take your eyes off him. He was simply magnetic. When Marlon Brando walked onstage in *Streetcar Named Desire,* no one who was there will ever forget it. When he stuck his head in the door and said 'Stella!' the audience was his. How do you account for that?"

I asked Tony if there was a specific moment when he knew he wanted to be an actor.

"Yes," he said. "I was twelve and I saw a play. As soon as I saw it, I knew I could do that. As soon as I saw them doing it, I knew I could do it *better* than they could. I have always felt that way. Almost all my life, I have felt I am better than any other actor. When I was a young actor working with people like Ethel Barrymore and Katharine Cornell, I'd sit there and think, 'I can act you off the stage.' I always had that confidence in my acting ability. Only two or three times have I felt, 'Oh my God, I could never do what you are doing. That would be impossible for me.' Three or four times I have felt that way, certainly about Olivier, and certainly about Brando, maybe about Paul Muni. It's the only area of life in which I have any confidence." Tony's voice suddenly changed and a certain wavering quality crept in. "I'm not a confident man. I'm a man full of insecurities and neuroses and all that. But about acting I am absolutely secure." Then the self-assured Tony was back. "I have always known I could do it."

What was so special about the acting of Paul Muni?

"He was an actor of genius," Tony said. "He had incredible intensity, powers of concentration. He had the entire range of human behavior at his fingertips. Anything that a man's gone through, he could act. He had an overwhelming voice. The greatest voice I ever heard—a piercing quality, unusually strong, with a tremendous range. A range I would guess of about three octaves. And he had an intimidating personality. He glowered. He was a strange, dark man. He liked me and he would kid with me in Yiddish, under his breath. He had that extraordinary quality of magnetism."

David Henry Hwang's play *M. Butterfly* is loosely based on

a true incident. A male Chinese opera star masqueraded as a woman in order to seduce a French diplomat and extract diplomatic secrets.

"They are both alive," Tony said, "and in this case, it would be useless to go into their lives." He waved his hand as if brushing something away. "The play is a complete fiction. It simply takes these fairly lurid facts and takes off. The play accepts the argument as truth, that the diplomat did not know [the opera star] was a man, whereas in fact he, of course, knew. The playwright is not talking about this case. The playwright is talking about faith. The play is about faith. Your faith means nothing if it's something easy to believe. Faith is only faith when you believe the impossible. That's what the play is about. It's not about a man not knowing the person he went to bed with for twenty years was of another sex. That's just the story. It's not what the play is about."

In the case of *M. Butterfly,* the audience knows more than Tony's character about the true identity of his lover. Did this present an unusual acting problem?

"No," said Tony. "Most audiences, even though they had been told, 'That's a man,' simply did not believe it. Even in the climactic scene, where the Chinese fellow strips down naked and puts on men's clothes, they wouldn't believe. You ask what makes audiences believe. Audiences *want* to believe. They believed that character was a woman. They did not believe the character was a man. They thought, there must have been some trick where they snuck a man in there."

Does an actor have to believe in the message of the play in order to act in it?

"Yes," said Tony. "Yes, he must. Every play has an ideological basis. If you are out of sympathy with that, you cannot act it fully. Somehow you have to convince yourself of the underlying message of the play. *The Odd Couple*'s basic ideology is about male bonding. It's very antifeminist. They say *horrible* things about their wives. Their wives have *ridiculous* names like Mimi and Beebee, and when you finally meet the two women, they're dingbats. The Pigeon sisters. The entire play has this bias against women, very much so, and all in favor of a world of men who love each other and get together to play poker, and need each other and don't need women. Unless you understand that that's what the play's about, you will just be playing the jokes."

Tony was the fourth actor to play *M. Butterfly* on the stage. I asked him if he saw any of the others.

"Yes," said Tony. "Gave me a lot of confidence."

In addition to switching back and forth from theater to film and television, Tony also has the ability to play both serious and comedic roles. Should comedy be played straight and not for laughs?

"That's right," agreed Tony.

If that's true, why is it that so few actors can do both?

Tony reflected for a moment, "I think I know the answer, but it may not be right. The actors who can play comedy, can play serious because it's the same thing. The actors who can play serious can't necessarily play comedy. The simple reason is that you must have a terrific sense of humor. Everybody thinks he has a terrific sense of humor. I've never heard anyone in my life say, 'I have no sense of humor.' But there are people who have very, very little humor in them. On the other hand, there are people who have a really good sense of humor. You've seen it in life as well as on the stage. In a party or a group, it immediately transmits itself. It sends out rays. People want to laugh, and a person who has a very good sense of humor knows he can make people laugh and that's it. Either you have a good sense of humor or you don't. You can't teach that to anyone. You cannot give a sense of humor to an actor." Tony looked me straight in the eye as he said this. His face was serious, but I had the feeling he would start to laugh at any moment. Then he added, "I think Paul Newman is a wonderful actor. Did you ever see him play comedy?"

I asked Tony which came first in his career, the ability to do straight roles, or his talent for comedy.

"I was such a fool when I was a young actor," he said. "I thought I was a romantic actor. It used to hurt me when audiences would laugh. Then I learned I could make a buck from that."

Comedy comes from extraordinary people in ordinary situations, and farce is based on ordinary people in extraordinary situations. But in both comedy and farce we still have to care about the people we are watching. What makes us care about a character in a play?

"In general, it's trying to do good," said Tony. "That seems to be it. But there are sympathetic personalities. This is a very interesting question. It's never been asked of me before. But isn't it funny, I had prepared the answer! Did you see *Grapes of Wrath* last year? There was something terribly wrong at the core of it. What was it?"

It didn't have Henry Fonda.

"Exactly," said Tony. "It didn't have Henry Fonda. You could *love* Henry Fonda. You could just love him. You wanted to die for Henry Fonda! You *cared* for him. Gary Sinise is a very fine actor, no question about it. But you didn't love him! Isn't that right? It was a beautiful production, well-acted, well-staged, but you couldn't love that guy. So there was a hole there in the middle of the production. You *loved* Henry Fonda! It just broke your heart when those terrible things happened to him. This guy Sinise seemed able to take care of himself. He was a tough guy. He didn't break your heart."

I suggested that the next level of humor, after comedy and farce, is black humor.

"No," said Tony. "There is no black humor. *All* humor is black humor. All humor is based on cruelty, suffering, aggression, hatred, bigotry. Everything that's ugly in human nature is humor. It's something terrible happening to someone else, and we laugh out of relief that it happened to him and not to us. That's humor.

"Comedy is something different. And wit is totally different again. I advise you to read Freud's book on wit, comedy, and humor. It's the best joke book you'll ever read, because he illustrates every point with a joke, and there are hundreds of jokes in the book and they are marvelous. Read it! You'll laugh out loud, and you'll steal from the book for after-dinner speeches. I'll tell you my favorite joke in the book: A man says to his wife, 'If one of us should die first, I think I'll live in Paris.' "

Tony broke up, laughing. "Think of the levels of meaning in that joke! He wants her to die. He's an idiot who doesn't think that *he* could die first. There are so many levels in it. Wit, comedy, and humor have almost nothing in common with each other. The only thing they have in common is that we laugh. They are totally different things. Humor is someone else's suffering. Real suffering. So it's all black humor. Something horrible. Someone slips on a banana peel. That's funny. Breaks his coccyx! It's funnier!"

When we laugh at something in a play, does that represent

a kind of enlightenment? Does our laughter help us gain insight?

"There are too many different kinds of laughter in a play to answer that easily," said Tony. "You sometimes laugh at big jokes, or you laugh at humorous or comic situations, but you frequently laugh in the middle of a tense scene, where a little joke has been added to break the tension. It's a technical way of telling a story and keeping the interest going, and you'll laugh much more because it's a relief from the tension that has been built up."

Tony is one of those people who has the mysterious ability to make people laugh. I asked him if his family found him humorous.

"That's the meanest question I was ever asked," Tony said. "I cannot make my wife laugh. Except if I cross my eyes. If I do that, she just giggles and goes out of control."

I was interested to hear Tony's assessment of critics—did he find them an asset or a detriment to theater.

"It's a difficult question to answer," said Tony, "because of religious prejudice. I'm forbidden by my faith. The critic should have a genuine function in the theater. If you read the theatrical criticisms of Shaw—there are three volumes of it—nine-tenths of the plays he writes about are long forgotten and the actors he wrote about are long forgotten, and yet his critiques are wonderful! You can read them just for the pleasure of reading Shaw, or you can read them to learn something about theater, about acting, about playwriting. The man was a giant. Who could write prose like that? I guess it's too much to hope that we have a Shaw. Most of our critics are pretty good. I wouldn't want the job, I'll tell you that. The problem is an unrealistic one and we're stuck with it.

"*Whoever* is the critic for *The New York Times* has inordinate power. You need that one review or your show closes. That's wrong. Even if he were Shaw! It doesn't matter who he is. It's Frank Rich now, but before that it was a man named Richard Eder, and before that it was Clive Barnes and before that Brooks Atkinson. The *New York Times* reviewer, whoever he is, makes or breaks a play."

I ended our session by telling Tony how grateful we all were for his work on behalf of live theater. I also told him I was grateful for his spending the evening with us.

"You should be," said Tony.

CHAPTER FOUR

WILLIAM HURT
AND
LOIS SMITH

"The mystery opened up through the theater is the imagination itself. That's the hero."

Lois Smith and William Hurt in "Beside Herself"

WILLIAM HURT was born in Washington, D.C., and spent his childhood in the South Pacific, where his father was director of Trust Territories for the State Department. When he was ten, his parents divorced and Bill's mother married Henry Luce III, the son of the founder of Time, Inc. Bill was sent to Middlesex prep school in Massachusetts. "I was a street fighter, a little punk kid," he recalls. One of Bill's teachers suggested he channel his anger into the theater. Although he enjoyed the challenge, he chose to study theology at Tufts University. However, at the end of his junior year he switched from theology to acting. After spending his senior year in London, he auditioned for Juilliard. Bill was accepted and studied acting with John Houseman. At Circle Repertory Company in New York, he has appeared in *Richard II, Childe Byron, Mary Stuart, Hamlet, The Runner Stumbles, Ulysses in Traction, The Fifth of July,* and *My Life,* for which he won the Obie and Theatre World Award. On Broadway, Bill was nominated for a Tony for *Hurlyburly.* His film credits include *The Doctor, Alice, The Accidental Tourist, Broadcast News, Children of a Lesser God, Gorky Park, The Big Chill, Body Heat, Eyewitness,* and *Altered States.* Nominated twice for the Academy Award, he won the Oscar for his performance in *Kiss of the Spider Woman.*

LOIS SMITH was born in Topeka, Kansas, and raised in Seattle. She majored in dramatics at the University of Washington and, after graduating, she came to New York to pursue an acting career. She got a job sorting checks in a bank from midnight to 8:00 A.M., and looked for acting jobs during the day. Lois made her Broadway debut in *Time Out for Ginger,* and then she met director Elia Kazan, who gave her a part in his film *East of Eden.* On Broadway Lois created the role of Josephine Perry in *The Young and the Beautiful* and appeared in *Blues for Mr. Charlie* and the original production of *Orpheus Descending* with Maureen Stapleton. She also starred in the Broadway revivals of *The Glass Menagerie* and *The Iceman Cometh* as well as the Circle Repertory Company's production of Corinne Jacker's *Harry Outside, Measure for Measure* at Lincoln Center, and the Steppenwolf Theater Company's production of *The Grapes of Wrath,* which eventually moved to Broadway. Lois's film credits include *Green Card, Fatal Attraction, Reuben, Reuben, Next Stop, Greenwich Village, Four Friends, Black Widow,* and *Five Easy Pieces,* for which she received the Best Supporting Actress Award from the National Society of Film Critics.

William Hurt continues to return to the theater, even though he has had major success in films. At the time of our series, Bill was appearing in an off-Broadway play called *Beside Herself,* and I invited him to be a guest along with his costar, Lois Smith. Before our session, I went to see the play, and afterwards I met Bill and Lois backstage. When I mentioned to them that, "Everyone is excited about our upcoming evening together; I know it'll be very rewarding," Bill gave me a wry smile and said, "That depends on *you.*"

Bill and Lois usually traveled together on the subway when they went to their theater, and they said they would prefer to continue that practice, instead of having me pick them up with the car and driver. We met at the restaurant near the New School. Bill still looked like the UPS man he was playing in *Beside Herself,* with his hair cut short and a heavy walrus mustache. Lois was effervescent, betraying none of the depressed impulsiveness of the lady she portrayed in the play.

In theater, both actor and audience participate in an illusion. The actor finds a way to believe in the character he portrays, and he gets paid for his work. The audience pays to watch the illusion. In our session, I asked Bill and Lois how the audience comes to believe in what it is watching.

"My job," said Bill, "whenever I enter a theater, is to suspend my disbelief, either as an actor or an audience member. That's my job. That's the first thing I do. That's the risk I take. That's the risk we all take. The mystery opened up through the theater is the imagination itself. That's the hero. As an actor, I don't *make* people feel things. I don't *make* people think things. If I did, I would be responsible for more than one person, and I can't handle the responsibility. My motive, when I go to the theater, is to enjoy and learn. The essential act of the theater is courage. There is no difference between me and the person in the last row, in terms of the courage it takes to come in here."

"When I go to the theater as an audience member," said Lois, "the magic happens to me. That's what I go for. Sometimes, if something is nagging me, I don't respond as fully as I might. I become critical instead of feeling something. When that happens, it's usually because I'm avoiding something. The real stuff for me to bring is my open and accepting self. That's when I'm likely to get the most from the experience."

Actors need to create a sense of spontaneity in their work. When actors work together over a four-week rehearsal period, and appear together in many performances, does this spoil the spontaneity because they know what to expect from each other?

"The depth and quality of your surprise in life depends on how much you are willing to know," said Bill. "If I have a dense and fully achieved rehearsal period, it *enhances* the quality of surprise in [my] performance, because then I can submit and trust the experience. When I trust, I am always surprised. I can look at the same pinhead ten thousand times, and I can always find something new about it. Acting is work, and the work helps me to trust the moment. The spontaneity and surprise come from that trust. Nobody does the same thing twice, ever. I'm not God. He may see repetitions, but I don't. I live way too short a life. It's all very exciting to me. Every gesture is different, even with a very disciplined actor. I always see something different."

When we sit in a theater as members of the audience, we do our best to imagine that the people we are watching are real, but we never forget who and where we are. If we fully believed the illusion, we would rush up onstage and warn Hamlet that Laertes's foil has been anointed with a deadly poison. This is also true for the actor. He cannot forget his own reality and start to believe he is the character. He has to remember his lines, and the stage directions, and how to project his voice, and at the same time he has to try to think and act like the character. How do actors learn to function on several levels at once?

"That's nuts and bolts," said Bill. "That's just stuff you learn. If you are a carpenter, the most fun you can have with a sixpenny or an eightpenny nail is to stroke right through it. You don't have to hit it twice. It goes right to the nubs. But you don't just start doing that, because you would lose all your fingers. You keep doing it. There is nobody I know who isn't in and out at the same time all life long, sleeping and waking. There is always a double presence. In any skill there is the essential human fact that we are all in the experience *and watching* it at the same time."

If the actor is aware of his own presence, how does he pretend to himself that he is someone else in a different time and place?

"What brings that about is the carefulness and completeness with which you structure an imaginative reality," explained Bill. "That's what you operate from. That's why you have to be very careful about it. It's a very special thing, because you build walls in your mind, you build skys and attributes for other characters. You build aspects of character in yourself. You build relationships, you build histories of characters, you build sensory work. It's not sixty-five degrees in that room, it's eighty-five. All that stuff becomes an imaginative reality from which you move, from which you execute your verbs. Verbs, not adjectives. Acting is *doing*. Surprise and spontaneity are structured things."

In *Beside Herself,* Lois was playing Mary, an unhappy woman with a dead husband and a dead lover who committed suicide, and Bill was Augie Jake, a UPS man with a strong Italian accent. How does an actor get inside the skin of a character who is so far away from his own personality?

"At this point," said Bill, "I get as calm as I can before the first rehearsal. For about a ten-year period, I worked very specifically. I had the order of my approach to my character, the history, the relationships, the sensory awareness, all of it down to a very exact science. That gives you the privilege to relax, because the people you are going to be working with are different from the people you worked with before, and the situation will be different. You have to reconcile all those variables to your technique. That's a big job, because there are a lot of people out there doing a lot of different things. So I get real calm so I can take, without judgment, the strongest presences in the working situation: the ones who are going to lead me to the heart of the material. I don't preorder it anymore. But I still use all the tools."

"Becoming calm strikes a great note for me," said Lois. "The first thing that has to be present is relaxation, and the second is concentration, if you can divide them. In the last few years I find myself making a large gesture or sketch, like a big painting. I need to try out the big shape of a character and just barrel through. For me, it's an outline. Everybody in rehearsal is making a structure together. You're weaving a basket so you can live in it, and we all weave it together."

Does the actor know how the character is going to sound, or look, or move before rehearsals begin?

"Not usually before rehearsal," said Bill. "Sometimes you have a flash or an image, and if it doesn't bother anybody, you go after it. But often it bothers people when you come in with a preconceived idea. Sometimes I'll have a really strong image, and I'll come in and say, 'Now look, this is going to work, so please don't bother me. You don't see it now, but it will work, I promise you.' "

Some actors use the technique of working from the "outside-in" when they are building a character. That means they start with the physical attributes first. Others work from the "inside-out," looking first for the character's feelings. How does the actor know which technique will work the best?

"There is a story about Spencer Tracy and Laurence Olivier," said Bill. "Olivier was preparing for a role, the quintessential outside-in guy. He was backstage with his five-hour make-up job, and Tracy, the quintessential inside-out guy, dropped by and asked if he was getting in the way of the sacred preparation. Olivier told him to stay, and after a while, Tracy said, 'I don't know *who* you think *they're* going to think you are . . .'

"There is validity to *any* approach, if you are going to let it be brought out of nothing into something." Bill spoke slowly, deliberately weighing each word. "The first something out of nothing is craft; some structure, some stick building, some technique. From that comes rules of behavior, ethics, and from that, morals. Morals are your conscious connection with a power in the universe greater than yourself that helps you figure out what's right and wrong. Fundamentally, it's all technique, because theater is a device. The mystery of humanity is revealed through theater. The hero has the ability that every one of us has to learn about ourselves by looking at refracted light through our imagination. We use metaphors to do that. You have to have technique to build a metaphor.

"The amazing thing is that the need to work, to discipline yourself, the need for repetition, for hard work, for the risk you have to take, for all the foolishness you commit yourself to, all the endless courage it takes to do this, is born of a need for which there is no name. It's all an audacious risk. That's why I would say it's the suspension of disbelief. We really *are* all equals in theater. It's the truth. We *are* created equal. That's what theater assumes. Shakespeare taught us that compassion is a function of character, not a right or a wrong. The issues of theater are not politics, not docudrama. The issues of theater are the conflicts of the human heart."

"For me, as an actor," said Lois, "the magic is what seems to come unbidden, after you have been working awhile." Her voice took on an upward lilt. "It comes because you prepare the ground for it. It seems like magic because the conscious work has been done, and then it seems to come unbidden. That's the fun."

Bill leaned forward. "It's so much fun working with Lois because she's ready, and it changes every night. This doesn't detract from the meaning of the play in any way. I always like to throw a little salt in there. Lois is utterly spontaneous. She doesn't check herself one little bit. She goes right with it, and that gives me stuff back so I have to be there. When I come out on the stage I'm generally frightened, momentarily, before I can figure out what to concentrate on. I need something real to get outside of myself—and for me that's always the other actor. I drench myself in the other actor instead of thinking about myself.

"I have to be awake to the subject of the play, and that means that it's about my life, because the play is not irrelevant to my life. If it were, I couldn't do it. That doesn't mean I'm acting out my life through it. I'm looking at it as much through my series of windows and metaphors as anybody else. We are all looking at it from a different point, but there is room for everybody."

If the actor's performance is constantly changing, is there a point at which the director comes in and says, "Wait a minute!" How does the actor know when he has gone too far?

"That's an interesting question," said Bill. "[The director] will say so."

"Directors do come in and check it out," said Lois. "Usually performances deepen and get better. There are occasions when somebody goes off the wall. It can happen. There can also be differences of opinion about it."

"That's a point of pride with me," said Bill, "that's hopefully a point of reasonable instead of false pride, that as you do it you get better. A lot of people do it and it gets worse. I think that's sort of pathetic. If you take another shot at it and you don't do it better, go back to school. Start again. For instance, the first film I did we had an average of twenty-two takes a shot. It was really important to me to be better every time. And if it had been an average of a hundred, that would have been true, because you never see it all. It's too interesting. You may look like you're doing one thing, but I see *something else,* and I go, 'No, no, not yet. Wait. Try this again.' " Bill pointed to his head. "You can play symphonies up here."

How does the actor know when he has found the truth about his character?

"You don't," said Bill. "It's not something you call truth. It's something you sit with. It's a breath. That's why they say about acting, dancing, or anything: Breathe, breathe. What is breath? It's spirit. Spirit means breath. When you are just riding on the breath. Acting is not dissembling, and it's not lying. That's one of the things that burns my butt in my life. That the equation exists. The common conception of acting is that it's like being a really good liar. I'm not a good liar. I'm a *horrible* liar. Thank God."

There is a story told by the Greek biographer Plutarch about the comic actor Parmenon who was famous for imitating the grunting of a pig. One of Parmenon's rivals placed a real pig onstage where no one could see it, and pretended that the pig's grunts were his own. The audience heckled the actor, saying the sound of the pig was not as good as Parmenon's. The actor threw the pig at them to show they were judging according to opinion and not truth. How does the audience know when it is watching something truthful?

"There is a different deal in every culture about what the norms of the truth are," said Bill. "Truth is an absolute, but every time sees it differently. That's what's great. Just because a writer is dead, is his work dead? Have there been definitive performances of roles? No. Those who put their finger on their pulse in their time, in their way, are called classic because the resonance of their honesty with themselves is what you hear.

"Everybody can hear the rhythm of the truth, no matter what language. You can hear it. It's honest. It doesn't have an ulterior manipulative motive. Your heart can hear it."

In the beginning, the playwright knows the most about the play, because he has spent all that time with the characters he's created; then the director takes over, and presents his concept to the actors in rehearsal. Eventually the play belongs to the actors.

"When it works," said Lois, "it goes past all of us, and belongs to the audience. Sometimes you know you have done it, and boy, is that great!"

"There is a time period when each participant has his experience with the play," added Bill. "It's not a question of who knows more. It's hard to find a writer who can write a play and then rehearse without getting in the way. Most of that is a reasonable defensiveness. In film, a writer sells his work. That's one of the worst things we do. Hollywood makes him sell his work! When I found that out, I nearly turned around and went home. I couldn't believe it—that you could take somebody's words and change them around any way you want to and still put the man's name on it.

"Playwrights don't sell their work. It remains theirs. I was taught as an actor to respect that. You don't change words to suit your personality; that's a copout. You're an actor. I was trained that, as an actor, your job is to serve the play. Something more important is going on than what *I* am. So I dedicate myself and my work to the play. If there is a lie in my work, the director or the writer will change it because that's *their* job. My job is not to write. My job is to act."

The actor looks at the other characters and events in the play from the point of view of *his* character. The director and playwright look at the total picture. I asked Bill and Lois if they have ever said, "I don't think my character would say this!"

"There's a lot of struggle that goes on in the working process," Lois answered.

If it's a collaborative process, would an experienced author and an experienced director realize that eventually the actor might make a valuable contribution to one of the lines because of his unique point of view?

"Sure," said Bill. "But you start out by respecting [the writer's] turf. I've been through many different kinds of experiences that way, from neofascist to free-for-all. They're all fun . . . I guess." Bill grimaced. "But I give him his rights. He wrote the words. I don't change his words. In fact, it challenges me to break up my cadences, to break my bad habits. It challenges me as an artist, not pointing attention to myself, but pointing attention to the work. Something greater is going on, which we are doing together. It's greater than what any one of us is doing separately. That's one of the intrinsic elements of theater."

Is it comfortable for the actors to have the author there when they are rehearsing?

"It depends on the author," said Bill. "Some of them work really well, some of them don't. Some of them come in and have a tough time saying good-bye to the play, because they have to sign off. At some point they must say, 'I'm not doing this kind of work on it anymore; now I'm bringing in other artists who are going to do many things.' You can have one word and ten different people will do it ten different ways with ten different meanings . . . with a hundred different meanings. The playwright must know enough about his own craft, and enough about theirs. To have respect is really key, right down to the lighting guy and the gofer."

What happens with dead authors?

"There aren't any," quipped Bill.

How far can one go in playing around with the style of a play that is not topical or modern anymore, like the works of Ibsen or Shakespeare?

"That's one of the things which is challenging for actors," explained Bill. "I remember this guy named Harry Richie when I went to college. He had this tremendous course. You couldn't get in the doors. And he would spit and drool and everything, but his course was great. It was called 'Introduction to Modern Drama.' He would get up there and he'd say, 'The first line of modern drama is, "Sit down, Torvald," from *A Doll's House.*'

"So let's take it further back, let's say Elizabethan, Jacobean, Restoration, something like that. Okay, you got to wear tights. I've stood in many entrances, just about to enter, going,

'*What am I doing standing here in tights?* What am I doing this for?' In those moments I didn't give myself a lot of credit for asking that, but, in fact, it's the right question. You have to wear tights *because the other guy's wearing tights*! The guy you want [something] from will look at you strangely if you wear Bermuda shorts! And you won't get what you want! So you have to convince him that you're in the same world as he is. Because you want something he's got."

In *Beside Herself,* Bill's character, Augie Jake, the UPS man, first says he has a girlfriend, then he says he doesn't. The playwright doesn't explain which is the truth, but the actor needs to know in order to play the part. How does an actor make that kind of decision about his character?

"Building an imaginative reality means there are a number of answers you have to have," said Bill. "Who, what, when, where, how, and why. That's acting. There are a myriad of ways to go about researching and answering those questions. One of the things I do is I make two lists: 'What does my character say about himself?' And 'What does everybody else say about him?' Then I make decisions when I think the time is right about which are true and which are false.

"That was only covering three percent of the written preparation. In fact, those are the shortest lists I make. I used to write books. Even for a spear-carrier. Really. Literally. Thick books about the imaginative history of the character, where he came from, brothers and sisters, exactly what temperature the room was, where the wind was coming from. I'd get that all down. Now I kind of run it through quicker. There's a tremendous amount of investigation. As an artist, you have a right to do something which you don't have a right to do as a human being: to second-guess a motive."

Do critics influence the actor's work?

"I pay attention to my peers mostly," Bill said. "The great critics were Hazlitt and Shaw. The educators. And also the ones who were willing to put themselves on the line. The ones who tried to scope out the concerns of their culture and the purposes of art, and to help artists accomplish their goals. A mutual goal. I have trouble seeing that there's a mutual goal these days between the artist and the critic. If you look far enough down the line, they're out of focus. They cross paths before they achieve what I would consider to be a compassionate goal.

"To the extent that anybody brings up a moment that was really great, next time it's going to be down the tubes. But what it makes you do is find another moment. So it's helpful to discipline your mind away from the expectations of others. It's useful for any human being to live in your truth now. Not that you become the characters you play, but that you're informed by the work that you do. Life first. Your work is *for* your life."

In order to act, actors need imagination, intelligence, sensibility, passion, and control over their voice and body. If an actor possesses all these abilities, does he also need a technique?

"No," said Bill. "The Italians don't think so. Someone described how most Italian productions work, which is that they prepare like crazy in every department *but* acting. And then they just say, 'Live! And I'll follow you around with the camera.' I haven't yet made a movie there. But it's a little bit like saying, 'Act orange. Be yourself.' *What are you talking about?* Be myself? Be myself? Okay. Pow!"

"Do you think that comes from *commedia dell'arte*?" asked Lois. "Where they would put up a couple of lines about what the scene was and then you'd go out and play it?"

"There's craft in all of it," Bill said. "It's a form. There's a stage. There are four walls here. It's something that we craft out of our imagination. We built the theater, we built the form. It's an indigenous art form. Like music. They rise out of things in us." As Bill spoke, a quiet intensity and passion informed his words. "The art forms that we subscribe to rise out of instincts for articulation in ways that cannot be articulated any other way. That's why they're sacrosanct. That's why they'll live beyond the attacks of any perturbed culture in the meantime.

"I've been reading *The Mask of Apollo,* one of my favorite books, by Mary Renault. I haven't read it in a long time, but I picked it up again. I got it from a guy who was selling books in the street in those rows, you know? I remember this sequence where [one of the characters] is walking into a new city. He's a Greek actor. He acts with masks. And he sees this *perverted* vaudeville. An awful, awful thing that just riles him. He's sickened by what he's seeing. This dirty play that mocks the gods. Sexy, bawdy. And then he says he sees something that offends him worse, which is actors using their own faces.

That offended him because it was a metaphor. In our time we do use our own faces. I'll try to change things as much as I possibly can, depending on the moment. Some people can't stand it, they don't know that you can change a lot and still not throw the line off."

I asked Bill what attracted him to the roles he chose.

"In scripts, structure. Whether there's a theme that you don't know the answer to yet, [or it's] written well enough to make it worth your time to spend your dowry on, your energy, your life—to place your body, which is all you got, in that place for that period of time.

"And I look for the quality of [the play's] structure. I try to hear the resonance of the theme and I try to look for the quality of the structure. And when it's there, it's just like a light. You don't read the part. You don't read the lines. I don't pay attention to any of that. I try to listen for something I feel in here," (Bill pointed to his heart) "a dynamic structure. 'Does this mean something?' I ask myself. 'Does it mean something for every human being on the earth? Does it mean something for anybody that I can imagine ever lived? Is there a subject here, an interesting enough question that every human being that has ever lived or ever will live would be interested in, that might be important in their life?' I can't really answer that question with one hundred percent certainty. All I can do is hope that I'm asking the best question I can about that today. That's how I do it."

When actors act they have a lot of assistance. There is a director and other actors to rehearse with. There are sets, lights, and costumes, and an audience prepared for illusion. When an actor goes to audition, he has to perform alone, and the audience is composed of his prospective employers. How does an actor convince a producer or director he can act when he has none of the usual help?

"I don't think I'm very good at preparing for auditions," said Lois. "I don't do much. I read the material. That's about all I do. I don't know how to perform a part in an audition. I have to trust that a fairly early impulse is all there's going to be time to deal with. I may be saying I'm really lazy. That may be what I'm saying at this moment."

"It's the most awful situation," said Bill. "It's just terror. The first thing you do is you figure out why you're doing it. It's one of those basic things like, Why do you want to be in this play? If it's the money and you're starving, that's a damn good reason. If you're hungry it's a good reason. *Get behind that reason.* If it's *The Seagull* and it's Chekhov, and he's going to teach you more about acting in six weeks than somebody else can do in six years just by being in the production, then that's your reason. Get behind that.

"Go in there with something that will defeat the fear of judgment. Go in there with something that validates you and that gives you a reason to respect yourself in an unbelievably difficult situation. It's humiliating the way most people run 'em. Try to find something that you love about yourself and your reasons for being there. The principles that you're there for will give you confidence and then you have to make a judgment call between whether you're going to give them what you *think* they want, or if you're going to use it for yourself. And that depends on lots of factors. Try to be clear in your head with yourself because that way you'll walk out with your self-respect. No matter what they do.

"A long time ago some guy wanted me to help him cast these two summer stock theaters. He was moonlighting and he hadn't told them yet. So I went and I had this big, big pile of résumés. I was an actor who hadn't worked for money yet. I was sitting there, seeing how many actors there were! (It's amazing how blessed my life has been.) I thought initially, 'God, you're only giving them two minutes? How dare you! You mean you're not going to give them more time?' But under those conditions all you wanted to know is whether the actor wanted to be there or not. And you could tell by the way he got up onstage. Then, beyond that, of course you want skill and accomplishment.

"Acting and auditioning are basically opposite things," explained Bill. "If you're coming up with some preconceived notion of that character without having worked through a process to achieve it, you're really spitting on your own process. And that is one of the most ruthless parts of it all. That's why I'll tend to pull way back. I can get a job if I need a job. But I make sure I'm damn hungry if that's why I'm doing it. I really make sure that if [that's why] I'm going in there, I'm really going to manipulate and control that situation. And that's a crime. Commit that crime for the sake of a greater good . . . the greater good had better be good."

When an actor becomes successful, he has more of an

opportunity to decide where he wants to work. I asked Bill and Lois which medium they preferred working in.

"For me, I think theater is the first and dearest love," Lois said, "but I find them all of great interest. I think I'd rather work on a terrific television show, with wonderful people that I wanted to work with, than a so-so play. So it's very hard for me to make a formula of it, though the theater in a way comes first."

"To me it's all theater," said Bill. "All of it, though not when I'm home. In a play, at some point, someone's going to say, 'Okay, the curtain's going to go up and come down in two hours, see you around.' In a film, you can put your hand on a doorknob in September and come through the door in December. Those are very interesting exercises mentally. You have to remember that you are responsible (within the limits of your control). If my hand is in the wrong place when I come through the door in December, I've done something very wrong. I have to nail that. I have to be very disciplined, not only to be in the moment, structuring my character contextually, but also remembering continuity. The continuity that the script lady is never going to be responsible for. I love and embrace those challenges because, to me, that's what it's about. Get down to the nitty-gritty.

"Ultimately though, there is no difference. It's the theater. The theater is a ritual, and the ritual is we come together to purge ourselves of fear so we can be free to live and enjoy life. That's just as true in a movie theater and, if you want to take it that far, to where the electrons bounce off the satellites and into individual homes on television. There is a communal experience taking place. I prefer it where people gather in a theater and agree quietly and bravely to sit there together, strangers, trying to solve their humanity together. That, to me, is what theater is all about."

CHAPTER FIVE

CHRISTOPHER WALKEN AND MADELINE KAHN

"When people enter a room, they're up to something."

Christopher Walken in "Coriolanus"

Madeline Kahn in "On the Twentieth Century"

Christopher Walken is a lifelong New Yorker who grew up in Queens, where he and his two brothers were child actors. He attended Manhattan's Professional Children's School, but didn't start thinking about a professional career until he was twenty. He and David Hartman landed parts in the off-Broadway chorus of *Best Foot Forward,* which starred Liza Minnelli. "I'd have been a choreographer," said Christopher, "if I hadn't made it as an actor." He danced in the chorus of *High Spirits* and *Baker Street* and played Riff in the touring company of *West Side Story.* Christopher's early theater credits include *J.B., The Lion in Winter, The Rose Tattoo,* and *Sweet Bird of Youth* opposite Irene Worth. In film, Christopher has appeared in *The Anderson Tapes, The Happiness Cage, Next Stop, Greenwich Village, Annie Hall, Pennies from Heaven, Heaven's Gate, The Dogs of War, At Close Range, King of New York, Batman Returns,* and many more. He won the Oscar for his portrayal of Nick in *The Deer Hunter.* Christopher's commitment to live theater takes him to the Public Theater for plays like *The Seagull* and *Coriolanus,* to Lincoln Center for John Guare's *The House of Blue Leaves,* and to Broadway for David Rabe's *Hurlyburly.*

Madeline Kahn was born in Boston and grew up in New York on the Upper West Side and in Queens. "When I was in my teens," said Madeline, "I spent some formative years in a boarding school, which I didn't like very much. I used to hide in the rhododendron bushes and pretend I was lost." She won a drama scholarship to Hofstra University in Hempstead, Long Island, and her big break came when she made her Broadway debut in Leonard Sillman's *New Faces of 1968,* where she did parodies of a singer doing Kurt Weill and Mozart. Other Broadway roles include *Two by Two* opposite Danny Kaye, David Rabe's *In the Boom Boom Room,* which won her a Drama Desk Award and a Tony nomination, *On the Twentieth Century,* which earned her another Tony nomination, the revival of *Born Yesterday,* and Wendy Wasserstein's *The Sisters Rosensweig.* Madeline's first major film appearance was in *What's Up, Doc?* with Barbra Streisand, and she followed this with her Oscar-nominated role of Trixie Delight in *Paper Moon.* She received a second Oscar nomination as Lili Von Shtupp in Mel Brooks's *Blazing Saddles.* Madeline's other films include *Young Frankenstein, High Anxiety, History of the World—Part 1,* and *Betsy's Wedding.* Off-Broadway, Madeline has performed in John Guare's *Marco Polo Sings a Solo* and the musical *Promenade.*

When Madeline Kahn appeared as a guest in our series, she was starring on Broadway in a revival of Garson Kanin's *Born Yesterday.* Her partner for our evening was Christopher Walken, who had just finished a run playing Coriolanus at Joe Papp's Public Theater. Madeline wore an elegant, short black evening dress (she was due at a formal dinner after our session) and Christopher wore a dark suit and black sport shirt. His buoyant charm gave no trace of the sinister psychopathic qualities he's displayed in such films as *Annie Hall, King of New York,* and *Batman Returns.* As Madeline and Christopher walked out onstage, they were greeted with generous applause.

When I asked them what makes live theater special, Christopher answered, "What just happened. I find it hard to ignore an audience. They are there. An old actor once said to me, 'What do you think they are, a field of cabbages?' The audience is there and that's what makes doing a show interesting."

Madeline said, "I find, for myself, that it's important to get back in touch with the kind of work you do in front of a live audience. In my film experience it hasn't happened that I get to do a whole role from point A to point Z. In theater you get to do it in one piece and you are in the moment and you get to explore yourself as an instrument. You don't get to do that in film."

"I grew up in musicals," said Christopher, "and I was used to performing in front of an audience. In *Pennies from Heaven* I had this dance number. I found that it was flat and it wasn't working. I said to the crew, 'Would you please just act like an audience. If you feel like laughing or making noise, please do.' And they did. And it worked. The element of the audience is cathartic and it's absolutely necessary. There is a scene in Tom Stoppard's *Rosencrantz and Guildenstern Are Dead,* when the player king says, 'I turned around and there was nobody there.' He's an actor. To turn around and have nobody there is not good."

"Had there been people there before?" Madeline asked.

"Yes," said Christopher. "They left."

"Because it could have been a rehearsal," said Madeline, "in which case there was *never* anyone there."

"No," said Christopher with a devilish grin. "They left. I don't know why they left . . ."

Is there an element of danger for an actor when he appears in front of a live audience?

"Depends on how you feel," said Christopher. "Look at Gunther Gebel-Williams in the circus. He gets into the ring with those tigers and he's perfectly comfortable."

"He knows those particular tigers, right?" asked Madeline. Then she burst into laughter. "Suddenly I'm asking the stupidest questions of you! What *is* this? We're going to become the George and Gracie show!"

Madeline made an attempt to compose herself, sitting with her back straight up. "I can say a word about the audience being dangerous. Having gone back to the stage from television and films, I find that in a comedy, every audience is different. Some people are very appreciative and happen to be quiet. It's an interesting phenomenon that audiences are different. Some are very noisy and vocally responsive, and others are not. But that doesn't mean they're not enjoying it. If you're surrounded by other actors who are going," (Madeline clenched her teeth and whispered) " 'Oh my God, it's because they're nervous that so-and-so didn't get a laugh. That's a sign. Now we're in trouble.' They stretch the message of the play out of line and the whole performance gets out of shape. That is a danger. So it's not the audience which is dangerous. It is seductive, since they're alive, to try and wring some response from an audience. [But] I don't think you should. You should let them be however they want to be. They paid. They're sitting there. Let them react or not react as the case may be."

Born Yesterday is a classic comedy that is fundamentally the story of an uneducated ex-chorus girl who rebels against the corrupt self-made businessman who is keeping her. In Madeline's production, there's a moment when she gets slapped, and then she cries. It's a serious situation, but the audience laughs. How does an actor remain in character and go on with the scene when she hears the audience laughing?

"That's part of the task of doing any comedy," said Madeline. "In a comedy you know the audience will laugh. It's part of the deal. You the actor might not feel that it's funny, but you're there because you know that it's supposed to be funny."

"Anything without jokes is not like life," Christopher added.

I asked Christopher if he found a lot of humor in *Coriolanus.*

He smiled. "A tragedy's got a lot of humor and a comedy's got a lot of darkness. I've seen different actors do different plays and it's funny what certain actors focus on. I went to see Richard Burton in *Private Lives* and I'd seen that play a number of times. In the second act he said, 'Death is a trick done with mirrors,' which is apparently a line from the play. I never heard that line before. I've seen the play many times, but I never heard an actor say that. And *that's* a comedy. A lot of Noël Coward plays, for example, like *Blithe Spirit,* are funny but also very dark. Somebody ought to do Noël Coward that way."

"I'd love to," said Madeline. "I would absolutely love to."

"He's got enough jokes," said Christopher.

Speaking of the mix of comedy and something darker, I referred Madeline to her own role in *Young Frankenstein,* and the scene in which she's raped by the monster.

"Yes," said Madeline. "What's funny about *that*? It's grotesque. I know when I'm in a Mel Brooks movie we're going to be doing some *low,* grotesque stuff. A lot of what makes sufficient numbers of us laugh, me included, is sometimes very broad, very low, grotesque, horrible stuff.

"*Blazing Saddles* was a lot of fun. It was a great collaboration and it was fun to go to work every day. You didn't want to go home. Mel Brooks was strong but he was tempered by Gene Wilder. Because they're opposites, you had a very harmonious collaboration there, one balancing the other."

Madeline herself seems to laugh very easily. Does an actor laugh on purpose to help make the audience laugh?

"You mean like my own laughter this evening?" asked Madeline. "No. I haven't contrived it. There are a lot of times I don't laugh at all when a lot of people *are* laughing. I'm someone who doesn't laugh a lot of the time. When I feel good and I'm in a certain energy level I do laugh a lot."

I asked Christopher if he looks for moments of laughter when he performs a serious role like Coriolanus.

"Sure," he said.

Coriolanus was done in a modern setting. Whose idea was it to stage it that way?

"Joe Papp wanted to do it and he made it happen," explained Christopher. "He got me and the other actors, including Irene Worth. Steven Berkoff, the director, had a way of doing it. That's the good thing in a collaboration. Nobody knows beforehand what it is, but if you're lucky, it turns out nicely. It's like cooking. You put things together and then you cook them and hopefully it's good. I never understand people who tell me what it is before. If you tell me, 'Look, this is what it is,' I think," (he snickered) " 'Good luck.' "

"You know there are directors like that," said Madeline.

"Of course," said Christopher. "I hope I never see them again."

"So you would tend to not want to work with them?" Madeline asked.

"Absolutely," said Christopher.

"And they probably would not be too happy working with you either," said Madeline.

"They wouldn't want anything to do with me!" said Christopher. "It's like animals in the forest. We stay away from each other."

"But what if," Madeline asked, "you happened, for some strange reason, to find yourself in a project with someone who *did* have a vision of what they were going to make it be?"

Christopher shifted in his chair. "Then I'd have to believe that they were so wonderful that I would surrender my own self. *Coriolanus* is an example of making a strange stew that worked out well. Sometimes it doesn't work out well."

"I have a feeling that your director had *something* in mind," said Madeline.

"Sure he did," said Christopher, "but it's especially difficult when you have a very specific idea and then you don't get cooperation. You never can tell what people are going to do. I saw Marlon Brando about twenty years ago on 'The Dick Cavett Show.' I thought he was being cynical when he said that acting was a roll of the dice. But in a way it is."

The revival of *Born Yesterday* seemed to be a stew that worked out.

"It didn't work out the way I hoped it would," said Madeline. "I wanted to take a new look at the play and focus on some of the values which weren't so important back in the forties, but which are now. My attitude was, let's find it, and it didn't turn out that way. I found new values in my own performance, but I wanted it to be true for the rest of the production."

Billie Dawn was originally played by Judy Holliday, whose appearance in the role still lives on in the film version. I asked Madeline how her concept of Billie differed from Holliday's legendary performance.

"There is a big difference," she said. "Judy Holliday comes from another period in time. She grew up in the twenties. She was informed by certain ideas of women which were different from the eighties. I feel that I'm more edgy and more aggressive, and I focus on different things in the play than she did. She felt much more comfortable with her softness and her femininity and glibly being the one who triumphed over everything. I don't feel that way about it at all."

It seemed to me that Billie had a lot of anger in this new production, which had the effect of producing a larger reality for the character.

Madeline nodded. "It's all in the script. It's what I find very interesting. I find her to be symbolic of someone who is very oppressed and who contributes to her own oppression because she doesn't see any other choice. Then she starts to see another choice, and she starts to change and finds it very difficult."

Is it harder for an actor to become somebody else on the stage than in film?

"There is a translation that happens in movies that doesn't happen on the stage," Christopher said. "On the stage, when people look at you, they are more apt to see *you.* If you meet somebody in person, you are more apt to get a true impression of them than if you see them on TV. A funny kind of translation happens by way of film. It has to do with your own attitude toward the camera, or the lack of audience."

Madeline was fired from the movie version of *Mame* on the first day she showed up for work. Lucille Ball, who was playing Mame, had seen Madeline looking frumpy in the film *What's Up, Doc?* and was surprised she didn't look that way in person.

"I was hired to play Agnes Gooch in *Mame*," explained Madeline, "and she would be different from me in appearance. I had come on the set and I had never met Lucille Ball. She saw me and I don't think she was pleased at all. She didn't give me the credit that maybe I'm really a good character actress. She reacted to me visually and she called me a Method actor in a derogatory way." She imitated Lucy doing a slow burn. " 'Oh, this is very dangerous, that you're going to develop a role slowly. If you have four weeks, you're going to develop a role slowly over the course of that four-week period, find your own way of doing it, and you're going to feel relaxed at rehearsal walking around the way you look. You're not going to be starting to perform on day one.' She didn't like that. It was her movie and she didn't allow it."

"It's horrible to have to perform prematurely," said Christopher. "I'm a member of the Actors Studio, although in all my years of going there, I've never understood what [the Method] was. I've tried. The only time I had a glimpse of what Method acting is, was when I was doing a scene for Lee Strasberg ten years ago at the studio. While you're doing your scene, the people who are going to follow you start setting up, so there's people arranging things. I thought I had done well, and afterwards Lee Strasberg said, 'Well, that was all right, but that man dropped a huge box of dishes during your speech.' I said, 'Yes, I know that.' He said, 'Well, you didn't even skip a beat. You didn't even notice him, did you?' I said, 'I noticed him but I didn't let on.' He said, 'You should never do that. When he dropped that big box of dishes, everybody in the room turned around and looked at him except you.' I said, 'I was rather proud of that.' He said, 'That's terrible acting!' I think that's true. You can't ignore life. That was my glimpse of what Method acting was and it was really the only time I ever thought I learned something."

For the actor to be successful, the audience must accept

what he is doing as truthful. How does an actor find truth for himself on the stage?

"Actors are unusual in that they are sort of like musicians," said Christopher, "but they carry their instrument around with them. You hear the expression, 'You're always acting, you're acting all the time.' I was always taken aback by that because I thought, 'I'm *not* acting all the time. I'm being perfectly like myself.' But on the other hand, if you are an actor, you've got your own violin with you all the time, so that if you're dishonest with people in a social situation, you are apt to be dishonest with them onstage, too. Actors have to practice all the time. In the last few years I've started to think about it that way. You have to remember that every time you talk to somebody, that's the quality you are going to bring to whatever it is you do when you work. Actors have to stay in touch with themselves. It's a cliché but it's true."

"*If* they are actors who want to bring truth to what they do," said Madeline.

"There's no other reason to be an actor!" Christopher stated.

"I agree," said Madeline, "but there are plenty of actors who 'do a good job' and they have a lot of fans."

"But it's not *fun*," said Christopher, "unless you bring truth to a role."

Madeline spoke quietly. "There are lots of other people who audiences of all types enjoy and who are praised. I don't know if you can judge such a thing."

"Maybe they have their own way," Christopher said. "I've met people that I didn't understand whatsoever. They were good actors. I can't even talk to them for five minutes. They're good actors but I don't know what they're talking about. But they're good actors."

Madeline looked thoughtful. "There's a kind of acting that has more to do with very skillfully constructing the outside portion of the character. They can do that and they are really *not* very in touch with their feelings, but they can *enact* feelings well enough . . . You may not be touched by it, but maybe you won't even know the difference. They have careers."

What is the most important quality for an actor to have in order to move an audience?

"Emotional power," said Christopher. "The power to emotionally move people. It goes back to the Greek theater, the whole idea that theater is basically a religious event in which you are changed, and when you go you ought to be altered. You come out of it knowing something you didn't know before. Otherwise, why go? It's like church."

When we are altered by an experience in the theater, does that happen because of the message of the play?

"It happens because of everything," Christopher said, "the whole thing, the script, the actors, the lighting, the music, the whole ritual."

If we go to see a powerful play such as *Death of a Salesman,* we may see it with an actor playing Willy Loman who touches us with his emotional power, or we may see it with an actor who doesn't.

"That's a matter of opinion," said Christopher. "I have my actors who give me that and you have yours. I don't think that there are definitive things about this. It's a matter of taste. A play like that almost carries itself. People tamper with Shakespeare, but the fact is Shakespeare will overwhelm everybody who fools with him. Do whatever you like, Shakespeare will be there."

Christopher once said that a Shakespeare play should be tackled as if it were a new play.

"That was one of the virtues of the production of *Coriolanus,*" he said excitedly. "It was produced as though somebody had just written it. I like shows like that. You're talking about your character. You have to look at it in terms of yourself. How else can you make connections? You have to look to your own life."

Can anybody be an actor?

"Anybody can do anything they want," Christopher said. "If you feel like being an actor, you can be an actor."

Are there any talents that are inherited, or can all the skills and all the tools be learned?

"I don't know," said Christopher. "You have to develop a skin that's very thick *and* very thin. I don't know how you do that."

"That's it exactly," said Madeline. "I'm still in the process. I suppose it's an ongoing process. I started off with a very thick skin, like, 'Wow, I know I can do this kind of a thing and I just want to get in there, into the marketplace!' In the very beginning that was my method of going about things. It was later that I felt, 'Gee, I'd like to round this picture out a bit. I'd like to use more of myself, and I really don't know how to use all these other parts of myself.' Then I proceeded to look into that and I was able to use more of my feelings in the parts that I did. I stopped performing so much and started to act more.

"I find that as I become more wholly myself, that I am more an actress than I am a performer. I don't really like performing. Acting does require, as Christopher just said, being vulnerable and honest and having a thin skin, so that everything does have an effect on you. At the same time, you have to be able to function in the world, and in the world of show business, which has a thing or two in it that makes you need a thick skin."

"In show business," said Christopher, "when they tell you they don't like you, it's not that they don't like your ice cream. It's not that they don't like the car you sold them. They don't like *you*."

"That's a rough one," agreed Madeline. "You have to live with that. You put yourself right out there. You're in business. Then if you are successful in having a life where you act, you are your own business. So part of it is that. You do have to have a strength, which is the thick skin, so that you can go, 'Ya, well, okay, fine, there was that review, and there is this and there's that going on and I'm just going to keep doing what I do.' You keep on exposing yourself, because there's something about communicating with people that you really enjoy, that you feel *compelled* to do."

In addition to the thick and thin skin, how important is formal training for an actor?

"I grew up in show business," said Christopher. "I was in musicals until I was twenty-five. That's my training. I went to different places and studied. Basically when you work with certain actors, like Irene Worth, that's the best. The good ones always show you everything."

"I studied voice a lot," said Madeline. "I was always terrified of acting class, so I avoided it as long as I possibly could. For whatever my reasons were, I just thought it was really scary. At one point I discovered this particular class I did go to, the Warren Robertson Actors' Workshop. I went in there and I was overwhelmed by what I saw and it really scared me. I thought, 'I really could use this,' at the time. So I did study there for a few years."

Because Madeline has a reputation for being funny, I asked her if directors ever just say, "Madeline, be funny!"

Madeline bristled. "If they do, I put an end to that very quickly."

Madeline has said that, "Comedy is created when someone is trying very earnestly to do what he feels is the right thing to do at that moment. For example, to eat the bottom of his shoes with great élan, as Chaplin did. When you see someone doing what they think is the right thing to do with their total self—when the audience sees that, and sees that it is not the right thing to do, from that comes the laughter." What *is* laughter?

"Laughter is a response that you can hear," explained Madeline. "It's a response that you yourself make at certain times. It's a spasm, and it comes through your vocal cords. There is this sort of staccato thing that happens with your voice. It's a spasmodic vocal reaction. Now what is that? Sometimes it's joy, but rarely. It's an expression of some sort of feeling about what's going on. As an individual, I have always been hypersensitive to what I see going on in front of my eyes. I think," (Madeline's eyes grew bigger) " 'Would you look . . . I can't . . . Would you look at that!' I have always been that way. I feel as though I came from some other planet half the time. It's all so amazing to me what goes on."

Christopher looked at Madeline. "Some people are just funny. I don't know why. You're funny! You're always funny, like even in the car you were funny."

"And that's all you can say about it?" asked Madeline with mock annoyance. "Can't you explain it?"

Christopher and Madeline had never met until their ride in the car to this session. Now they were rolling along like a pair of experienced vaudevillians. Madeline had become the straight man but there was humor in her sincerity. The fun came from her earnest search for the truth. Christopher seemed to stumble onto punch lines as he spoke with her. Comedy was being created while we talked about it.

"I think that's true," said Madeline, agreeing with Christopher that she was naturally funny. "But I don't know what *that* is."

Christopher began to egg Madeline on. "Who knows *what* it is?"

"Does that mean I can't do a straight play?" she asked.

"Of course not," he laughed.

"If there's any humor in it," said Madeline, "they're going to laugh."

Christopher said, "I read in Laurence Olivier's book that when he plays a tragedy, he looks for the comedy."

"I remember in college I did *27 Wagons Full of Cotton,*" said Madeline. She paused for a moment and then added with great dismay, "Did they laugh! There was a lot of humor in it . . ."

"There is," said Christopher emphatically.

"There is?" she asked.

"It's a hilarious play," he exclaimed.

"Oh," said Madeline, "okay, fine. I thought I failed."

"It's a scream, believe me," said Christopher. "It's never been done right."

Madeline cocked her head toward Christopher. "Either you're putting me on or you mean what you say."

She was having the same problem I often have with actors. She couldn't tell if Christopher was acting or being sincere.

"I'm deadly serious," said Christopher.

Does a comedy start to come to life in rehearsals?

"It depends a lot if the rehearsals are fun," said Christopher, "and that's almost what a director does best. If I was a director, and I never have been, I would try to make the rehearsals fun. By fun I mean that when people got there in the morning, they'd be looking forward to it, and when they left in the afternoon, they'd be waiting to come back the next day. The best rehearsals are always like that. No matter what it is, you enjoy yourself."

Can an actor recognize the comedy in a play by just reading the script?

"No," said Christopher. "You see it when you stand with somebody and they do something and you do something. That's what happens. Plays are not like books. They're not meant to be read. They're meant to be played."

"You don't see the potential comedy in a script?" asked Madeline. "Or the potential non-comedy in a flop script that's not funny?"

"Of course," said Christopher. "That's a professional way of looking at it. You never really know whether that's going to actually happen because you may get there and say something that you think is hilarious and the other actor looks at you like—" (Christopher made a quizzical face) "Then it won't work."

"Then it won't work," agreed Madeline. "But you can see it there in the script. I do believe you can see it on the page and you can also see when it's not there on the page."

Is it possible that reading a play can be very funny, and then when it's spoken out loud it's not?

"Look at the same play done by different actors," said Christopher. "One can say something and you don't even hear him say it, and another can say it and it rings a bell. Lines really finally amount to what they mean to you. Shakespeare is a particular instance of that, because in many of his plays the language is archaic. It's stuff that isn't even said anymore. Elizabethan English. In *Romeo and Juliet,* a lot of Mercutio's stuff. In *Measure for Measure,* a lot of Lucio's stuff. There are references to things that people don't speak of anymore. And yet, audiences are sometimes bowled over, laughing. When that happens, it's because *the actor* knows what he's talking about. The audience doesn't know what he's talking about. All they know is, 'If you're having a good time, I'm having a good time. If you think it's funny, I do [too].' "

Even if actors can't tell how a project is going to turn out, is there a moment when an actor realizes he's involved in something special and that his performance will be part of that?

"I know exactly what you mean," said Christopher, "and you're right. But I don't like to talk about mystical things. I think you're absolutely right. There is a point in special things but I can't possibly name or articulate or describe that."

Even when a script is brought to life by experienced actors, directors, and producers, it may still turn out to be a flop. Does an actor know when she is involved in a project that is *not* going to make it?

"I usually know pretty soon," said Madeline. "But I'm not in control of it. So why am I in it if I know that it's not going to succeed? I'm not including *Born Yesterday,* which obviously works. I've been in some movies that haven't worked and I knew that they were not good from the minute I read them. What I knew was that I needed to work and I knew it wasn't terrible. It wasn't embarrassing. It had some merit and some class, something going for it. If, in fact, it was done to a tee, it could be all right. Very few things are done to a tee.

"Why does it go forward? Boy, you got me there! I just really don't understand why some people can look at a project and put down the money they put down on it when it's just not there. *I* knew it wasn't there! I'm not the one who's in the position to make it happen. I say, 'Well yeah, I'll do this job,' because I feel I can do this job and kind of float away unscathed. And that, unfortunately, has been what I've done sometimes. I am amazed, myself, that they can't see that it's just really not there."

"It's funny how people think that actors make all these career choices," added Christopher. "They say, 'Why did you do this movie?' It's a job, you go to work. There's this notion that actors sit around making these artistic choices. I don't think that's true. Maybe some do, but that's a very, very rarefied group. Most actors act first to be busy. Everybody likes to go to work. You go to work to make a living and you go to work to go somewhere. It's funny how people think, 'Why did you do *The Ninja from Mars*?' I did it because I wasn't doing anything else!"

An actor goes through many stages of getting to know his character before he actually performs the role. Before rehearsing with the director what does an actor do on his own to begin working on his part?

"I read the script about one hundred times," said Christopher. "I focus on my own lines, and I think about how I would say it. In other words, I paraphrase it for myself. I look at what everyone else has to say. I try to understand what's going on. One of the things they tell you in acting class is when you go into a scene, ask yourself, 'What do I want?' Usually in life when people enter a room, they're up to something. Even if it's very subtle. They want a sandwich. They want a divorce. They want *something*."

"If you don't have an intention, you're very boring," said Madeline.

Does the playwright specify what each character wants in a scene?

"Sometimes," said Christopher.

Can an actor choose a goal for his character that's different from what the playwright has written?

"Absolutely," Christopher stated. "It's shown in the great plays because they get repeated—Shakespeare, Tennessee

Williams, etc. As many times as you see them, you see different interpretations. It's like music."

Do different actors pick different goals for the same scene?

"Sure," said Christopher. "And it wouldn't be worthwhile unless they did. You don't want to see somebody repeat something. It's funny how many actors choose to enter the same arena that other people do, that other people do much better than they do. It's always been curious to me. I see actors who are very interesting and then they go and do something and they try to do what other people do and it's pointless because, in fact, all they have to offer is what's theirs."

"But what if they feel that that's a part of them that they haven't explored?" asked Madeline.

"It's funny to see people doing things that they're supposed to do," said Christopher. "It's always interesting to see how many fascinating actors there are who never pursue their own 'fascinatingness.' They just try to repeat what someone else did. They don't tell the truth."

If actors are expected to be truthful, what happens when they experience stage fright? How does an actor deal with that?

"Acting onstage has to do with a state of grace," Christopher replied. "There's no telling how you attain it. But if you don't have it, you can't do it. There's an act of faith in walking on the stage, because you can never tell when your mind might turn on you. You have to be comfortable with yourself about your part. I find that I either have stage fright or I don't. I don't have it, period, or I have it a lot."

"You can take that energy and use it," suggested Madeline. "If you can find a way in your part to use, 'Ooh, my character *would* be afraid at this moment,' then you're kind of pleased that you have that on hand."

Christopher laughed. "You play a really scared person."

"You work it right into the role," Madeline said, her voice building with enthusiasm. "Then, when it's gone, you're left hanging with—*nothing*!"

What happens when an actor forgets the lines?

"I haven't blanked out," Madeline said. "I've been caught when something happened unexpectedly, like a loud explosion or the lights going out. Other people have no problem ad-libbing. I just stand there. I don't know what to do."

"The audience is very interesting," said Christopher. "It

sometimes doesn't realize when something's wrong. I was onstage once [waiting for] a guy who didn't show up. I said to the audience, 'The actor who is supposed to come on isn't here and I'm going to go get him.' It was one of those theaters where you had to take an elevator down to the dressing room. So I took the elevator down and walked into the dressing room and he's playing checkers with another actor. We went back up onstage and played the scene and after the show I said to some friends of mine, 'I'm sorry that happened.' They said, 'What? What happened?' "

Many of Christopher's roles have been dangerous people. They have psychological and personal problems. Do actors make a conscious choice to get involved with these kinds of roles?

"Movies are so expensive to make that if you do something that works, you're apt to get asked to do it again," he said. "So in answer to your question, that's why I play psychopaths. I kind of got a ball rolling in movies. Theater isn't like that because the stakes aren't so high and people tend to take more chances in terms of casting. The truth is, I've been married for over twenty years, I've got two houses, I pay all my bills, I have cats, and I drive a station wagon. There is *nothing* eccentric about me. I'm a model citizen. All I'm saying is, I would love to play a part like that with a girl and jokes and no guns."

Even if it's easier for an actor to avoid typecasting in the theater, once he is cast in a role, the show's costs require that he work eight times a week. What can an actor do to give himself the stamina for this?

"You have to get sleep and eat and not stay up or smoke cigarettes," said Christopher.

"You don't have a shot unless you take care of yourself like an athlete does when they're in training," said Madeline. "Then you have a chance to do it eight times a week. What I find difficult is my mind sometimes does not want to do this now." She began speaking in a robotic monotone, " 'I do not want to do this now.' "

How does an actor get into a performance when she doesn't feel like doing it on a particular night?

"It's really a mind thing," explained Madeline. "Because physically I'm okay or, even if I'm not quite okay, I can kind of function if I'm a little under. It's never physical. If it is, you deal with a specific problem. It's usually mental." She became robotic again, " 'My mind does not want to do this part right now.' And you have to adhere to a rigid schedule on Broadway. You do it eight o'clock, two o'clock on all the designated days. Mostly it's fear that I won't be able to do it because I don't *want* to do it. It's fear I won't be able to. I've done the preparation. I really have prepared very well. All I really have to do is take the first step, like get myself ready, go over there, just take that first step. Put one foot in front of the other and then the play is so good that point A leads to point B. It leads to point C and before you know it, sometimes it's one of the better performances and I come out of that performance saying, 'That was very interesting.' "

"Do you find that sometimes when you're finished at night you don't wanna go to bed?" asked Christopher. "It's terrible. When you've finished a show, what you should do is go to bed, but you can't because you're all jacked up."

"You're wound up," Madeline agreed. "You have to wait for a few hours."

Do established actors still have sleepless nights before auditions?

"One of the first things I ever did was *The Lion in Winter*," said Christopher. "I was a dancer before that. I was dancing in the chorus and for some reason I got a job in the original production of *The Lion in Winter*, which was done on Broadway with Rosemary Harris and Robert Preston. It wasn't a very successful show but it got made into a movie. It opened in the early spring and it was closed by the summer. I went to a famous summer stock producer who was doing *The Lion in Winter*, and I auditioned for the part that I was just in on Broadway. After the audition he said to me, 'You're not right for the part.' "

By the end of the session, I found myself thinking like a producer. It's always interesting to cast actors in parts you would not expect to see them in. If I could find a script where I could use the seriousness of Madeline Kahn, and the humor of Christopher Walken . . .

C H A P T E R   S I X

KATE NELLIGAN
AND
CHARLES BUSCH

"If I really knew why I did it, I wouldn't want to do it."

© MARTHA SWOPE

Kate Nelligan in "Plenty"

Charles Busch in "The Lady in Question"

© CAROL ROSEGG/MARTHA SWOPE ASSOCIATES

KATE NELLIGAN comes from a fourth-generation Canadian family of Irish descent. At sixteen she won a scholarship to Glendon College, York University, in Downsview, Ontario. After the rehearsal of a school play, she switched her major from English to the dramatic arts program. "From that day forward, I never thought I would do anything else. I remember feeling comfortable for the first time in my life." One of Kate's professors persuaded her to apply for one of the two places reserved for North Americans at London's Central School of Speech and Drama. Kate won the place and within three weeks of completing the program, she was signed by the Bristol Old Vic. Her London debut came in David Hare's *Knuckle,* for which she won the London Critics' Most Promising Actress Award. She created the role of Susan Traherne in David Hare's *Plenty* and won the London Critics' Best Actress Award. Kate re-created her role in *Plenty* for her New York debut, earning rave reviews and a Tony nomination. She received two more Tony nominations for *A Moon for the Misbegotten* and *Serious Money*. She also appeared on Broadway in *Spoils of War*. Kate's films include *Dracula, Eye of the Needle, Eleni,* and *Prince of Tides,* for which she received an Academy Award nomination.

CHARLES BUSCH is the son of a retired record store owner who used to take him to community opera productions in Westchester. Charles was fascinated by the nineteenth-century artifice, from the paste-and-glitter costumes to the painted backdrops. His fascination with old movies fueled his desire to act. Charles attended New York High School of Music and Art, followed by the Northwestern University School of Drama. After graduating, Charles traveled nationwide with his one-man show *Alone with a Cast of Thousands.* The show had narratives that ranged from a film-noir murder mystery to an Irish ghost-story saga. Charles wrote "a little skit for friends" and called it *Vampire Lesbians of Sodom.* He staged the show at the Limbo Lounge on Avenue C in New York, with himself in the lead as a sacrificial virgin in ancient Sodom. The show eventually ran for over five years off-Broadway and led to the formation of Charles's own company, Theatre-in-Limbo, for which he has written and starred in *Psycho Beach Party, Times Square Angel, Theodora, She-Bitch of Byzantium, Pardon My Inquisition,* and *The Lady in Question.*

After Kate Nelligan agreed to be in our series, I went to see her in Michael Weller's Broadway play *Spoils of War*. Kate played a sexy, hard-drinking, divorced mother of a teenager in the 1950s. In the words of Frank Rich, she was "a voluptuous figure in scarlet—from her Rita Hayworth pile of hair to her full lips to her drop-dead high-heel shoes." Charles Busch was equally voluptuous when I saw him as Gertrude Garnet, "the leading concert pianist of the international stage" in his original stage spoof of 1940s Nazi war films, *The Lady in Question*. I was amazed at Charles's ability to so totally transform himself. I was struck by the difference between the slightly built, rather shy-looking actor with sandy hair who arrived at the New School and his stage persona. In full costume, industrial-strength makeup, and raven-haired wig, he *was* Gertrude Garnet, commanding the stage as if wholly possessed by this vixen of his imagination.

Charles had said he was a fan of Kate's and I thought it would be fun to pair them together. On the evening of our session, Kate said she would have to leave early because her husband, who is a musician, had an important audition and she needed to be with him. Charles agreed to stay on afterwards.

The week of our session, Kate was appearing in A. R. Gurney's two-character play *Love Letters*. In the New York production, the cast changed every week, affording the actors very little rehearsal time. I asked Kate why the cast kept changing.

"Because none of us sell enough tickets to run more than a week," she said. "That's the honest truth."

Was it possible that another reason was that it's hard to get stars to commit for a long period of time?

"I'm sure that's the press-release version," said Kate, "but I think the real version is something different. It's very difficult to sell that piece, two characters *reading*, unless you keep changing the flavors."

The play is about a relationship between two people over a long period of time and it's told entirely through the funny, revealing, profoundly moving letters they write to each other. The actors read the letters aloud. But they are still two actors simply sitting on a stage. Can an actor build an effective performance when her partner keeps changing?

"He doesn't keep changing every night," Kate said. "I did it for a week with Treat Williams. Then tomorrow I do it for a week with David Dixon. I don't think [changing partners is] too much of a problem, because it's not in the strictest sense an acted piece. For instance, Pete Gurney, in the stage instructions, says it works best if the actors never look at each other. I never see who I'm talking to, and he never sees who he is talking to. You never look at each other, so there's absolutely no interplay in the conventional sense with the other actor."

The director says to the cast, "You must *read* each letter. This play is not about acting out each letter." Does that mean that the director and the author are asking the actors to improvise?

"No," said Kate. "I can't think of anything less improvised than *Love Letters*. It's almost actor-proof. It's like a little vehicle and it really doesn't matter who's driving it. It works so beautifully. That's why they can keep changing the cast and have it work again and again no matter who does it. I wouldn't be doing it if it was improvised. I'm really no good at that."

"I have a theater company," said Charles, "Theatre-in-Limbo, and we've been together about six years now. We are the world's *worst* improvisers. If somebody forgets a line, the other actors walk off. You can't depend on anyone! It's each man for himself. We are not Second City."

We believe an actor when he appears to be unpredictable, when we don't know what he will do next. Effective acting has *the look* of improvisation. Rehearsals make it possible for the actor to acquire that kind of freedom by setting up the structure within which he will operate. How much rehearsal time is there for *Love Letters*?

"There's no rehearsal in the conventional sense," said Kate. "Today David Dixon and I met on our own in my apartment, and tomorrow night we go in front of an audience. Under-rehearsed isn't improvised. They are two quite separate things."

What is the difference between improvisation and acting? Is it possible to improvise with a script?

"No," Kate said. "Improvised means no script or text, doesn't it?"

"That's what I always thought," replied Charles. "People ask me in our plays, 'Do the actors come up with their own roles?' No. I write every word of it. In some companies or plays, the actors sort of develop it in rehearsal, and they just kind of invent their own things and they freeze the best stuff, but we are strictly by the book. We don't change anything."

Would a play like *Love Letters* benefit from more rehearsal time?

"I don't think so," said Kate. "It's not an 'acted' piece. What Gurney is saying, when he says that, is: 'Please do not lead the audience to expect acted scenes. Please do not lead them to expect *that* convention, because we can't fulfill it. And we don't intend to fulfill it. So please read these things and allow that convention to remain intact throughout the evening.' That's what he's working within and he doesn't want it to be broken."

The characters in *Love Letters* are Andrew Makepiece Ladd III and Melissa Gardner. Typical Gurney, may we say WASPs?

"Oh, I think we *must* say WASPs," said Kate.

May we say rich WASPs?

"We may say *filthy* rich WASPs."

The conflict in the play seems to come from the different ways Andrew and Melissa deal with their feelings.

"She expresses her feelings right, left, and center," said Kate, "and it leaves him absolutely paralyzed. He doesn't know what to do with her, because he is so proper and respectable and restrained and controlled. He is a typical product of his background, and she is absolutely atypical, and a real rebel."

Actors have the chance to become people who are different from themselves, but some roles are specific physical types defined by the playwright. Do the actors in *Love Letters* have to have a WASP look?

"I'm trying to think of the people who have done it," Kate replied.

"Lainie Kazan hasn't done it," said Charles.

Kate laughed. "I think it's less important for the woman because they are playing kind of an offbeat version of that background. It's more important for the man because he is much more conventionally the product of Connecticut."

Actors seem to love being in *Love Letters.* Is it just as fulfilling as being in a regular play?

"It's different," said Kate. "It's not as satisfying to go into something which you haven't prepared together with a group of people, and that you don't have an enormous stake in when you open, and all of that. There is something a little saddening to me about two people who come together, do something for a week, and go away again. It's not what I think of as the theatrical experience. The theatrical experience is about people who don't know each other working their guts out and then failing together, and having an awful lot at stake in common. So I miss that part of the experience with this. On the other hand, it's a lot of fun to do and the audience loves this show. They have so much fun at the show, almost more than any other play I've ever done. If it can be called a play."

Kate has had a long association with the playwright David Hare. Hare wrote *Plenty* specifically for her.

"No he didn't!" interrupted Kate. "I have spent my life explaining this. He wrote it with no one in mind. In fact, the play was offered first to Diana Rigg, who is a player at the National Theatre. She [had] just had a baby and she didn't want to come back to work and David was going to wait for Diana to come back. His agent Peggy Ramsay was determined to get the play into a slot that Peter Hall had open at the National, and [she] said, 'Give it to Kate,' and he said that I was too young for it and that I was wrong for it, and Peggy, who is a legendary literary agent in London, just throttled him into giving it to me. So David put a script of the play underneath my door with a note saying, 'I don't think you can do this. If you think you can, you must take full responsibility for it!'

"And that was the confidence with which I entered this production. In no way did he have me in mind for it, although it is so associated with me that I can't seem to convey that to people. You know why that happened? Because there is a dedication at the beginning of the play. David has dedicated each of his plays to his children and his close friends and people like that, and that play was dedicated to me, but it wasn't written for me."

What happens to relations with the rest of the cast when a play like *Plenty* becomes a star vehicle?

"That play was produced first at the National Theatre," said Kate. "We played in repertoire three nights a week with other shows. I worked in other shows the other nights of the week. We were not a success there. We did not get good reviews and we did not get good houses. People assumed because it came here that some enormous hoopla had taken place there. So I never saw myself as the star of anything. I saw myself as one cast member with a great part in a play that nobody seemed to get.

"When I came to New York, it was very peculiar because I was brought up in the industry somewhere else. There aren't stars in England in the same way and you're not paid a lot of money and you're not made a great fuss over. I came here and I didn't even know I was being made a fuss of. I didn't even know what had happened. People started sending me telegrams, people I didn't know. I didn't know this behavior.

"There was some kind of political campaign on at the time and there was a Republican candidate called Lew Lehrman. And I got a telegram from this guy inviting me to a party. It turned out to be from Leo Lerman, who ran *Vogue* magazine. I never even answered it. What I'm trying to say is that for me, only in retrospect did I even know what was happening. I had no idea. I knew no one. I went to the theater. I went home. I didn't know a single person in New York except the people I was working with. I had no idea what was happening! I'm sure the American cast members knew but I was totally in the dark."

I asked Charles if he had specific actors in mind when he wrote his plays.

"I write the entire show for my group of people," said Charles, "every part, and I have now written seven plays for these same eight people. It's very real to me. I can't help but think that some of that must convey itself across the floodlights. There is such a deep affection there because we have worked together six years. But I have known them all a long time before that.

"I [originally] just called up some friends and said, 'What are you doing Saturday night?' There has to be some kind of subliminal message going out because we are all so close. We work so quickly that we rehearsed *The Lady in Question* in a week and a half. I don't think you could do that unless you had worked together. The actors didn't need coaching because they knew the style of the play, which is sort of a tricky one. In some sense they had actually played their roles before with different accents in other plays. It's delightful and it's very comforting to be surrounded by this wonderful feeling of well-being."

Do playwrights who are also actors ever write with themselves in mind?

"Every play I have ever written," said Charles. "I wouldn't know how to do it any other way. It's a terribly egotistical thing. I need to work. It's a wonderful position to be in. It's kind of an old-fashioned way of writing a play. If I was a great serious writer, I would have something compelling to say, and a vision, and I would torture myself for years, trying to write this play and then I would cast it with different actors. But from the beginning of my career, I was an actor as much as a writer, so it was just a question of coming up with vehicles for me.

"I was criticized by *The Village Voice* after *Lady in Question.* They asked, why would I be content playing in overproduced star vehicles? I think it sounds *fabulous.* I would think *anybody* would want to do that. So I write for myself and for this group of very special actors, and it's interesting to try to develop them as personalities. In each play I like to get them to do the things they do best, and yet also give them an opportunity to stretch in different directions. So that's very exciting for me."

Kate is Canadian and began her career in England. Are English theater audiences and critics different from ours?

"What I remember of the English audiences," Kate said, "is that they are far more restrained than American audiences. Here you're innocent until proven guilty in the theater and that's wonderful. People respond very warmly and that's nice. The main critical difference is that we had *ten* critics. It took ten critics to close a show there. You could get five really bad notices and run. Because five other people disagreed."

Is there a major difference between English technique and American technique?

"Oh yes," said Kate. "When I came to New York, I came to do *Plenty* and I stayed. I have lived here for many years now. Edward Herrmann is a very distinguished actor who played my husband, and just before we opened I turned to Edward and said, 'I think this company is better than the London company.' And he almost fainted. He's a very sophisticated man and he could not believe that. It struck me as extraordinary. There is as much bad work in England as there is here.

"English actors use the language better. They are taught to use the language well. It's the cliché that the feeling can ride through language; that language is not the thing that strangles the emotion, but rather the thing that expresses and frees the emotion and allows you to share in it. That's a great strength that English actors have. American actors are far more inventive and spontaneous and take a lot more responsibility for themselves.

"The business here is so much rougher than the business there. English actors have a very, very nice life, which no one can ever claim an American actor has. That's the main difference. You have a really nice life where you work all the time there and you don't have to think up projects. English actors aren't forced into creating opportunities for themselves, like Charles writing for himself and his friends. Here people say, 'What do you want to do? What plays do you want to do? What projects? Who have you got writing for you?' I think, 'Are you nuts? I'm an actor, I don't know about these things.' In America, you better know about them. You better know about them because the game is so rough here. And I don't. I spent too many years having projects just sent to me and I showed up and acted in them, and so I'm very bad at keeping my career going, because I'm not a producer. But it's nice to have worked in both places. It's nice to have seen what the two sides of the story are."

Why is it so much easier for the English actor?

"Because there's so much work," said Kate. "There are many more theater companies. I started working in 1973 and there were dozens and dozens and dozens of very high-quality repertory companies that you worked in. And it seemed the BBC was an organization that put out a hundred and fifty programs a week. Fine quality plays that real playwrights wrote and that were not filmed but taped in five-camera television. There was just an awful lot of theater in that country. Good television too, so everybody worked a lot. And that has to do with state subsidy."

What is the main difference between English and American actors?

Kate paused. "I think that English actors work so much more. You don't have to be a huge success there to work fifty weeks a year. If I had to define the difference, it would be that when you work with actors who work fifty weeks a year, they have a great deal more confidence and self-respect than American actors who never work. I mean American actors are treated so appallingly that it's very, very difficult to maintain your self-respect and your confidence as a performer. It takes so much more guts here to do this. That's my view anyway."

Why do American actors have to work harder to find jobs?

"It has to do with the much larger employment of English actors," said Kate. "There's a lot more jobs and a lot fewer actors in England. That's the other startling thing about America—*everybody* is an actor! In England it's as rare as being a racing car driver. You don't talk to fifteen actors on the street in one block. It's a very rare thing to do! The culture did not engender this notion that if you don't know what you do, you're an actor. It's a real skill and it's a real rare one. That's just accepted. It may have changed in the eighties, because I'm not current [about things over] there now. [Still,] it was an amazement to me to come here and have everybody I meet call themselves an actor! I couldn't believe it. And there's only four jobs in town."

If everyone fancies himself an actor, is that one of the reasons theater is not treated with the same respect here as it is in England?

"I have a theory about that," said Kate. "The theater is one product of a whole society and the rules that apply to industry also apply to the theater and television, and the restaurant business, and everything. I think that our society is in a crisis and that we're no longer prepared to demand quality in anything. It's a tiny thing about everything. People here used to make great theater and a lot of it. They used to make a lot of great things, but people stopped asking for it.

"I have a wonderful career and a wonderful life, but it is frustrating to see the swing in the New York theater that's happened in the time that I've been here since 1982. When I came here, theater actors worked in the theater, people who had paid their dues and learned how to do it. And that's not true anymore! That happened in seven years! The minute people stop going and say, 'It's not good enough,' it'll stop happening. But right now, they are selling tickets.

"I'm not at a place in my life where I audition. I'm at a place in my life where people either say, 'We'll give it to her or we won't.' It's not like at an earlier stage where you can sort of campaign for a part. I don't hear about something until it's offered to me. Or until I go to the theater and I look at somebody else doing that thing, and I think, 'Oh, I wish I had a shot at that!' "

The purpose of acting is for the audience to feel something, rather than the actor. When Kate appeared in George Bernard Shaw's *Heartbreak House,* at the National Theatre, John Gielgud told her not to cry so much onstage because, he said, "If you do, they won't." Was Gielgud saying that the more the actor feels something, or shows it, the less the audience will feel?

"No," said Kate. "What he is saying is, it may be a lot of fun for you to indulge in your sorrow and you may feel full of integrity and self-congratulation, but you leave me cold. That feeling isn't sufficient. You have to have enough of an outside eye to say, 'What is the effect I'm having on an audience here?' I am not of the school that says this should be more fun for me than it is for you. This should be an awful lot more fun for the audience than it is for the performer. It's a great deal of fun to go out and show how broad your emotional range is, and how deeply you feel, but for me as an audience, I can't bear it. I can't bear it. I don't believe it either."

"It just seems indulgent," added Charles.

The great nineteenth-century debate on emotion in acting centered around the question of whether an actor needed to feel the emotion he was portraying. Does an actor have to be grief-stricken in order to produce that effect in the audience?

"It seems to me that adjectives are really a bad thing for actors to have," Kate said. "Verbs are the things that actors need. What is the action? What is the verb? 'She *turns* away.' 'She *blushes.*' 'She's *avoiding* the question.' 'She's *pretending* she doesn't know what he means.' This is far more useful to me than 'She's shy.' "

Kate first trained at London's Central School of Speech and Drama, which was the alma mater of Laurence Olivier and Peggy Ashcroft. In those days, they only allowed two students from North America. Is that still the case?

"One now," said Kate. "When I went it was one. I was the North American entry. I was their token North American."

When Kate was in *Spoils of War,* she said that it had taken her eight years to be accepted for being herself with her own voice.

"Yes," she said. "It's the first time I got to use my own voice on the stage in this country. I'd never spoken in my own accent. I'd always impersonated English people. It was a great relief."

At this point Kate had to leave because of her husband's audition. After she walked off the stage to much applause, Charles looked in her direction admiringly and turned to me as if to say 'Wow!' I asked him if he could write a play for Kate, now that they had officially met.

"That would be a dream," he said.

Charles majored in drama at Northwestern. Did his training prepare him for a serious career in the theater?

"I grew up in New York City," explained Charles, "and I've been obsessed with the theater for as long as I can remember, so I was taking acting classes as a kid through school and through college. I'm sort of a throwback to vaudeville. After I got out of college, I wrote a one-person show, and I actually had a whole repertoire of different pieces that I did by myself, and I booked myself all around the country doing this act, so it was really kind of like Bert Lahr and Jack Benny and all those performers who did vaudeville. In a sense I learned the most in those eight years that I toured around doing that.

"I was brought up in New York and I had been going to the theater since I was a kid. I always had a pragmatic view of the theater as well as being enraptured with it. Starting from when I was in college, I got this feeling that maybe I was an offbeat type or it would be hard for me to pursue a traditional career as an actor. I always loved to write too, and yet I didn't take it seriously. There weren't that many roles that I was just dying to play. And that terrified me, because if you're going to go into the theater, which is such a crazy life with no security, surely there must be a whole slew of great roles that you're just desperate to play. And I couldn't think of those. So I started to think [about] creating roles for myself, where I could be unique and have something special to offer.

"Since the writing was always important to me, it just seemed the natural way to express myself and that's what I enjoyed most. Then it was just a realistic thing that I had to produce myself because I was unknown and I couldn't find management.

"So with great ingenuity and perseverance I booked myself around the country doing this act. And then, me and my good friend Ken Elliot (who I knew from college and who had been directing my one-man show when we started doing these little plays in the East Village), we realized that what we had and what we were doing just for our own amusement perhaps had commercial viability: *Vampire Lesbians of Sodom.* We just went around and learned and made mistakes and ultimately succeeded, thank God, in producing it ourselves."

In most professions workers use the same tools. Acting is different because the actor's instrument is himself and every actor, like every human being, is unique. I asked Charles if he gave a name to his particular acting technique.

"Just throw yourself into it," he said with panache.

How does a male actor learn to play female roles?

Charles smiled. "What I really learned was I didn't have to do that much. When I first started playing female parts, I'd watch myself on video after we'd taped it and I'd think, 'My God, I'm moving around so much and moving my shoulders and women don't do that unless they have Saint Vitus's dance.' So it was a question of cooling it and doing less. Maybe there's not quite so much difference between the sexes as we are led to believe. So I just had to calm down. The other thing is that I don't use a fake voice." Charles began talking in a falsetto voice. "I don't talk like this, which would be kind of monotonous and unnecessary. Look at Lauren Bacall, there are a lot of famous women who have husky voices. So I can sound much more like a realistic woman if I modulate my voice for use with the characters. It's not all that difficult.

"When I play female roles, it's kind of a liberating thing. It seems that women are *allowed* to be more emotional than men. They don't have to think so much about restraining [their emotions]: 'Oh, I got to be macho and can't show too much enthusiasm and I can't show too much sadness.' I don't have to be thinking about suppressing things. I can be more expressive. It's more flamboyant. It's more colorful. More fun."

Is it easier to express emotion as a woman on the stage?

"There are many women who I think are probably uptight or can't express emotion," Charles said. "That's not a strictly male province, to be uptight."

Is it more enjoyable to play women's parts because there's a greater opportunity to become emotional?

"If I really knew why I did it," said Charles, "I wouldn't want to do it. If you're good at something, you don't really want to quit. It seems to be something that I'm getting pretty good at, so why give it up?"

Charles's play *Theodora, She-Bitch of Byzantium* was based on a play that was actually performed by Sarah Bernhardt.

Charles explained, "I have read just about everything there is to know about Sarah Bernhardt. It's one of my hobbies. I find her fascinating. She was an incredible woman. In reading about her, she used to do all these plays that were written for her by Victorien Sardou. He was a very popular writer and he wrote wild melodramas for her. A lot of them we know as operas today, like *Tosca.* So he wrote a play called *Theodora* for Sarah Bernhardt, and it was a huge triumph for her around 1886, and I read all about it. It sounded like such a fascinating play. She kills somebody with a gold hairpin. It's just wild and you can see why she would love to do it.

"When we were first doing plays at this strange little East Village after-hours bar/art gallery called the Limbo Lounge, I just thought you could do anything you wanted. Everybody had this Mohawk haircut. They didn't care what they saw. I thought, 'Well, if they're so wild, there is no way I can be wilder than the audience.' I thought, 'I'll be Sarah Bernhardt and I'll do *Theodora,*' so I wrote a parody.

"In the nineteenth century, plays were very long. *Theodora* was a *popular* play. It wasn't a great classic play. It was like six acts, and it must have been about five hours long. The audiences had much more stamina in those days, as I think actors did. So I distilled it down to forty-five minutes, kind of 'The Highlights of *Theodora*.' I got the whole story in. We moved quickly. It was really fun, so I got to live out my fantasy and be Sarah Bernhardt with the hairpin."

Charles has written and performed one-man shows, which were actually plays where he performed all the parts, and most of them were male roles. He's done female impersonations and now he writes plays where he takes the leading female role. I asked him if he's acting or impersonating when he plays a role like Gertrude Garnet in *The Lady in Question*.

"I can't really be concerned with labels," he said. "Some people get very fussy about what they should be called if they perform in drag—a male actress? I just do it and hope you pay money to see it. I consider myself an actor. I play the part. I really don't see the great hoopla and difference between playing a male part or a female part, as long as you are believable and entertain your audience and have some truth in it.

"If I was just doing Bette Davis, I would think of myself as a female impersonator or something like that. But I like to feel that I have some integrity in the character. I don't think that I'm playing it very much differently than a female comedienne like Maggie Smith would have played the part. I'm sure that there's a level of satire just inherent in the fact that it's a guy playing this part that wouldn't be there if a real woman was playing it. But I learned a very interesting thing: When I first started doing these plays and playing female parts, I thought there would be a certain amount of humor that I could derive from reminding the audience from time to time that I'm a fella. But then I noticed that those jokes just fell flat whenever I would do that. I began to think that maybe the audience accepted the fact that, 'Okay, you're a lady, we buy it, go on with the story.' They didn't really like me to remind them that I was a guy, so I thought, 'Okay, that's fine, I prefer that. Just play it and try to play it with truth and believability and do it that way.' I hope I'm an actor. I hope I'm not deluding myself."

What is the difference between impersonating and acting?

"Usually," said Charles, "when they say female impersonator, to me it's something that you do in a nightclub and you're doing impersonations of a famous person. I don't do a specific person. I'm playing this original character, and a woman who has her own mannerisms that don't belong to a famous person."

When Frank Rich reviewed *The Lady in Question,* he said Charles had found his "most assured style as a writer." He also said, "*The Lady in Question* mimics its source material so accurately and affectionately that it is as much homage as parody." Clive Barnes called the play "serious, loving parody." Are these critics suggesting a new kind of theater has been invented?

"I don't think so," said Charles. "I'm a product of many things that went on before. Maybe I'm a new adaptation of an old tradition. What was interesting about *The Lady in Question* was that it was an anti-Nazi war melodrama from the forties, and it was like a lot of those old Joan Crawford pictures, where a selfish, glamorous lady gets involved in all sorts of Nazi intrigue and gets the best of everybody and learns a lesson at the end. What was fun about it was that we kind of had our cake and ate it, too. On the one hand it was a spoof of these movies, and you could enjoy it as that. But at the same time, we were trying to make it really suspenseful and touching, like the original movie was—and it seemed to work. It seemed that people could actually take it on both levels. They could laugh, and at the same time they could really get involved with it. I loved that. That was thrilling, sometimes it really felt like you were in this movie."

The reviews were ecstatic, but they all gave different names to Charles's style. Charles's work has been called "high comic characters in low farce."

"I have been beloved and reviled," said Charles, throwing his head back like a true diva. "It ain't easy. And they turn on a dime. These critics are wild. Frank Rich seems to be a figure of controversy. He *hated Psycho Beach Party.* What he wrote about me in *Psycho Beach Party,* Mengele didn't deserve. Your worst enemy you wouldn't wish to open a paper and see yourself described in the most horrible, horrible ways. So then we found out he's coming to see *The Lady in Question,* and you've got all your investors and you've got two hundred and fifty thousand dollars, including my Aunt Belle's money, in the thing. And your fate is in the hands of this man, who clearly loathes you. Forget it! So then the review comes out where he says," Charles paused as if in a trance, rather like Bea Lillie as Madame Arcati. "I have it memorized. (Well, you would too! I'd be rich if I had a nickel for every time I read that last line.) He said, 'It doesn't matter that *The Lady in Question* is a man. What matters is that the performer in question is a star.'

"So you can imagine the shock when this person who hates you says that. Now, I'm such a terrible hypocrite, because when people mentioned Frank Rich, I used to say, 'Don't get me started. He's destroyed the theater! Anything that he likes I hate!' Then he writes this and I say, 'He *knows* theater. He is *so* astute!' But of course they turn on a dime, so next time who knows what kind of list I'll be on?"

Who are the theatrical ancestors of the Limbo Lounge? Are they the East Village playwrights like Ronald Tavel, or Tom Eyen, or Harvey Fierstein? Or are there other more classical influences like Shakespeare?

"Ah, Shakespeare, yes, yes," said Charles. "That's who I'm really based on. I read a lot. Bernhardt . . . Nineteenth-century boulevard popular theater fascinates me. I've read so much about that. In a crazy way, that's a big influence.

"The first theater I ever saw was opera, because my father was a frustrated opera singer. He used to appear with these awful, awful opera companies in Westchester, sort of amateur groups. I just thought it was fabulous. So the first stuff I saw were these little theater companies. The extras were painted on the backdrop. The food was painted on the backdrop. I just loved that cheap theatricality so much, and the glamour.

"He did a *Traviata* and the woman who played Violetta, I just thought was the most beautiful, fragile, glamorous lady. And then I met her afterwards and she was this real big fat school teacher. A lot of kids my age might have been disappointed, but not me. I just thought it was fabulous that she could transform herself, and make us believe that she was this other thing. I guess in a crazy sense I'm doing that. I try to make audiences believe that I'm something so far removed from me. I love that kind of cheap theatricality. Critics used to say, 'He loves trash.' I took it as a terrible insult. Now I think, 'Maybe I do.' I love popular entertainment, pop culture and old movies, and that sort of thing."

There is nothing new about men playing women's roles. They did it in Shakespeare's time. But Charles is doing more than providing a vehicle for performers. In *The Lady in Question,* Gertrude Garnet goes through a series of transformations.

"I didn't realize it until much later," Charles recalled, "but I remember reading somewhere that most playwrights have basically one story to tell, and then they keep retelling it until they finally get it right. I tend to think that's true. I'm beginning to learn that. Basically I always tell the same story, and I have certain themes that mean a lot to me and that I identify with. *The Lady in Question* was a pure example of this kind of story, of someone who is battling against a closed view of life and is so involved with their own neuroses, and is being forced to see that the world is a wider place than just their own narrow concerns. *Vampire Lesbians of Sodom* is a wacky play, as it would have to be with a title like that, but yet there is a real heart to it. I like to think that it has a little insight into human behavior, and the need for friendships and for relationships."

Where does the initial inspiration come from for an actor to write a play?

"I'm really spoiled," said Charles, "because I've almost never sat down to write a play. We have a joke that I get the booking first and then I write the play. And it's often true. Kyle Renick runs the WPA Theater on Twenty-third Street—it's a marvelous theater. It's where *Little Shop of Horrors* started and *Steel Magnolias.* It turned out that he liked our shows a lot and I had dinner with him and he said he'd love for us to do a play at his theater. Since we had the booking I said, 'What kind of play would you like?' I have blueprints for a million plays. I wanted to do something in French music hall 1900, and he didn't like the idea. I had this big gown made for this big benefit that I was appearing in and it was this fabulous 1940s costume and I wore it once and then it was sort of hanging up in the closet. And the thing is, I can't just wear it to the Rainbow Room . . . I can't! If I don't wear it on the stage, that's it. So I didn't know what to do and then *boinggg!!* Forties. So I said to Kyle, 'What do you think about a 1940s anti-Nazi war melodrama?' And he loved it!"

CHAPTER SEVEN

HUME CRONYN AND JESSICA TANDY

"I'm going to pretend it's the first time!"

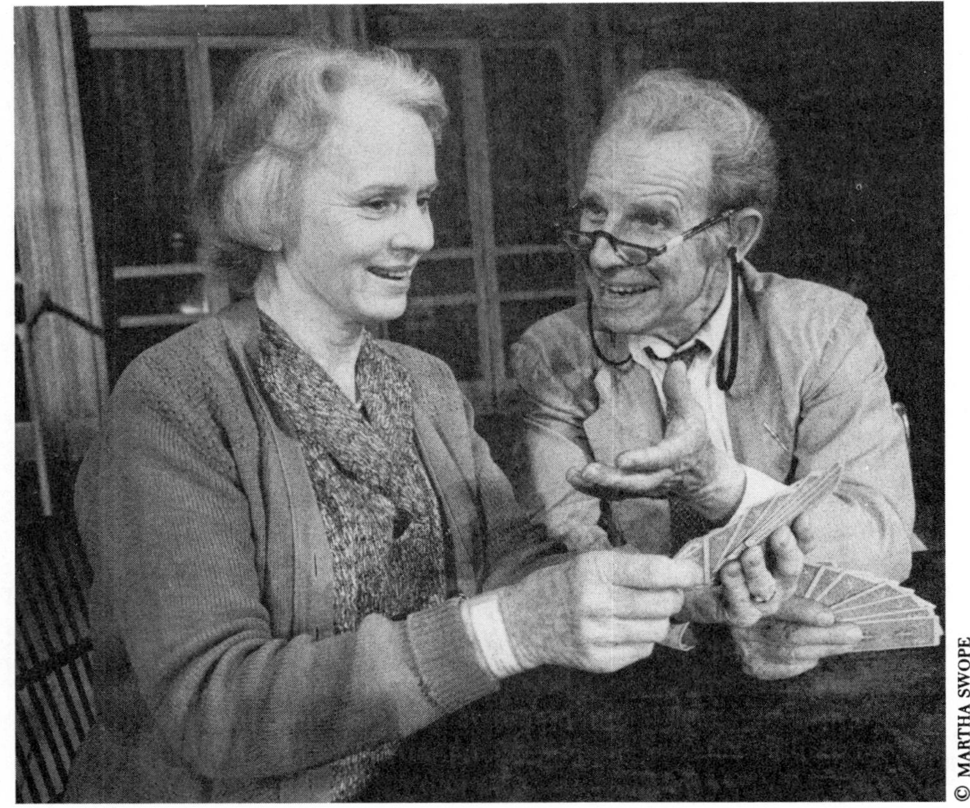

Jessica Tandy and Hume Cronyn in "The Gin Game"

HUME CRONYN was born in London, Ontario, into a distinguished upper-class family. His father was a member of the Canadian Parliament and his mother belonged to a noted Canadian brewing family. Hume was the youngest of five children and thirteen years separated him from his next-oldest brother. By the time he was six he was acting as a means of dealing with feelings of loneliness. Hume studied acting at the American Academy of Dramatic Arts in New York City. He made his Broadway debut in *Hipper's Holiday*, and obtained his "first really big part" when George Abbott cast him as Erwin Trowbridge in the national company of *Three Men on a Horse*. Hume has played everything from the prison guard in *Brute Force* to Polonius in Richard Burton's *Hamlet*, directed by John Gielgud. For this performance he received both the Tony and the New York Drama Critics Circle Award. His range encompasses plays by Tennessee Williams, Noël Coward, and Samuel Beckett. In film he's been directed by everyone from Alfred Hitchcock to Steven Spielberg. Hume has won awards as a writer, producer, and director. In 1979, in honor of their contributions to the performing arts, Hume and his wife, Jessica Tandy, were inducted into the Theatre Hall of Fame.

JESSICA TANDY was born in London, England. When Jessica decided as a teenager to be an actress, her mother "endorsed the stage as a dignified way for me to break out of my bleak life." She made her professional debut at eighteen in a small back-room theater as Sara Manderson in *The Manderson Girls*. Too poor to afford the five costumes required for the role, she sewed them herself. After joining the Birmingham Repertory Company, Jessica made her debut in London in *The Rumour*. Eventually, Tennessee Williams cast her as Blanche DuBois opposite Marlon Brando in the acclaimed Broadway production of *A Streetcar Named Desire*, directed by Elia Kazan. Jessica has played over 150 roles onstage, in film, and on television. She has acted opposite Laurence Olivier, Alec Guinness, and John Gielgud in plays ranging from Shakespeare to Shaw. She has won three Tonys, for *A Streetcar Named Desire*, *The Gin Game*, and *Foxfire*, and the Oscar for her performance in the film *Driving Miss Daisy*. Recent films include *Cocoon* and *Fried Green Tomatoes*. At last count, Jessica and her husband Hume Cronyn have appeared together eleven times onstage and seven times in film, in productions such as *The Four Poster*, *A Delicate Balance*, and *Happy Days*.

I had never met Hume Cronyn and Jessica Tandy, but like most of us, I had seen them many times on stage and screen. I was amazed at how compact they were physically. They had brought so much power and variety to so many different roles! Where did it come from? Hume spoke in a somewhat gruff yet reasonable voice that seemed to have its origins in the lower part of his body. It contrasted with Jessica's beautifully enunciated, slightly English accent. Jessica's was a delicate beauty, with her angular features and fine white hair, but one could sense a power emanating from her silence and economy of movement. They are America's premier acting couple. I asked them if anyone has ever come up with a useful definition of acting.

Hume answered, "I can quote you one. Lynn Fontanne said, 'You speak loudly enough to be heard, and you don't bump into furniture.' I don't know that I could improve on that."

"There's more to it than that," said Jessica.

Since she did not elaborate further, I quoted Laurence Oliver, who said, "Acting is the art of persuasion," and George Bernard Shaw, who said, "The function of the actor is to make the audience imagine for the moment that real things are happening to real people."

"For George Bernard Shaw, the function of the actor was to read Shaw's lines *as written,*" said Hume.

"With all the punctuation correct," added Jessica.

A pattern was developing of Hume answering my questions and Jessica adding brief rejoinders. I resolved to try and change this, although something told me it might not be wise to interfere in the rhythms of this happily married couple. I looked directly at Jessica for my next question.

It is the actor's job to make the audience believe that what it is looking at is real and happening for the first time. How do actors create the illusion of *the first time,* especially when they act together a lot and are also husband and wife?

"But," said Jessica, "when we are playing, we are not Hume and Jessica. We are two other people. The most important thing is always to listen. If you don't, it gets very stale. You cannot give the illusion of the first time if you don't listen to what the other person says, which brings forth your response. If you are thinking about what you are going to have for lunch while the other person is talking, the audience will know it."

"There is a distinct difference between listening and simply hearing," Hume stated. "Poor Jessie has heard this *ad nauseum*—"

"But," said Jessica with a twinkle in her eye, "I'm going to pretend it's the first time!"

The tables had been turned with this remark. Jessica was displaying the strength I knew she had.

Hume continued, "Our longest series of performances together was eight hundred performances in *The Gin Game.* We have been married for forty-seven years and Jessie has had to get used to a lot more than eight hundred performances."

By the time the eight-hundredth performance of a play comes around, the actors know each other's dialogue and what is going to happen. They also know what to expect from each other. What can an actor do to keep her performance from becoming monotonous?

Jessica said, "You have to pretend to yourself, while you are listening to what he says, that he is saying it for the first time, and that you don't know what you are going to say next. You do know, of course, what you are going to say next, but you have to believe that it's the first time. Each night is a separate challenge. It's a whole new set of people out there. Also, neither one of us will play with exactly the same inflection every time. We will change it. The words will mean exactly the same thing, but the shift in inflection keeps it fresh and newer."

"Changing inflection is okay," added Hume, "but do not

change the words, do not improvise. Improvisation is a wonderful tool, absolutely wonderful and valuable, but once the performance is set, and once you come to an agreement with the director on what the interpretation should be, it's your job to reproduce *that,* performance after performance after performance, as truthfully as you can. It's almost impossible to answer your question precisely because you've got to listen, and listening is a very active matter. You can be absolutely still. In fact, it's better if you are absolutely still, but listen. To make yourself do that, performance after performance after performance, is one of the hardest jobs that an actor ever has. To find something fresh in what threatens to become horrifying routine takes a degree of concentration that is really exhausting.

"That's what's exhausting about a very long run, because those people who are out there tonight, they haven't seen it before, they paid (God help them) the impossible prices we pay today, and it's the old business of the illusion of the first time. You must maintain the illusion of the first time. How do you do it? *Listen. Concentrate.* An actor's awareness on the stage becomes very acute. Any experienced actor can tell that there's a lady in the sixth row who's got a paper bag, that there is somebody in the second row who's asleep, that the light on the third pipe has gone out. You can be aware of those things, but God help you if you stop to really consider them.

"It's that insistence on concentrating on your character's intention, your action. What is that character after? What does he want? What does he *not* want? Whatever the action is, you've got to glom onto the intention and not let it go. You'd be dead if you weren't aware of the extraneous things, but they may not interrupt."

When we watch two actors in a scene, and one is talking, we watch the one who's listening. This is the moment when the magic click occurs and we begin to believe the actor. We say to ourselves, "Anyone can memorize a speech and put on a costume and pretend to be the king of France. I did that in camp. But to *listen* as someone else—that is something beyond my understanding." I asked Hume and Jessica how they manage to continually listen to each other when they perform the same play night after night.

"Hume and I have a great advantage in long runs," explained Jessica, "because we're not threatening each other in any way . . ."

"You threaten me constantly," interrupted Hume.

Jessica continued, "In a long run you very often find that you cannot change the intention but you can simplify and do less. You can make it better. You're not just going to repeat it every night, repeat it every night, repeat it every night."

Is the illusion of the first time created differently in film?

"You don't get a chance to do it as well in film," said Jessica. "I need that time of rehearsal, of trying, of experimenting, of getting past the stage of saying, 'How am I going to do this? How am I going to implement whatever it is I need the audience to know?' I need to get past that, to know why I am doing it as the character, not as *me.* I don't think you ever have the time to go as far as that when you are doing movies. First of all, you do things completely out of sequence. You may do the beginning of a scene today, the end of it three weeks from now, and the middle of it two weeks after that. How can you sustain anything? You're guessing."

How does the actor compensate for the lack of an audience when she is making a film?

"You are very concentrated on whoever it is you are playing with," said Jessica. "On the other hand, you have a lot of distractions with the camera moving, and people moving cables or other things. To shut them out is very difficult."

"You have to learn to shut them out," Hume said. "I find it less difficult than you do."

"I'm more sensitive," said Jessica.

Hume nodded. "Right on the button."

Although Hume and Jessica were not working from a rehearsed script, they displayed a perfect sense of timing. It was hard for me to believe they would enjoy film work as much as the stimulation of working in front of a live audience where the response to what they were doing was immediate. I asked Jessica which she found more fulfilling, theater or film?

"I prefer the theater," she said. "In the theater, if you don't get it right tonight, you can try again tomorrow, and every night until you finish. You can aim for an unreachable perfection. But it's very important to do film and television too, because the percentage of people who go to the theater now is so tiny. Also, who tours anymore? You don't do what we used to, which was to do a play on Broadway, and then take it on the road for a season. You don't get exposure to a lot of people anymore, which is very important."

Can actors work together on the stage when they have different approaches to preparing for their roles?

"I defy any two people to go about it the same way," said Hume. "Because we are all different. Yet we all aim for exactly the same thing. I was playing a complicated emotional scene with Olivier in *The Moon and Sixpence* on television, based on Somerset Maugham's novel about Paul Gauguin. I had a wonderful scene with Olivier, which was highly emotional. I said, 'Larry, what do I do with this?' I was expecting some careful, meaningful, inspiring analysis. He thought for a few moments and he said, 'Just give it a bash.' That's not bad advice. Sometimes you just plunge in. It's the adventure of taking the plunge which sometimes leads you to a triumph—or to disaster. There is no way of guaranteeing the result, but you have to take the plunge."

How does technique help the actor get inside the skin of the character?

"Technique," said Hume, "is a word which is often translated, particularly by young actors, to mean the more mechanical aspects of acting: speaking loudly enough to be heard, not bumping into the furniture, having proper control of your voice, knowing how to use your body, and other aspects of *the craft* of acting.

"The Cronyn definition of technique is: That very personal and very private means by which the actor gets the best out of himself or herself. That means you not only have to be a very keen observer, but you also have to be enormously aware of all the emotional currents that go on about you, even in the most mundane conversations.

"Almost all of us act all the time. I'm acting right now. I'm hoping to make a satisfactory impression on this audience. It's not the real me. I don't go around worrying about that. Underneath the performance that people give, there is always a current of some sort of emotion. If you become a keen observer, you will listen to what really goes on. It is generally quite contrary to the impression which is being given by the speaker . . . The big question is not how, it's *why.* To understand what motivates is all important. It's what makes the character tick.

"Let's assume you have the voice and the knowledge of movement and a sense of the stage. If you understand the *why,* the how will generally take care of itself because it will dictate what form it takes. One man who is in a rage" (Hume began to speak very quietly) "will control himself to a point where he talks very gently, and another" (he began to roar) "WILL GIVE YOU ALL SORTS OF HELL! It depends on the nature of the character; who he is. It's not difficult to fool people, but it is very difficult to be true. An audience will recognize the difference between when they are being fooled watching somebody who is simply accomplished (which any competent actor should be), or when they've seen an actor who has at least a smattering of the artist in him."

How does an actor begin the process of getting to know the character he will portray?

"The actor clutches so desperately for some sort of security that he may start with the character's *hat,*" explained Hume. "If he's got the *hat* right, he's got something. If he's got the shoes right, or if he understands the way he smokes his pipe, he's got something. Little by little, you absorb.

"Jessie works from the inside-out, which is what is generally admired. But I have some good company: Olivier used to work a lot from the outside. Fredric March, who I have directed, worked from the outside. It doesn't really matter where you start. The important thing is to end up with a persuasive truth. I get irritated with people who say, 'This is the path you must take.' How dare you say there is only one path to heaven and the person who is taking another path won't get there! It depends on each personality and what little by little gives you the building blocks.

"When I directed Fredric March in *Now I Lay Me Down to Sleep,* all he could talk about, to start with, was the general's uniform. I remember going backstage and seeing Larry Olivier as Othello and the first thing he did was show me his contacts. Larry had blue eyes but he had brown contacts made. You couldn't tell in the audience what color his eyes were, but they made *him* feel that he was more the Moor."

"For me, it doesn't work that way," said Jessica. "There is a great danger in that method for me. Once you get those superficial things, you are liable to get stuck with them, and you won't let go of them when you have found that you don't need them anymore."

"I threw away that hat," Hume said proudly.

Her mouth tightening in a smile, Jessica said, "Sometimes you don't."

Hume explained, "In some respects we do work differently, but the end result is precisely the same . . . Inner truth is absolutely essential. Without it, one is lost. That's what Jessica homes in on right from the word go. That works for her. I'm sometimes frightened that I cannot discover that inner truth immediately, so I say, 'I can see how he moves, I can hear his voice,' and I will get there eventually.

"I'm happier in film and television than Jessie is. The nature of the endeavor is one that gives you very little time. I have the gift—and the danger—of facility. I can do things quickly. Jessie can too, but she takes another approach. When I have worked with her in a play, after the second week, I will say to myself, *come on, come on.* Meanwhile, Jessie is already up there, because she has latched onto something true which gave her all the other things which I hit on first, which she considers superficial. Eventually, hopefully, I will catch up with her. I hate it when someone tries to say this is the only way. I don't believe it. There is no only way.

"To repeat: it's the personal and private means by which you get the best out of yourself. The best of the best is not the externals. Here we agree. It's the inner life, the emotional life, the core of the character. I can't read a play and immediately hit on that. I can't always discover what makes this man tick. I'll find out the how. You tell me *why* he does this. *Why* does he stutter? *Why* does he lie? *Why* does he laugh so easily? Why Why Why. It takes a lot of exploration sometimes to find that out. Jessie will home in just on that why. If I can sometimes get a sense of exactly what his laugh is, that can be very helpful. It gives me a security blanket."

"Supposing I am playing somebody who is very old and who has lived a different kind of life from me," said Jessica, "such as Annie Nations in *Foxfire.* If I go about it by saying, 'Oh, well, she's old, so this is the way she will walk' or 'this is the way her shoulders will bow' or 'this is the way she walks up the steps,' it doesn't work for me. I find that as I know more about the character, my body will do it. It will happen and I don't have to think about it."

With his voice rising, Hume countered with, "I'd like to suggest that, by the same token, if you find yourself walking up those steps," (Hume hunched over and spoke with a frail, weak voice) "as a genuinely" (he took a long pause and started gasping for breath) "old man, and you have to use the rail," (he grasped an imaginary rail) "and you find every step hurting in your knees and your hips," (another pause for breath) "that *that* physical thing will inspire in you some of the feeling with which you insist on starting."

I was beginning to feel like a referee in a boxing match. Hume and Jessica were competing with each other as they represented their totally different approaches to acting. Hume was using his body and forceful personality to physically prove his point while Jessica watched him, waiting for the right moment to have her say. It seemed that Hume was getting the upper hand, so I asked Jessica if she was okay.

She reassured me with, "I'm okay. He's off the rails but I'm okay."

Hume and Jessica are a wonderful example of two actors who work differently but successfully together, each preferring his own technique. But where does that leave the young actor? There are schools that insist, 'This is the way, work from the inside-out,' and others that advocate working from the outside-in. How does the young actor decide which technique will work best for him?

"Hopefully," said Jessica, "if the young actor goes to a school, there will be many different teachers who won't agree with each other. And that's fine, because that actor has to learn to work in this man's method and that man's method. Eventually, he will take the best and work in his own way."

Elia Kazan directed Jessica as Blanche DuBois opposite Marlon Brando in *A Streetcar Named Desire.* In an interview Kazan once said, "I have always felt that one of the most fascinating things about Jessica's performance as Blanche was that she made me realize what a lady the tramp character is. It was brilliant, totally intuitive acting." How did this interpretation of the part come about?

"I never thought of Blanche as a tramp," said Jessica. "To me, her behavior was dictated by her upbringing. She had been taught to expect that when she grew up someone would take care of her. She had a terrible experience when she was married, far too young, to somebody she discovered was a homosexual. She felt guilt for having said something so cruel to him that he blew his brains out. I think that guilt has been driving her behavior to try and get it right. That's why I think she had so many young lovers. She was trying to relive it and make it come out differently. So I never thought of her as a tramp, no matter how much sexual experience she had."

Elia Kazan also said, "Both Jessica and Hume have that extraordinary ability as actors to express the dimension of a character through a natural discovery process that does not involve a lot of neurosis . . . With Hume Cronyn and Jessica Tandy, there is no sloppy self-indulgent spillover into their personal life. It's the miracle of great acting. *They* don't get taken over by the characters. *You* get taken over by the characters." Does this mean that some actors have to believe they are the people they portray in order to act them?

"You have to believe, for the moment, you are the person you are portraying," said Jessica. "You have to believe in the truth of that. However, some actors are very self-indulgent."

"There is a marvelous story," said Hume, "which touches on that, about Olivier and Dustin Hoffman working together in *Marathon Man.* Dustin was playing a scene where he was supposed to have been running for miles and miles and miles. He is a very careful actor, who prepares meticulously, and he came to play this scene after he'd been running up and down, up and down" (Hume puffed, pretending to be out of breath) "and he was ready to play," (Hume began to pant) "and he said, 'I just ran around the block, let's go.' Larry looked at him and said, 'Did you ever try acting?'

"Acting is *not* reality. It's *the illusion* of reality! Am I going to come on and play Oedipus and have my eyes put out? Am I actually going to commit a murder? Am I actually going to die onstage? No! It's a performance. But it must be done so persuasively that at least within my imagination I've created a very, very vivid reality. Sometimes it's a painful process."

Does the actor need to feel what he is expressing?

"At some point," said Hume. "But do you think I can feel it for eight hundred performances? No way. Night after night, to say nothing of matinees, you have to come on and persuade the audience that" (Hume began to contort his face) ". . . you're close to tears. That what you have to say . . ." (he spoke, as if choking back tears) ". . . is very painful." The next moment Hume calmly asked, "Do you think I could put myself through that at every performance?"

To feel or not to feel, that is the question.

"You *must* feel," said Hume. "At some point you must feel it with a passion, and it becomes you. It's a very dangerous thing, because you can become indulgent and then it's not within your control. I can play that same fragment that I just played and burst into tears and it would be way over the top, and it's not what's needed. What's moving and touching is the terrible struggle *to contain it.* It's *the illusion* of reality. Behind it, one must have the experience, and awareness, the sense of what it actually is like to feel that kind of pain; it is almost impossible to reproduce.

"When I was about fifteen years old in physics class, I heard the science master talk about Kirchhoff's law of radiation. The hypothesis is that the best absorbers are the best emitters. Actors are in the job of emitting. *But you can't emit what you haven't absorbed!* Part of the actor's job is to embrace life, to discover as much as you can about how people feel. The broader the experience, the richer you are. It really doesn't matter how many flops you're in, if your aim is to become a really skilled actor. It matters a lot if you don't listen, if you don't watch, if you don't expose yourself to all the other arts. Some of the best advice I have ever heard about acting was written by Picasso in some of his letters. And the same thing with da Vinci. Other artists are constantly throwing things out which are fundamental to all the arts."

Actors have to believe in the truth of what they are doing, but they cannot completely abandon themselves to the character. They cannot totally forget their own identity or they would no longer be able to function on the stage. Does it ever happen that an actor feels *too much* and forgets his own reality?

Jessica replied, "The only role that I ever got out of control with—and I used to pray to God every night before I went on that He would let me break my leg or something so I wouldn't have to do it—was in a play of Beckett's, which was called *Not I.* All the audience saw was my mouth. Beckett doesn't say exactly where the woman is or what the circumstances are. When Beckett talked about it, he said that the mouth was constantly spewing out and couldn't stop. It was not in control of the brain. The woman is in absolute panic for twenty minutes. I couldn't move my head because the spotlight had to hit my mouth. They strapped my head in and I had to hold on to something so that my body wouldn't move. There were a couple of times when I think I had a small stroke in there. I was not in control of it, which was what he wanted. It was not like any other experience of acting."

When an actor creates a role in a successful play on the stage, it would seem logical she would be the best equipped to re-create it on film, as Jessica did with *The Gin Game.* But very often the person who does the play does not get the film role.

Both Hume and Jessica nodded. "It is a disappointment," she said.

"Bitter," he added.

"Yes," said Jessica, "particularly for *Streetcar* because everyone else in the original cast did the film and I didn't. But Warner Brothers needed a film name and I wasn't a film name."

"Neither was Marlon," said Hume. "Not then."

"You get chosen to do a film role for different reasons," Jessica replied.

"Frances Sternhagen gave a wonderful performance onstage in *Driving Miss Daisy,*" said Hume. "Jessica Tandy's playing it in the film."

Jessica smiled. "I think the only reason that I got the film was that they were very sure that what they wanted was an actress who was closer to the age. Miss Daisy goes from seventy-two to ninety-four, and I'm in the middle. Frannie's a lot younger than me and they probably would have doused her with so much makeup. Frannie's done an awful lot of wonderful work."

"But *you're* better known," Hume insisted.

"I've been at it longer," said Jessica.

It is often said that Marlon Brando should be credited with giving the American actor a style of acting, and that all contemporary actors have been influenced by his style.

"Marlon's style was so much Marlon," said Hume. "When you start aping a style, I would say, almost immediately, that that's bad. Don't copy, *steal*! If you see somebody do something brilliant, say, 'I must remember that. That was marvelously done.' But what you steal must be interpreted in your fashion.

"Years ago, during the days of 'Omnibus,' Jess and I did a play on television which was really written for Jessie by

William Inge. It was called *Glory and the Flower* and there was a young actor in that and I had a scene to play with him. When he first came on, he had real presence, real quality. There was no question about that. But, boy, he was all over the place, imitating Marlon from the very first day that I saw him. The stance, the intonation, the voice, it was Marlon, Marlon, Marlon. I thought, it's embarrassing. The director will stop that. It was like some sort of parody, very well done, by a very talented actor.

"I had a scene to play with him and this was live television. Live television is hair-raising because there is an element in it that does not exist on the stage—and that is the clock. At a certain point, it's over. If you extend pauses, if you embroider or God help us, if you cut, you have a frantic stage manager standing beside the camera, going" (Hume comically combined the gestures for speeding up and cutting, weaving his hands in the air and then drawing his hand across his throat) "and it can drive you absolutely crazy.

"I was playing the owner and manager of a sleazy bar and they had a little dance floor, which was crammed with kids. A fight broke out and I had to break [it] up and I found that I had to confront this particular actor that I'm talking about. I went on in the dress rehearsal" (he started looking around) "and suddenly a voice said, 'Here I am,' and he was behind me and I said, 'Get here!' I was a lot older than he was and better established. I said, 'Be where the hell you're supposed to be! We gotta be on the air in twenty minutes and I don't know about you, but I like time to have a pee.' He stood there and the director said, 'Knock it off, both of you!' So we played through and afterwards when I was coming out of the men's room and we had about ten minutes to go till air time, he came up to me and said, 'Mr. Cronyn, you shouldn't talk to me like that. I respect your way of work and you should respect mine.' I said, 'I know, I apologize.' The actor was James Dean.

"He met me on the street a couple of weeks later and he came up and he said, 'Hume!' and he threw his arms around me and I said, 'Jimmy, I'm very sorry about "Omnibus,"' and he said, 'Th-th-that's all right. You were nervous.' Boy was he ever right."

"I don't think it's true that all American actors follow in Marlon's footsteps," said Jessica. "There are many styles of acting. The best ones were influenced, but then they found their own way."

When a play is in rehearsal, which is better for an actor: to have the blocking imposed by the director or to leave it up to the actor?

"I could go either way," Jessica said. "It depends on the director. There are some directors who have to block. But I also want to feel free, after we have done this blocking, to say, 'Can I try something else?' Some of the directors will say, 'No, that's it,' and others will say, 'Okay,' and they'll let you try it and [then] they'll say either yes or no. The ones that feel threatened will be nervous about having any changes. Some directors, who are wonderful directors of the content, will be hopeless about directing traffic and then you can help. You have to learn to do it either way."

"You have to learn to do it either way," repeated Hume. "I personally, infinitely prefer to be allowed to discover my own moves, but I may discover a move that takes me far stage right, and the actor I am playing with has also decided that she wants to be far stage right. There has to be, at the very least, a referee."

"I want to be upstage center," Jessica resolutely announced.

"Of course you do," said Hume, "and you generally are." He paused. "I did a play by Irwin Shaw, which was a failure and was the last play the Group Theater ever did. It was directed by a brilliant director named Harold Clurman. Harold spoke about character, about what made the people behave as they did, more brilliantly than I've ever heard any director speak. He gave you such a sense of the life of the character you were playing that it was enormously enriching and you couldn't wait to put it on the stage. But he was not good about traffic, and people bumped into the furniture and into one another.

"So, in the last few days of rehearsal they brought on a stage manager from the Group Theater to help straighten out the traffic. When Harold had more than three people on the stage . . . things which other directors like Tyrone Guthrie did well, were not Harold's forte. I don't think it even interested him very much. So this stage manager came along and he moved us around and he sorted us all out, which was fine. And the stage manager's name was Elia Kazan."

Because of the collaborative process of the theater, the final product doesn't reveal itself early on. When did the cast of *A Streetcar Named Desire* realize it would become an important piece of theater history?

"I don't think you're ever aware until you play to an audience," Jessica said. "But it was quite obvious to all of us that it was a very special piece of writing and a great challenge. But you don't know. You can have a feel when you're working on it that it's a worthwhile play. Whether it will be successful, you just don't know. I've been in plays where, during rehearsal time, all of us know in our hearts (we would never admit it) that [it] isn't going to work. But you still go on psyching yourself up that it *is* going to work and you're going to make it work and then very often it fails. You can never be certain of success. But that was a special play."

Because Hume and Jessica are so secure in their different techniques, I thought it would be important to find out where they began their acting lessons. I asked Jessica what kind of training had prepared her for the stage.

"My training was to go to a theater school in London where the teachers were all working actors," said Jessica. "All of them were, and they were all different. We worked very differently in those days. We started off by doing scenes as well as the ordinary vocal training and so forth.

"I understand that now you don't ever do a scene until your second year. I would find that very difficult. One thing which was very important to me was I learned that there were many ways of going about it, because all the people who taught us had a different approach. We also did the classics. We got on with our Shakespeare. That's very good training. If you can do that, you can do other things."

I asked Hume and Jessica how they met.

"Well, I was working at the time," said Jessica, looking at Hume mischievously. "I was in a play on Broadway and Hume came backstage to see another actor who had been born in his same hometown. Hume *wasn't* working at the time, actually, and so we were introduced. That's how we met."

"And it was disaster," added Hume. "This actor invited me out. He had an eye on Jessie and the three of us went out to supper. I sat at the table and made some (I thought reasonably amusing) comments about the nature of the British and their idiosyncrasies. Jessie was silent for quite a long time. When

I finally finished my witty sally with a flourish, she gave me a long hard look and said, 'You are a fool.' " Hume looked to Jessica and asked, "True?"

"Well, sort of," said Jessica.

"Absolutely true," Hume said. "You don't remember. It's written in blood in my memory."

"I just looked it, I didn't *say* it," explained Jessica.

"It took me a long time to recover from that," said Hume.

I asked Jessica how she had been able to keep a relationship going so strong for so long with another actor.

"I think it's wonderful to be in the same profession," Jessica said. "If I had married a doctor, for instance, or a lawyer, whose hours were so different, our lives would have been pulled apart. I think one of the reasons it's been so successful is that for both of us it was a second marriage. Both of us had been married far too young before and had maybe wrong expectations. My first marriage lasted ten years. The second time I had a different way of looking at it. The first time, I thought it was all going to be lovely. The second time, I knew there would be ups and downs and they must be weathered. Also, he's a good actor. He's a very generous and kind man. I admire him enormously as a person and as an actor. All those things help."

"You want to know how it worked?" asked Hume. "She made it work."

Actors come and go, and get older, like the rest of us. How is it possible to continue constantly working in such a precarious profession?

"That has to do with the fact that Hume has been a great organizer of projects," said Jessica. "So that when a play ended, he was already thinking about what are we going to do next, and *making* opportunities. I was never allowed to sit back at home and just wait for the telephone to ring. There was always something in the future that he would be working on. So that's really his contribution to our longevity. And I think that we try to take care of ourselves. The more you do, the more you *can* do."

"Use it or lose it," said Hume.

CHAPTER EIGHT

ELI WALLACH

"If tears were important, my Aunt Minnie would be Sarah Bernhardt."

Eli Wallach in "Cafe Crown"

ELI WALLACH was born in the Red Hook section of Brooklyn known as Little Italy. "We were the only Jews in a sea of Italians. I grew up feeling Italian as well as Jewish." His parents ran a candy store and Eli's brother and two sisters became teachers. Other family members were doctors and lawyers. "Being an actor to them is like joining the Foreign Legion," said Eli. After majoring in history at the University of Texas he earned an M.S. degree in education at City College of New York. Eli decided not to become a teacher and began studying acting at the Neighborhood Playhouse School of the Theatre in New York. He made his first Broadway appearance as the crew chief in *Skydrift,* which lasted seven performances. After appearing with Eva Le Gallienne's American Repertory Theatre on Broadway, he acted in *Mr. Roberts* for two years, and then created the role of the Sicilian lover, Mangiacavallo ("Eat a horse" in Italian), opposite Maureen Stapleton in Tennessee Williams's *The Rose Tattoo.* For this performance Eli received the Donaldson, Drama Critics, and Theatre World awards and he also won the Tony as Best Featured Actor. Other Broadway plays include *Camino Real, The Lark, Mademoiselle Colombe,* and *The Teahouse of the August Moon.* Eli met his wife, the actress Anne Jackson, in an off-Broadway production of *This Property Is Condemned.* Together they have performed in *The Typist and the Tiger, Luv, Rhinoceros, The Waltz of the Toreadors, The Diary of Anne Frank, Cafe Crown,* and many more. On screen, Eli has been seen in *Baby Doll, The Magnificent Seven, The Misfits, The Good, the Bad, and the Ugly,* and *The Godfather, Part III,* to name just a few. In 1988, Eli was inducted into the Theater Hall of Fame.

I've known Eli Wallach for many years, even though we've never officially worked together. Offstage he's very different from the evil bandits and devious characters he's portrayed during his career. Eli is short and cuddly with a permanent twinkle in his eye. He seems to constantly be looking for the humor in life. On the day of his appearance with us, Eli was inducted into the Theater Hall of Fame, in a ceremony that had taken place earlier at the Gershwin Theatre.

"You know what I said when I received the award?" asked Eli. "I said, 'I don't know if I deserve this, but I've got arthritis and I don't deserve *that* either.' "

In the Baseball Hall of Fame, you can see Babe Ruth's bat and Lou Gehrig's glove, but the actor's instrument is himself. What can they take from an actor? Maybe one of his costumes, or a false nose?

"I did wear a [fake] nose in the play *Camino Real*," Eli recalled. "It was lit and it looked like a Ping-Pong ball painted red. At the end of the second act, as the lights were going down, they were torturing me, and I pressed the button and kept lighting my nose and the house lights went down. It was beautiful. The first film I did was called *Baby Doll* by Tennessee Williams. In it I appeared with an actor named Karl Malden. We had an argument in the film and we stood face to face, nose to nose, and I called my wife afterwards and asked her, 'How was it?' She said, 'Never have two noses filled one screen so well.' "

A well-known actor said, "It does sometimes seem that acting is hardly the occupation for an adult. False noses, lots of makeup, and gum on my face. I can't stand it anymore. I hope I'll never do another play."

"Who said that?" asked Eli.

I told him it was Laurence Olivier. Then I quoted Marlon Brando, who said that an actor's life is "a bum's life in that it leads to perfect self-indulgence. You get paid for doing nothing, and it all adds up to nothing."

"Marlon Brando often says that acting is not an adult's occupation," said Eli. "But he does that because he's a genius. I like acting. I enjoy it. I have an appetite for it. Otherwise I would stop doing it. Hiding behind noses? Yes, that's one way of working. I spent a day with Sir Laurence after he opened in *Othello* in London, from morning tea till the performance. It was extraordinary. He had gym, vocal lessons, and then we spent two hours with him making up and then he took a shower to wash it all off. It was remarkable. He likes to hide."

Is there an exact moment when an actor knows he wants to make acting his life's work?

"I hated mathematics," Eli said, "and knew I could get out of trouble by acting my way out. The first part I ever played on the stage was an old man who didn't believe in God anymore because God had taken his son away. His son had died. I had this long beard stuck on and two kids in the front row said, 'That's not an old man, that's Eli.' I wanted to jump off the stage and poke them, so I figured I'd better learn to act."

Do actors ever wonder if the audience is believing them while they're performing?

"I played an Oriental for two years in *Teahouse of the August Moon,*" said Eli, "and I used to peek through the curtain to see who was out there. One night there were four Japanese men in the front row. I had to speak half my role in Japanese. The captain in the play would say, 'Tell 'em there will be rice for everyone,' and I would repeat it in Japanese. He'd say, 'Tell 'em there will be a democratic institution,' or 'Tell 'em there will be a school here with five sides like the Pentagon,' and I would repeat those words in Japanese. That night, I was sure those four Japanese were going to stand up and say 'Faker, liar!' So all the lines went out of my head except how to say, 'The school will have five sides,' in Japanese. So the captain said, 'Tell 'em there will be rice for everyone,' and I said, 'The school will have five sides.' The Japanese in the front row thought I was crazy—as did the cast."

When Eli appeared in our series, he was playing the egomaniacal producer, David Cole, in an acclaimed revival of

Cafe Crown at the Public Theater. The character of Cole has a dashing theatrical appearance.

"There's a line in the play just before I come on," said Eli. "[A character] says, 'He was sitting there in the aisle and all you could see was his hair.' And the other character says, 'What hair! Like snow on a mountain!' My wife Anne Jackson, who's also in the play, puts my hair in hot curlers before the curtain goes up every night. She says, 'I wish somebody would take a picture of this.' There I am with my hair in curlers so it will look like it's more."

I had been to see Eli's performance, and the moment he made his entrance, I found myself believing he was the character. How does an actor make the audience believe so quickly?

"The director said a wonderful thing," explained Eli. "[He said,] 'It's a cafe and there are six tables. I want the audience to feel they are occupying tables seven, eight, nine, and ten, so they are peeking in on what's happening.' It's as though I'm walking into a cafe. It's the Jewish Sardi's. I come with a plan in mind: I want the busboy, who has money, to invest in a play. So when I come on, it's with the premeditated intention of getting this young man to invest in my play.

"When they ask me, 'How do you do the same thing night after night after night?' I say, 'If I did, I'd go crazy.' I've been in plays that have run two years. The audience is always different, every night. I can tell in the first five minutes what kind of an evening I'm going to have. I go to the theater to have fun and enjoy, and I hope that's communicated to the audience. Some nights Bob Dishy plays the young busboy as sleepy and not interested. Some nights he's eager. It's wonderful, because he's never predictable. I don't know what the hell he's going to do!"

There's a lot of humor in the play about Jewish waiters and how they intimidate the customers.

"They certainly do," said Eli. "The guy says, 'I think I'll have the chopped herring.' The waiter says, 'It's *your* stomach.' "

In spite of its humor, *Cafe Crown* is about the weighty issues of family, betrayal, and tradition. The [characters are] loosely based on the Adler family, which included the actors Luther and Stella Adler.

"It's an amalgam," said Eli. "The part of the young actor

who goes off to Hollywood is really based on Paul Muni. It's a play about a conflict between a father and a daughter.

"I myself have two daughters and both of them are actresses. They live in California. I almost didn't do the play initially because one of them auditioned for the play and didn't get the part. She flew all the way to New York to audition for the director and Joe Papp and they didn't choose her. I thought, 'Wouldn't it be interesting to have the real conflict on stage? To have my real daughter there and to *really* take it out on her.' I like the girl who's playing it. She's a lovely girl. But this would have been an added element. They chose not to take Roberta, who's a wonderful actress. My wife said when she was rejected, 'Why do we have to live through it twice?' When Annie and I were rejected it was all right because we thought, 'They're making mistakes.'

"I once went to audition for *The Madwoman of Chaillot* on Broadway. I've studied movement and mime, and I went in for the part of the mime in the play and Alfred de Liagre, who was directing it, said to me, 'All right, act out in mime: it's a beautiful afternoon.' So I acted it out and then he says, 'Well, I don't know. It looks kind of *rainy* to me.' So I didn't get the part. I sat in the outer office and Julie Harris went in and two minutes later she came out so angry she slammed the door and broke the window in the door! That was a rejection I could cope with. I lived through it. Later on I became very friendly with Alfred de Liagre."

In *Cafe Crown,* Eli's character expresses an anger at his daughter that seems very real. How is this achieved?

"Part of it is the scheme of my Machiavellian character. He wants to put on this play. He wants to unite with his wife, whom he hasn't seen in three months. He's been out having affairs. After playing the part for six weeks, I suddenly realized what one line meant. The wife in the play says, 'Where do you live?' and he says, 'I just arrived and my bags are still at the station. I'll pick them up on the way to your house.' After six weeks of playing the part, I realized it's an alibi and a cover-up, because he's been sleeping with some young girl somewhere, and his wife knows it. It took me all that while to discover that. That's one of the mysteries of theater. It takes six weeks to discover what you are really saying and what the other person is really saying."

In *Cafe Crown,* the character of David Cole wants to improve on Shakespeare by giving *King Lear* a wife and an apartment on Riverside Drive.

"The Yiddish theater often did that. Jacob Adler played Shylock or Lear on Broadway in Yiddish. The rest of the cast played in English. I made spaghetti Westerns for seven years and there the cast spoke whatever language they spoke. In one of them, *The Good, the Bad, and the Ugly,* there was a man with one arm. He was Italian, and he said to me, 'I don't like Americans.' I said, 'Why?' He said, 'I lost my arm in the war.' He had to say something in this scene we were doing and he wasn't an actor. So the director said to him, 'Count from one to ten in Italian, angrily.' So the man said to me," (Eli's voice grew louder and more menacing as he recited each number) " 'UNO, DUE, TRE, QUATTRO, CINQUE, SEI!' When they put it in the movie, he looked brilliant. He was just counting in Italian! That's the difference between movies and being on the stage.

"*The Good, the Bad, and the Ugly* was the third of a trilogy. The first movie focused on Clint Eastwood, the second on Lee Van Cleef, and the third on my character. I got the part because I was in California doing a movie and my agent said to me, 'There's an Italian director who wants to see you about being in a movie.' He'd seen me in *The Magnificent Seven.* I said, 'An Italian Western? That's like Hawaiian pizza!' The Italian director and I communicated in French. He said to me, 'Just come and see some of my movie.' They showed two minutes of his movie with the credits. I said, 'I'll do the movie. Wherever you want me to go, I'll do it.' He said, 'I want you in Rome.'

"I arrived in Rome and the director, who is a two-hundred-and-eighty-pound man, has suspenders on and a belt. I say to him, 'I want to have suspenders and a belt.' He said, 'Okay. But I don't want you to ever carry your gun in a holster.' I said, 'What do I do?' He says, 'I want you to carry the gun around your neck on a rope and it dangles between your legs.' I said, 'Come on!' He says, 'Ya. When you want the gun you go like this and it's in your hand.' I said, 'Show me.' He pulled on the rope, it missed, and the gun hit him in the groin. He said, 'Put it in your pocket.' So for the rest of the movie I put it in my pocket.

"On the film I met Clint Eastwood, who didn't say very much, didn't talk very much. This was long before he directed. He said to me, 'I'm never going to come back to Italy and do another one of these movies. I paid my dues.' You work from sunup to sunset. Your lunch consisted of a piece of chicken stuck between two pieces of bread and a bottle of wine. That was it. He'd had enough. Clint was wise and on to all of this. What was ingenious about the filming was that they did their homework.

"We shot a sequence about the Civil War and they went to all the Matthew Brady prints so all the clothes and everything were done exactly as they were during the Civil War, including the cannons, the guns, and the trains. They were all real Civil War relics and Clint was very observant. He'd done six years in the television series 'Rawhide,' and now he'd done this movie. Until I *saw* the movie, I thought, 'He doesn't really act very much. He's a movie star like Steve McQueen.' When I acted with Steve, he kept saying, 'Cut my lines. I don't want to say very much. The fewer lines I have, the better.' "

How does an actor decide when to do a film and when to work in the theater?

"My first movie was a glorious experience," said Eli. "I won the British Academy Award. I thought, 'How insightful the British are!' But I didn't do a movie for two years. I decided, 'No more, I've had the movies, I'm going back to the theater.' Finally, they called me and said, 'Do you want to do this movie? It takes place in San Francisco. It's a lovely location.' I read the script and I said, 'I can't believe this! I kill five people in one day! I'm a hit man with an attaché case and a gun with a silencer.' Every time I was going to kill somebody I'd open the latches like this" (he demonstrated in mime, making the noise of the latches opening). "I said, 'I can't do this movie.' Then, as a joke, I said, 'Okay. I'll do it. Ten grand a killing.' This was thirty years ago. They said, 'Okay.' Now I was stuck and I had to do the movie!

"My wife went to see the movie, [in which] I trailed a woman and her child. I opened the case and Anne said, 'If you kill them I'll walk out of this movie.' To atone for my sins for what I did, I flew to London and for the British Broadcasting Company I did a wonderful play by Elmer Rice, called *Counselor-at-Law*. Live on British television. Then I flew with my wife to Rome and I did a lecture at the Teatro Quirino with Anna Magnani on the Method. Then I flew back to New York and did a play with Sir Laurence Olivier and his wife

Joan Plowright called *The Chairs*. So I washed away my sins. Then I was ready to do more movies.

"I'm not in penance now. I haven't done a movie in a year. The last movie I did was *Nuts* with Barbra Streisand. In the movie I testified first at the hearing. It's a room and we're going to shoot six more weeks in the same room as other people testify. So I go to the director and I say, 'Listen Marty, I testified first. Why do I have to hang around now?' He says, 'What do you mean? If I turn the camera around from her or the judge, I want to see you.' So I said, 'Okay.' After three weeks I went back to him and I said, (I'm playing this psychiatrist), I said, 'I can't stay anymore.' He said, 'Why?' I said, 'I have other patients.' He said to me, 'Like hell you have. She's getting five million dollars to do the movie. You'll stay right there!' And I did."

We have all heard the phrase, "the spine of the play" and "the super objective," meaning what the play is all about. How does an actor deal with the spine or super objective of his character?

"You can't play a concept," said Eli. "Take crying or tears. If you watch television and you see someone discussing the murder of their child, they try *not* to cry. They don't say, 'I'm going to go on television and cry.' It's your stifling of the emotion which releases the tears. That's what makes it happen. The actor who says, 'I'm going to cry in this scene,' is defeating himself.

"Bobby Lewis just directed me in Florida in a play about Noah called *The Flowering Peach*. He once said, 'If tears were important, my Aunt Minnie would be Sarah Bernhardt.' How do you play a king? The only way you play a king is if the other people around you say, 'Your majesty, your majesty.' The king doesn't say, 'I am being kingly today.'

"I played for the Queen of England. The only request she had when we did the play was that no one sit directly in front of her. She didn't say, 'I'm a queen.' When I make my entrance in *Cafe Crown*, I'm the maestro, the entrepreneur, the great director. If I start to play that, it won't work. But everybody on the stage gets up and says, 'Oh, Mr. Cole. How are you, Mr. Cole?' I'm very modest, and that kind of fake modesty is what makes him powerful and in command."

Eli makes acting sound easy. The actor comes onstage with a premeditated intention, which he works out with the director. Then, even though the lines are the same every night, the actors react differently to each other and the audience is always different, which makes what is happening seem spontaneous. Does that mean that anyone can learn to act?

"People are acting all the time. Everybody is an actor. Only *we* get paid for it. It takes a thick hide, and an ego and a drive to do it. Today acting is like instant coffee for most actors. You don't brew [it] anymore, you don't age it right through the process of brewing, you don't perk it; you add hot water and you get coffee.

"I tested the waters in a TV series. I played the head of the Mafia and I used to go in on Monday and say to my son, 'I want you to look into this, you understand?' Then I would come back on Friday, and I'd say, 'Did you look into it?' I was getting twenty-five thousand dollars a week to do it, and I felt terrible. I said, 'Write something, let me do *something*! Let me earn my money.' They said no. After twelve weeks it was over and I was glad to get out. I would rather make three hundred bucks a week playing David Cole off-Broadway and enjoy it, than make that money and not enjoy it. We've only got a short time in our lives and in our careers, and you better do what you enjoy doing. Fortunately, I've got Social Security and a pension from the Screen Actors Guild. And Toyota trucks, God bless 'em.

"I'm often asked, 'Would you want your children to go into the theater?' It's as though they are saying, 'Would you push your child off a cliff?' My answer is, 'If that's what they choose to do, and they have the guts to stay with it, that's what they should do.' The greatest gift you can have in your life is to pick what you want to do, know what you want to do, enjoy doing it, and find the right partner to share it with. I've been fortunate that I've had that.

"I'm on the board of a school called the Neighborhood Playhouse School of the Theatre. You can't just wish to go into a career. 'I'll go and make the rounds. I have a nice face, etc.' You've got to do your homework. You've got to go in the lab. You've got to work. I don't care where. I appeared anywhere there was a stage. Anywhere! Whether I understood what the hell I was doing or not, I'd appear. My wife teaches at the Berghof Studio and then when she comes to [the theater] at night, she's invigorated by what she's been doing, teaching. It's good to take classes while you're trying to work in the theater and make the rounds. You get something from them."

Is it necessary to have a technique to be an actor?

"No. There are some brilliant actors who don't care about it. I like what Charles Laughton said to me. He gave me a part in a play called *Major Barbara.* I had been studying, and I was in that new wave of actors who were in the Actors Studio and the Method. Laughton said to me, 'You are going to play the greatest comedy creation since Falstaff. And furthermore, I want no Stanislavski shit from you!'

"The value of technique is that it gives you an ability to enter each evening with a feeling that you *want* to do it. When you are dry. When it's income tax time or somebody is ill or different problems arise, and you've got to go on and play a happy man.

"When I was playing *Teahouse of the August Moon,* one of the stagehands died of a heart attack right there, and we couldn't move him because the coroner hadn't come. I had to step over him and come out on the stage and be this cheerful little guy. I loved that old man who passed away. We had had a wonderful chat just before the show started. The audience knew nothing of what was going on in me, and I had to play as though I was cheerful. I had to do the same play in front of Winston Churchill and he had a hearing aid and he did something to it and I didn't know if he turned it off or not. I spent the rest of the play looking at him to try and find out, and he never changed his expression."

It's amazing to hear an actor say technique is not necessary, especially when that actor is a charter member of the Actors Studio.

"I certainly am," said Eli. "I'm an original member of the Actors Studio, founded in 1947. Two groups got together, one under Elia Kazan and one under Robert Lewis. The Group Theater went out of existence in 1941. In 1947, Cheryl Crawford and Kazan and Bobby Lewis formed the Actors Studio because they wanted a laboratory or a gym where trained professional actors could come, even though they were working, and try other roles. I did Hamlet. I would never have gotten the opportunity to do Hamlet. This was long before Joe Papp. I would be able to do Hamlet now, but I'm seventy. I can't do Hamlet anymore. It would be an *old* Hamlet . . .

"My wife and I do a poetry reading and we do a scene from

a play by Terence Rattigan called *Harlequinade* about an old couple. There's a ladder on the stage and the old couple are doing *Romeo and Juliet.* They're long past their prime and we do the actual scene from *Romeo and Juliet.* At one point, she says, 'O Romeo, Romeo, wherefore art thou Romeo,' and I say, 'Shall I hear more or shall I speak at this?' I do a little leap and Anne says, 'O Romeo . . .' " (Eli did an imitation of Anne's nasal Brooklynese) " 'are you going to do that?' I say, 'What?' And she says, 'That little jump.' I say, 'Why not? Does it bother you?' 'No,' she says. 'Just as long as I know.' I say, 'All right, let's go on.' 'No, no,' she says, 'I'll tell the stage manager.' And she goes over and says, 'He's going to do a little jump. I know he never did a little jump before but he's just put a little jump in.' I say, 'I don't want to do the little jump.' She says, '*Do* it if it makes you feel *young*!' I say, 'I don't want to do it. I'm going to deliver the line standing as still as the rock of ages. And looking just about twice as old.' She says, 'It's all in your head.' I say, 'I WILL NOT DO THE ROLE!' We did this in China and we have a tremendous fight at the end of the scene. The Chinese thought we were really fighting. They were very upset. At the end of the scene I drag the ladder offstage and she says, 'I'm reporting you to Equity!' "

After a pause Eli asked, "Did I answer your question?" Then without prompting, he went on:

"This is Mike Nichols's brilliance as a director. I did a play that he directed called *Luv* by Murray Schisgal. The curtain goes up and *Luv* takes place on a bridge. There's a bench, a garbage can, and a lamppost. Mike Nichols says, 'The audience is going to be stunned. They're going to say, 'Where's the furniture? Where's the telephone? When are the actors going to sit on that bench?' So he said to Alan Arkin and me, 'Stay off the bench as long as you can.' So we began improvising. We sat on the edge of the stage. We sat on the railing. We sat on the garbage can. We stood near the lamppost and all during this time Alan said, 'You know, sometimes I have these fits. I go deaf. What? What?' I said the line a little louder. He said, 'Sometimes I get rigid and stiff and I fall over.' Then he said, 'Sometimes I go blind, blind,' and I led him to the bench. I sat him on the bench. He said, 'You bastard!' But that's bright directing because it *engages* the actor's energies, the actor's inventiveness with the director's overall baton. In

Cafe Crown, what was wonderful was Martin Charnin's ability to orchestrate all these people coming in and out of doors and sitting at tables and getting up. It's wonderful."

The Actors Studio is associated with the Method. What *is* the Method?

"It's a system of evaluating a role," said Eli, "and learning how to bring to that role your own experiences. For example, my first movie was *Baby Doll.* In that movie, my cotton gin has burnt down and I suspect someone of arson. I have to turn around from the ashes of my cotton gin, and the camera is right there, and I have to be furious. So I thought to myself, 'What do I do? They could burn all the cotton gins in Mississippi, I don't give a damn about a cotton gin. What do I do? How do I find something in my personal experience which would equal what the audience is supposed to see in me?' I chose something which is very private. It's my private moment, and I chose to do that. The director was very impressed and bright enough never to say to me, 'How did you get that?'

"The same director directed me in *Camino Real.* He said, 'I want you to go onstage and make friends. I know how to make friends my way, you know how to make friends your way. Different people do it differently.' What he didn't tell me is he told all the other actors, 'He has bad breath, don't go near him.' So every time I approached an actor and started to speak, they moved away.

"It's a game. The actor is playing in a game. When I was in *Androcles and the Lion,* I once said to a wonderful old character actor who never knew anything about technique or the Method, I said, 'Boy, do I get a laugh there!' He said, 'You do?' I said, 'Yes.' He smiled. And the next performance, I didn't get the laugh. It was a valuable lesson. It's like the pitcher is throwing the ball and there is a catcher and there are seven other men behind him. All of them are involved in the throwing of that ball, not only the pitcher. That's what acting is about. You are *reacting.*

"It's the same as what I said about my experience in *Cafe Crown.* I'm finally listening to what the other actors are saying. It took weeks. That's all part of the technique. Trying to anticipate how you're going to react to something is like trying to pick up a piece of mercury. It splits and you can't quite pick it up. The height of a great technique is to be relaxed enough to react and respond to something else.

"I made a movie called *The Misfits* with Marilyn Monroe, who had begun to study the Method. She had to cross the road. She had to go from here to over there. She left me and Clark Gable in a truck and she started to walk across the road. She began to think, 'What about the past relationship with my husband?' because she was on the way to a divorce in the movie. 'What about my husband, and the divorce, and the ring on my finger?' and she would get halfway across the road, and then she would stop because she had left out one of the things. She had assigned herself seven things [to think about]. We did ten takes. Finally, I said to Marilyn, 'You are going to get run over! Go across the road!' and she got across the road.

"John Huston was a brilliant director and had great insight into the actor's problems. The first scene I had with Clark Gable, I kept staring at him and thinking, 'Oh my God, this is the king of the movies!' He kept looking at me as though he was thinking, 'Who is this guru from the East with this mysterious Method?' We just stared at one another and Huston gave us each a drink and said, 'Knock it off! Say the lines!' And we did."

At this point I told Eli I was a little confused.

"I do tend to confuse people," said Eli impishly. "It's part of my charm."

We are trying to understand what the Method is all about. The story about Marilyn Monroe and Clark Gable and Eli working on *The Misfits* seems to suggest that the Method doesn't always work. How did Montgomery Clift manage on the film?

"Montgomery Clift was a very sensitive, wonderfully talented actor. He worked this way: He was to play a rodeo rider. He went out a month or two months before we started the movie and went to rodeos and *rode* in them. When he reported to work on the movie, he had fallen off a horse or been stuck by a bull or something and he had a big scar across the bridge of his nose. The first scene he did in the movie he had to go into a phone booth and do two pages of dialogue, which is an enormous amount in a movie.

"Clark Gable, Marilyn Monroe, Thelma Ritter, and I are in a car and we drive up and stop and he says, 'Gay, how are ya . . .' and there he is in the phone booth, and he did the scene and he'd been preparing it for two months. And Huston said, 'Cut! Print it.' And Monty Clift said, 'Wait a minute. Do you mean that I don't get to do it again?' 'No,' Huston said, 'you'll never do it better than I just saw it.' And Monty was terribly disappointed and anxious. Sometimes he'd have to be drunk or he'd be thrown off his horse. In the ring Monty did sixteen turns in a row, like a whirling dervish, and fell down. Some actors don't do that.

"Monty and Marilyn were neurotic and haunted. The act of life was very demanding on them. Some people can cope with life, some people can't. Some people get lost in drugs, in alcohol, in the occult, in anything to escape the reality of life. Both of them were vulnerable and weak in that sense. It was *painful* for them. Marilyn's marriage was breaking up while we were doing the movie and the movie consisted of a valentine to her. So everything we said about her only deepened her anguish and her anxiety and her pain.

"We had a scene in it where we danced. I love to dance. We used to dance a lot together while we were filming this thing. One day while taking a shower I looked at my shoulder and it was black and blue from her digging her hands into me [from our scene together]. She said the line, 'You dance very well!' I said, 'Well, I like it.' She asks, 'Did you dance with your wife?' I said, 'No, she was clumsy.' She said, 'Why don't you take the time to teach her to be graceful?' I said, 'Well, I don't know . . .' She said, 'We're all of us dying every minute. Why don't you take the time to share with her?' And it *killed* her to say those things, because her life was in shatters."

How is the Method helpful for actors who choose to use it?

"I did *The Diary of Anne Frank,*" said Eli, "and in the end, as the Nazis come trooping up the stairs to get us, I turned and looked at my two real-life daughters who were playing my daughters in the play. I turned and looked at both of them. I didn't have to think anything, but my eyes would fill up with tears. And then we would do the epilogue of the play where I would read about what happened to Anne Frank in the concentration camp. Even if I did it now, my eyes would tear up. My daughters have never been in a concentration camp. I don't know what deposits I have made emotionally, but when the right buttons are pressed, out come these tears.

"If I put a bowl of oatmeal under your nose, without saying

a word to you, out would come all kinds of memories. Locked in your brain are all these things you have stored away. It comes out at odd times. You find yourself arguing with your wife about something. It's *not* what you are arguing about *at that moment.* All the resentments that have been stored away in the bank come out now. The computer opens up and out it comes. The skill of the actor is to say, 'I'm not going to anticipate being emotional. I'm not going to cry. If I have to cry, it's going to be very difficult to do it. I'm going to *keep* from crying. I'm going to resist it.' And you'll cry."

In 1888 such distinguished actors as Ellen Terry and Sarah Bernhardt responded to William Archer's questionnaire on the craft and psychology of acting. Here, a century later, Eli had just described a practical way for the actor to cry onstage, providing the answer to one of Archer's first questions about acting and the emotions. I thought that now was a perfect opportunity to put a few of Archer's questions to Eli. For example, next on the questionnaire was: "Supposing that in the same situation, on one night [you] shed real tears and speak with a genuine lump in your throat, and on the next night [you] simulate these affections without physically experiencing them. On which occasion should you expect to produce the greater effect on the audience?"

"I can answer that by telling the story of Joe Jefferson," said Eli. "When Joe Jefferson, who played Rip van Winkle for sixty years, came off the stage saying, 'God, I was wonderful tonight! I gave *such* a performance,' people would say, 'I wonder when he's going to retire.' When he came off the stage saying, 'I don't know how I was tonight,' they thought he was brilliant. *The actor really has no measure of knowing what the audience is thinking.* Some nights at *Cafe Crown,* the audience is very outspoken. Some nights, when it comes to curtain calls, the applause is there but it's not great. When they are quiet and hooked in and listening, then at the end their response is much stronger. You can't denigrate an audience.

"I'm farsighted and I can see pretty good. I had just made my entrance in a play called *The Typist and the Tiger* and there in the front row was a guy who looked like he was asleep. While I was doing the play, this is what went on in my mind: the two sides are arguing. One side says, 'Why the hell is he falling asleep, I just came on!' And the other part of me is saying, 'Wait a minute, he paid, he has a perfect right if he wants to sleep here.' And that part of me says, 'Maybe he had a late dinner and he had a bad day at the office.' And then the other part of me says, 'No, goddamn it, I can't be *that* dull!' All during the play this man appears to be asleep. At the end of the play, I'm taking off my makeup and the stage manager comes back and says, 'Somebody wants to see you.' I thought, 'If it's that guy, I'll kill him.' And it was. He comes back and he says, 'I had the most marvelous evening!' I said, 'Oh, thank you,' and he was blind . . . That taught me a valuable lesson. Don't stick a label on anybody in the audience about their response."

Eli's story also applied to another of Archer's questions: "Can you give any examples of the two or more lines of thought which must coexist in your mind while acting? In other words, can you describe and illustrate how one part of your mind is intent on the character, while another part is watching the audience, and a third perhaps is given up to some pleasant or unpleasant recollection or anticipation in your private life?"

"I feel like I've cribbed for this," said Eli. "My wife Anne sits in the car with me when we drive, and she goes, 'Uh! Oh!' We're driving to the theater and I've had enough. Finally I say, 'Goddamn it, you take the car!' and I stop the car, get out and leave her, and take a cab to the theater. She doesn't have her eyeglasses, so she arrives at the theater as angry as I was when I left. We sit at the makeup table, and we have a dresser who helps us, standing between us. My wife says, 'Tell him I never want to speak to him again!' And I say, 'You tell her she should keep her mouth shut when I'm driving the goddamn car!'

"Then I bring her on the stage. I have a raincoat thrown over her head, I'm tying her in a chair, and I'm going to rape her. That's the play. It's called *The Tiger*. She says, 'I have a husband and two children!' I say, 'Shut up!' (That night it had a special quality.) I don't break up onstage, I have very good concentration. She has a line, she says to me, 'Isn't there someone you love?' My line is, 'Besides myself?' She says, 'Yes, like your mother.' I say, 'Ich . . .' She says, 'Isn't there *someone* you love?' I say, 'No!' Then she looks at me and says, 'You have kind-looking eyes.' While she is saying this, my eyes are *twitching* as a result of our fight."

Theater historically was always supposed to have been

cathartic for the audience. We purge ourselves of fears, anxieties, and unholy desires by projecting them onto the characters we are watching. Is theater also a healing for the actor? Do actors get rid of their hostility on the stage?

"Absolutely," said Eli. "We saved on all the psychiatrist bills. It's not been easy. They asked Anne in a recent interview, 'How do you do it? You have three children. You have a career. You have the house to do. How does a woman do it?' And Anne said, 'I'm a saint.' "

Another question from Archer: "In scenes of laughter, do you feel genuine amusement, or is your merriment entirely assumed? Have you ever laughed on the stage until the tears ran down your face, or become so overcome with laughter as to have difficulty in continuing your part?"

"I don't," said Eli, "though my wife does a strange thing. She breaks up, and then appeals to the audience to understand it. She was onstage with Alan Arkin, and he winked at her or did something. Some man in the third row fell out into the aisle, he was laughing so hard. They had to take him out of the theater. She began to break up, and then she did this, which was unforgivable: She said to the audience, 'I can't help it!' I came onstage and said under my breath, 'You amateur!' And she broke up again. She is able to do that. She laughs easily onstage. I can't."

My last question from Archer: "Do you ever blush when representing bashfulness, modesty, or shame, or turn pale in scenes of terror, or grow purple in the face in scenes of rage, or have you observed these physical manifestations in other actors?"

"Yes," said Eli. "Hume Cronyn. I did a play with him. He can turn absolutely red onstage. I tried it holding my breath, and I almost passed out."

I asked Eli what was left for him to accomplish, since he seems to have done it all.

"No, I haven't," he said. "That's what's wonderful. I don't think I've solved the human dilemma. Annie and I have been playing for forty-two years. We've been married forty, and I still haven't figured it out. I can't figure out how the marriage works. That's the mystery of a relationship."

Are there any roles left to play?

"For years I lied. And Sidney lied with me. Sidney Poitier and I were going to do *Othello.* Sidney was going to play

Othello and I was going to play Iago. We thought, 'How comfortable it is to say, "Yes, I will do Iago." ' And I never did it. The American actor doesn't have to go over those hurdles. The British actor does.

"It's a strange thing in this country. In England you're knighted. In France you become a member of the Legion of Honor. You join the Comédie-Française. In Russia, you become an Honored Artist. In America, if you're successful, you acquire an agent, an accountant, and ulcers. What happens is the original drive, the interest, the ego, *the love* for what you're doing gets off to the side and they talk about numbers. The gross and the cost, and so on, so that the original reason you went in to explore what happens in acting, *the fun* or *the difficulty* [of it] gets waylaid. It's so *refreshing* for me to be in the theater, not only with my wife when we do two-character plays, but in *Cafe Crown,* where there are eighteen actors.

"The other night one of the actors left to go on tour to make some money, and we all sang good-bye to him. It's like a family. I thought, 'We'll miss that.' I love doing the play. I dread the next three weeks because I know it's going to end and I don't want it to end. I like playing a long run."

I asked Eli what he would do if he were not an actor.

"I'd open a little clock shop somewhere," he said. "I collect little clocks. Don't ask me why. My wife has no concept of time. I get to places twenty minutes before and she's always late. Groucho Marx once wrote a book, saying, 'This book was written while I was waiting for my wife to get dressed.' I would be happy opening a little shop called 'Ye Olde-Time Clock,' and selling old clocks. But I would design them."

William Archer said the best advice ever given to an actor was written by William Shakespeare in Hamlet's speech to the players. I handed Eli a copy of the speech. He took out a pair of glasses and moved to the edge of his chair, holding the speech in one hand and using the other to gesture gracefully. He looked out at the audience and for a moment he became a worldly-wise Hamlet, addressing a band of players. His voice took on a quiet modesty as he read:

"Nor do not saw the air too much with your hand, thus; but use all gently: for in the very torrent, tempest, and—as I may say—whirlwind of passion, you must acquire and beget a temperance, that may give it smoothness."

CHAPTER NINE

EARLE HYMAN AND FRANCES STERNHAGEN

"I cannot remember when I didn't want this life of illuminated emotion, this other world."

Frances Sternhagen and Earle Hyman in "Driving Miss Daisy"

Earle Hyman was born in Rocky Mount, North Carolina. His parents were teachers and they moved north when Earle was six years old so their four children could receive a better education. "When I got to Brooklyn and saw my first professional play at the Brighton Beach Theatre, I just lost my mind. It was Ibsen's *Ghosts,* with Nazimova as Mrs. Alving. I knew theater was for me." Earle made his stage debut as a teenager with the American Negro Theatre. In 1943, when Earle began acting, it took great courage for a black man to attempt a career in the theater because there were so few parts available. Fortunately, just at this time NBC began doing radio shows about black history and they started using black actors. After appearing on one of these shows, Earle was asked to do the Broadway musical *Run, Little Chillun* and his career was launched. Earle's roles run the gamut from Shakespeare to Fugard, from Chekhov and Shaw to Hansberry and Albee. He received a Tony nomination for *Lady from Dubuque.* In addition to his roles on Broadway and off, Earle appears with the New York Shakespeare Festival, the Roundabout Theatre, the Lincoln Center Repertory, and in Scandinavia, where he enjoys great popularity. His television work includes playing Russell Huxtable, Bill Cosby's father, on "The Cosby Show," which won him an Emmy nomination.

Frances Sternhagen has been nominated five times for the Tony Award, which she won for her performance in Neil Simon's *The Good Doctor.* Frances is a Vassar graduate who established a reputation as a serious actress off-Broadway, winning the Clarence Derwent Award, the Drama League Award, two Drama Desk Awards, and two Obies. Frances's off-Broadway credits include *The Admirable Bashville, Misalliance, The Pinter Plays, Ulysses in Nighttown, The Red Eye of Love, The Return of Herbert Bracewill, Little Murders,* and *Driving Miss Daisy.* She was a member of APA and Lincoln Center, where she performed in *Cock-a-Doodle Dandy, The Playboy of the Western World,* and *Enemies.* On Broadway, Frances appeared in *Equus, On Golden Pond, The Sign in Sidney Brustein's Window, Angel, Grownups, You Can't Take It with You,* and *Home Front.* For many years she was the spokesperson for Colgate, dipping chalk in blue liquid in their toothpaste commercials. Her films include *Fedora, Hospital, Starting Over, Outland, Independence Day, Bright Lights, Big City, See You in the Morning, Misery,* and *Communion* with Christopher Walken. Among her numerous television credits are *Resting Place, At Mother's Request,* and "Cheers."

Watching Earle Hyman and Frances Sternhagen in *Driving Miss Daisy* was like attending a concert. Earle and Frances had been playing their roles for a year, having taken over from the original cast, and because it was a two-character play their voices had established an almost musical rhythm together. Earle was capable of pianissimos and loud crescendos that resonated throughout his whole body. Frances's voice had a delicate but firm vocal presence. I wondered how much rehearsal time they had had in order to achieve this.

"Not much," said Frances. "We did have the opportunity of seeing it done. Earle's a quick study. Before he came into it, everybody said to me, 'Don't worry, he's a quick study.' I felt the burden was on Earle when he came in. We both would have enjoyed it more to have started the play and worked on it. When you are replacing, they never give you enough rehearsal."

Earle and Frances performed so well together that I was curious if they had previously been familiar with each other's work.

Earle nodded. "I first saw Frances as Amanda Wingfield in *The Glass Menagerie,* in the original Arena Stage in Washington, D.C. It was the only theater that was going at that time in Washington which blacks and whites could attend. I thought Frances had to be very old. So I went backstage, and by God she was a little bit of a girl, twenty-seven years old! It was an unforgettable experience."

"I first saw Earle in *Mister Johnson* on Broadway," recalled Frances, "which was a wonderful production of the Joyce Carey novel. He was extraordinary."

Does it help a performance for actors to know one another well off stage?

"In our private lives," said Earle, "I'm very afraid to get to know Frances so well that we laugh a lot. If I knew Frances that well, I would know what is funny to her. I am so terrified of breaking up onstage. I'm very easy to break. Not knowing exactly all the things that make Frances laugh helps me. When Frances is on the stage, I do not see or hear or think of Frances at all. She *is* Miss Daisy."

"I find that when I'm into a play and into the role," said Frances, "that it really doesn't matter. I don't think about what's going on privately with my co-actor while the play is going on. I've often felt that an actor is like a computer. Once you start pressing whatever it is that starts all that machinery going, that's what you're doing, and you don't really think about the other person as anything except what he's playing."

Frances replaced Dana Ivey and Earle replaced Morgan Freeman in the show. The director was Ron Largomasino. How much leeway did the director give in a situation like that? Did he ask for the replication of the performance of the original cast or were the actors allowed to start from scratch and invent on their own?

"I got the blocking," Earle said, "but I didn't feel that if I wanted to change it for some reason that I couldn't. I didn't have Ron's direction very much. His mother was ill and he was on the Coast, so the author, Alfred Uhry, and the stage manager, Frank Luchesa, got me up into the part, and they were both absolutely wonderful. I knew one thing I had to abide by and that was, 'Earle, step by step, there's no point in panicking! You've only got ten days but don't think of it as ten days! One of these nights you're going to be out there and you will be in the show. Just don't panic! Just breathe.' And that's all I did was breathe deep. I was rehearsing with Frances's standby and I just let it happen. My first reaction was, 'You're crazy. I can't do this in ten days!' But inside I said, 'You may not have this chance again.' "

"I have replaced quite a number of times," said Frances. "I remember, for example, in *Equus,* when we were all replacements. John Dexter was using a very basic plan that had worked already to great acclaim at the National Theatre in London. He was essentially bringing that plan over and we were going to fit into it, which is what happened. He got us up on our feet the first day, which is what happens when you are replacing.

"In *Daisy,* I got the blocking right away and started moving around with it. If the play has worked with that blocking, you're a little silly to start objecting to it before you try it."

Can an actor actually bring about changes in the concept for a particular scene?

"There were two moments that I definitely changed in *Daisy,*" said Frances. "In the graveyard scene with Morgan, who was in it before Earle, I had in my script a line after I have given this whole lesson about how to spell the name on the tombstone, and I say, 'Go off and find it,' and he turns around and says, 'Miss Daisy,' and she says, 'What now?' like 'Get on with it!' I said, 'What now?' and Morgan walked off the stage. I said, 'Is that the wrong line?' He said, 'If you say that, I just can't stay.' I said, 'It's in the script.' And Morgan looked down and said, 'Is that line in the script?' I said, 'Yes, Dana never said it but it is in the script.'

"I had to persuade Morgan because it did seem like a put-down and, of course, Miss Daisy would not feel abashed at all about putting somebody down. It was like, '*Now* what?' I said to Morgan, 'You know, it takes more courage for Hoke at that point to actually say "Thank you," ' which is what he does. He says, 'I really appreciate this.' Then she says, 'Oh well, it was nothing.' And Morgan accepted that, but at first, simply because it wasn't what had been done, he was all ready to reject it. I don't think Earle knew that or had any problem with it. So I got my way. There was a whole scene that had been played slightly differently before I did it and I just said, 'I don't want to play it that way because I don't think that it is clear enough.' So we played it the way I needed to have it played and everybody seemed to accept that. You have to present your case logically and without emotion. You have to know why you think it works better the way you want to do it."

Did anything similar happen for the role of Hoke during the rehearsals for *Driving Miss Daisy*?

"No," said Earle. "But I have the joy of being able to relax and know why I say this and what the beats are and what my intention is. A lot [of that] you're just not going to know by the time you open. You just hope you know your lines."

When Earle spoke, he drew out the syllables of certain

words for emphasis, letting a word sail on the breath to illustrate the meaning of what he was saying. For example, "able to relax" became "able to relaaaaax."

Frances has a dazzling smile. In fact it's a famous smile. There was a period in her life when she was paid for it as the spokesperson for Colgate toothpaste. One of the things the director asked her to do when she took over in *Daisy* was not to smile.

"Yes," said Frances. "And it was a very good thing that he did because I have always tended to smile at some point in a play. It was wonderful because Alfred Uhry, the playwright, showed me how his grandmother smiled. This is how his grandmother smiled." The corners of Frances's mouth began to droop down. "He said her mouth just went down a little bit and that's how she smiled. It was a wonderful challenge. It really is fun because then the warmer she becomes at the end of the play, the more touching it is when you've seen a woman who just isn't going to give an inch. Ron even said, 'Anytime you have your picture taken as Daisy, don't you dare smile.' "

Earle once asked Michael Redgrave what to do when you see a perfect performance.

"And you're offered the part," added Earle. "He said, 'Copy it, dear boy, copy it.' "

"That's just wonderful," said Frances. "That's so right."

"And he *was* very right," Earle said, "because actually you can't, and he knew that. You can start. I know exactly what Morgan did as Hoke the first five minutes. After that, I can't remember. Each time I saw it, I was carried away by the play and the people in it, Morgan and Frances, and I just don't remember what he did."

Earle developed a very recognizable voice for Hoke, especially when he said a line like, "That's my business, Miss Daisy."

"That was just my father," said Earle. "That's the way he spoke. When I read the play first, before I'd seen it, I saw him, and my grandfather, in that character. I could hear them and see them. The two of them together were Hoke. So that's all that is. I'm imitating the way my father talked."

Does that mean when an actor takes over a role he still can go about building the character in his own personal way?

"Right," said Earle.

What about Daisy?

"Daisy is a composite for me of a couple of teachers that I had as a child," said Frances, "and strangely, as she gets older, [she's like] my father rather than my mother. My father was an invalid. He suffered from palsy."

In the beginning, the author knows the most about the characters in the play, then comes a period when the director is the one most deeply involved, and finally it's the actor who gets to know the character best by inhabiting his or her skin.

"There have been times when I wanted to tell an author to get out of the way," said Frances, "that he didn't know what he'd written, and that I was beginning to know what he'd written. I'd say, 'Don't tell me to do it this way because it doesn't work that way.' I have gotten into a couple of fights with authors in the process of rehearsal and I've won because there are times after the author has had the initial enormous inspiration when he simply doesn't know. Putting on a play is a very mysterious thing. I remember working with Harold Pinter. At one point, Hank Forsythe said, 'Harold, what does he mean when he's saying this? I don't understand. What am I saying?' And Harold said, 'I don't know. I just wrote it.' It's as if playwrights are transmitters."

Tennessee Williams said he found himself following his characters around during the writing of his plays. Many playwrights have said the characters start leading them after the initial creation.

"I love what Ibsen said one morning to his wife," said Earle. "Ibsen said, 'You know, Nora came to me today. She was wearing a blue dress.' He was writing *A Doll's House*."

When the actor makes a decision about a part she wants to play, does she take into account how long it may take her to get into the role?

"It can vary," said Frances. "There have been times when a character has come to me very easily and I've known that I could get into that character quickly. Other times I have taken on a character because it was a challenge. It's been a kind of fun mistake. I've decided, this character's going to be tough for me to find, and I feel like digging in. Then I can be waffling around for quite a while, wondering whether I'm doing the right thing. I heard from André Bishop that even in previews Joan Allen in *The Heidi Chronicles* was saying to the director and producer, 'Don't worry, I'm still finding out what I'm doing. I'm still finding Heidi. So if I'm not there yet, don't worry.' I think that's very courageous on her part. She had the confidence that she was going to find her, but she didn't quite know how, and it took longer than another character might in another play."

"It does vary," said Earle. "The first time we read a script as actors, we have to read it as an audience. We don't know what is going to happen on the next page. It washes over us. As actors we have to relax into that and be aware of that and let it do just that, wash over you. Then having done that, before you read it the second time, you take a few seconds to ask what did happen, if anything. Were you drawn to a certain role or did you say to yourself, 'I know something about that situation.' Beginnings are very important."

When I saw *Driving Miss Daisy,* I was drawn into the action of the play and started to care about the characters almost immediately.

Frances said, "Many people in reading the play did not feel that way. It's interesting the number of people who read the play and didn't like *Daisy* before they saw it."

There is a moving moment in the play when Daisy and Hoke touch hands and Daisy says, "You're my best friend." What is *Driving Miss Daisy* about?

"Most plays are about very few things," said Earle. "It's about love. It's as simple and as complicated as that. That's all it's about."

In the 1920s a great French actor-director named Charles Dullin said, "The actor is an athlete of the heart. . . . The actor's body is supported by his breath whereas the athlete's breath is supported by his body." What do actors do to keep themselves in physical shape when they are appearing eight times a week in a two-character play, which runs for ninety minutes with no intermission?

"It's hard," said Frances. "I find that after a year I feel more tired, not while I'm on the stage, but the rest of the time. If people ask me to do other things, my tendency is to say no. I need one day off. I try to do exercises, calisthenics or yoga. I try to walk to work from Grand Central. I try to do things that will be a kind of exercise. Otherwise, you spend the rest of your time paying bills and doing the laundry and cleaning the kitchen, which isn't really good exercise. It does drain you."

"I have never had a more easy work experience," Earle said. "I could have done three or four performances in one day."

"But you live across the street," said Frances.

"True," said Earle. "All the things I've been told—'Earle, you work too hard, you're struggling, you're forcing, you're overacting'—all that stuff I *had* to go through. Somehow this one was easy. I really was not exhausted physically at all. But I agree with Frances. After a year you need more energy to concentrate so that the right words come out, because I could almost put it on tape and it would do itself. The words would come out, and the movements, because they are in me, in my body. But that's dangerous. You come out doing that for about two minutes and suddenly something comes out of your mouth which wasn't even English, just a ridiculous noise, and you think, 'Oh my God.' I'm using energy so that doesn't happen and I am a little bit tired afterwards."

Apparently such a catastrophe actually happened to Earle when he played Othello.

He explained, "I lead a double life. Half my time has been spent in Scandinavia and the other half here. For twenty years I was very lucky. For six months I'd act there and for six months I'd get a show here. I found it the ideal and perfect life, although I knew it would have to end sooner or later. The first time I was offered Othello over there, I said no because I can't do a part if I can't think in that language. Some actors do it phonetically. It doesn't work for me. They gave me the script and they said, 'Take it with you and read it. If you change your mind, call us and let us know.' I had no intention of changing my mind. I was playing Othello in Cleveland and Laurence Luckinbill was Iago. I had been looking at the manuscript and even memorizing some of the words. Some of the lines came out great. I said to myself, 'By God, now I can prove in Norwegian that some of the things that Othello says are *funny*,' like the big speech to the Senate. There are funny words about "the Cannibals and the Anthropophagi." No American or Englishman ever laughs because they don't know what the hell they mean. In Norwegian you have to translate them into words that mean something and they are funny. Cannibals, for example, became *menskeeder* and it means people-eaters. I thought how fascinating, and that night while I was performing, I suddenly went over from English into Norwegian. I was *terrified.* So that night I sent a cable and said I would come and do it."

Because of Earle's Norwegian connection I thought it would be appropriate to ask him one of William Archer's questions. (Archer was Ibsen's English translator.) His question reads, "A distinguished actor informs me that he generally perspires freely while acting but that the perspiration varies, not so much with the physical exertion gone through as with the emotion experienced. Do you find the fatigue of playing a part directly proportionate to the physical exertion demanded by it or is it dependent on other causes?"

"I think it has to do with the physical," said Earle. "Certainly with *Othello* I've never been able to get through that without being bathed in sweat, whether the feelings were flowing or not. Just the physical demands. It's like getting on a roller coaster, and once that roller coaster starts there's no turning back. I think it's the most difficult part ever written. I agree with Olivier and I don't often agree with him. He said that King Lear was an easy part compared with Othello. With Othello, it's a combination of the emotional and the physical."

When I saw *Driving Miss Daisy,* what Earle and Frances were doing seemed effortless. I was not aware of any exertions.

"The only thing that makes me perspire in *Miss Daisy* is the heat," said Earle, "which is fierce in the summer, even with the air conditioning. For me this has been an entirely new experience. I like to feel that because of Frances and working with her and the manner in which she works, perhaps I've graduated and have found that thing that I have always been looking for, which is truly not to have to work so hard to have things happen. Things *should* flow. Acting should be a continuous flow of emotion and thoughts.

"We're like jugglers. The best actors always seem to be able to juggle the character's thoughts, the character's feelings, the actor's thoughts, and the actor's feelings all at the same time. If you're up there and you don't know that you're there at all, that you're really *not* the character, then I think you should call for the ambulance to Bellevue. Believing is one thing and knowing is another."

Because theater is a bigger risk for actors than film and television, most of today's actors will not commit to long runs.

Frances and Earle are exceptions. At the time of our session, they had not only been in *Driving Miss Daisy* for a year, but they had just signed up for another six months. I asked them about the danger of appearing in a long run, and of the possibility of becoming tired of a part.

"I turn down the things that I could potentially get nauseous about," said Frances. "I have turned down things that I know I wouldn't want to stay with for a long time. But in terms of getting tired of a part, if the character and the play are good, I don't get tired of a part. I don't get bored, I get better. I don't change the blocking or the intention or what I'm doing with another actor, but I just feel that it's getting richer, that it's getting deeper as I go along.

"It's strange, but in the last three months, there's a certain scene in *Daisy* where I can almost guarantee that I'll get tears or near tears. I don't think the audience knows the difference as to whether I do or I don't. I used to have that happen quite rarely. It doesn't matter whether it does or not, but the more I do it, the more I am likely to get the genuine emotion. I'm glad to say that I think I approximated the genuine emotion quite early on, but it makes it easier to play when the emotion gets closer to what you're acting and some of it is real. Some of it is because of what we do together and some is because of, yes, the way I'm feeling that day, what has gone on in my week. I may not even quite know what that is, but it leads to that moment where an emotion will break through.

"I don't think the audience really knows the difference because what I actually do is so imperceptibly different. I don't think it's different enough to notice, but what I feel is just a little more flowing. I have had times when I have acted it and approximated it quite accurately, but I have been playing the part so long now that, strangely, the emotions that would really be there tend to be there a little more often than some months earlier. I think that's because of the growth in the character.

"If you *act* as if you are having a legitimate emotion," said Frances, "that's what will make the audience feel it. *You* don't have to feel it necessarily. Paul Newman once said, 'An actor has to feel it at least once in rehearsal.' You have to *feel* what you are going to approximate so you know *what* you are going to approximate. Sometimes you can achieve that with improvisation.

"In *The Good Doctor,* Marsha Mason and I had a scene that we couldn't figure out. We didn't know what was happening in the scene. Marsha and I had to play a scene that came from a Chekhov short story and it was only by improvising it, meaning you put yourself in a comparable situation, that I knew what had to be in that scene. Sometimes you don't even know what that improvisation scene is until you try it several different ways and you say, 'Ah, I think that's the emotion that I need for this scene!'

"At some time in the rehearsal or in the early playing, you have to find the appropriate or correct emotion for a scene, and then once you've found that and you can act it, you can act *as if* you're having that emotion. That's the important thing. You don't have to feel it every time. But it's nice to feel it, because it's actually easier to play when you're feeling it than when you're tired and you're just going through the motions. That's really more exhausting."

In his book *On Acting,* Olivier says that he has never cried or felt any grief on the stage. He says the important thing is not to weep on the stage, but to *make people think* you are weeping. For Olivier, that is the essence of acting, a total illusion of the reality. Is it possible that both methods of acting are equally effective?

"Look at his work in the theater," said Earle. "That's what comes across. I am constantly aware of an extraordinary technician. He's like a great circus artist. He's doing something that is extremely difficult extremely well, but I am constantly aware of the fact that that is what he is doing. To me, just me, the great artist is the one who makes me totally forget for a while that he or she is *doing* anything. He or she *is.* Then, after it's over, I say, 'My God, how the hell did she do that? How the hell did he do that?' Those are the two kinds of actors. They have always been with us and both are equally great. You pays your money and you takes your choice."

Does your personal feeling toward an actor affect your performance?

"Sometimes there are actors who are hard to work with because you just don't get along," said Earle. "Once in *Anna Lucasta,* which is the only one of two, now three, hits I've ever been in, we went to London. I'd been playing it here. I was nineteen years old and more than just a little bit in love with Hilda Simms, who played Anna Lucasta, and I desperately wanted to go to London. My whole dream was to play on the London stage. Wow! I had to go.

"The producer said, 'I don't care who you bring over as long as you have Hilda Simms. She has to come. She's the one we want.' Hilda was in love with a guy who wasn't even an actor. She said, 'I'll go but why can't Dick come over and play Earle's part?' Well . . . Even though we did not speak off the stage we had to do the love scene. It was the first time that blacks ever played a love scene. It was not allowed. You could live with them but you never made love in terms of falling in love on the stage. It was the first time it ever happened. I had to play that scene, which was one of the high points of the play, and still mean it when all I was thinking was, 'Hilda, how could you do this to me!' The reviews said it was a moment of perfection, even though we weren't speaking."

More people watch Earle playing Bill Cosby's father on "The Cosby Show" than have seen him in his whole career on the stage. Earle tapes the show during the day and acts in *Driving Miss Daisy* at night. Do actors have to make a conscious adjustment when they move back and forth between the stage and television because of the different technique required?

" 'The Cosby Show' is very easy for me," said Earle. "I'm not called upon to act. I'm called upon to be Earle. That's what Bill wanted, and whatever Bill wants, he gets. We have a wonderful time and I'm not knocking it. I enjoy it immensely *but,* to me *Miss Daisy* is where I basically am, all of me. And that is what means most to me. If you want to use the word work, that's where the work is, in the sense of a sensible life work. Television is very nice, enjoyable and all that, but it doesn't demand very much."

Acting is something that comes most easily to children. A child has no problem believing her doll really exists. Is there an exact moment when actors know they want acting as an adult occupation?

"I'm crazy, just nutty," said Earle. "I cannot remember when I didn't want this life of illuminated emotion, this other world, this magic. I always wanted it since I was four years old, when I saw the church plays. Ministers preaching was the greatest theater I ever knew and I got that when I was two years old. I'll never forget it.

"After preaching on Sundays, they came to our home for fried chicken and potato salad. I was scared to look at these men. *They were God!* When a preacher said, 'My sermon is from Isaiah, the second to the fifteenth chapter,' I *knew* it was! From the movies I remember the all-black minstrel show called *Silas Green from New Orleans.* They put up the tent in back of our house! And my grandfather, who was an electrical expert for the whole town, helped them put up the lights! Their big star, called Princess White, the most beautiful woman I'd ever seen, asked if she could come into our house and iron her dress and sleep on my grandfather's bed before the show! It was divine!"

"I didn't think that I was going to go into the theater at all," said Frances, "because it was too much fun and you didn't do something that was fun and earn a living at it. So I started teaching when I left school. I taught for a year and I discovered I was performing for the kids. I got into a little theater in Boston near where I was teaching. A woman helped me prepare audition material because I had decided I would audition for some theaters.

"I auditioned for the Brattle Theater (which I didn't realize was on its last legs) because I had seen some wonderful stuff there. I prepared five very different women for this audition. I auditioned for a young man who smoked a pipe. My husband has since said, 'Beware of a director who smokes a pipe, because all they are interested in is keeping the pipe lit.' I did Sonya from *Uncle Vanya,* and Juliet, and *The Country Wife* and two others, and he watched, puffing on his pipe the whole time. Then he said in a very Harvard accent," (Frances gritted her teeth and spoke through them) " 'Miss Sternhagen. If you're interested in being an actress, I would advise you to give up teaching because you do everything as if you're leading the Girl Scouts onto the hockey field.' That got me so mad that I quit my teaching job and went into the first theater that would have me."

I had resolved never to ask any of my guests to perform anything in one of our sessions, but in the case of Earle and Frances I couldn't resist, since they had been in their show for such a long time. I asked them if they could give us a few of their lines in character.

Frances said, "My stepfather came from a period where people recited quite easily, and once at the dinner table with guests he said, 'Frannie, do that speech from *Equus!*' I said, 'Bernard, I don't remember it.' And he said, 'What do you mean, of course you remember it!' Well, I didn't. If we had been asked to prepare a scene tonight, I think we could have done it, but we're not ready. You can't do it off the top of your head. So I think we have to turn you down. I'm sorry."

Earle said, "When we met earlier this evening, David spoke about the magic of the theater, and the magic of the work of the actor. When David used the word magic, I thought, it *is* magic. Who really knows how it's done? Truly, at this moment I don't know my first line from *Driving Miss Daisy.*"

"When I'm putting on my makeup and I've got my hair up in pincurls," said Frances, "Earle will come into my dressing room and say, 'No. She's not there yet.' And when I put my wig on and I have my shoes on and my dress, then Earle will say, '*There* she is!' I wore my pretty, sort-of-younger clothes this evening. For me to get into Daisy without the wig and everything, it just feels like it isn't enough. I'm not her."

"It *is* magic," repeated Earle.

C H A P T E R T E N

FRANK LANGELLA AND JUDITH IVEY

"From low self-esteem to insufferable arrogance, we are the seesaw kids."

© MARTHA SWOPE

Frank Langella in "Dracula"

Judith Ivey in "Hurlyburly"

© MARTHA SWOPE

Frank Langella comes from Bayonne, New Jersey, where as a child he realized he wanted to act even though his Italian ancestors were businessmen rather than performers. After studying acting at Syracuse University, he was one of the thirty charter members in the Lincoln Center Repertory Company's first training program—and one of sixteen *not* asked to join the company. However, shortly thereafter he made his New York debut, starring in an off-Broadway revival of *The Immoralist.* He won his first Obie for *The Old Glory,* and two more Obies followed for his performances in *Good Day* and *The White Devil.* Other off-Broadway productions include *The Prince of Homburg* and *After the Fall.* Frank made his Broadway debut and earned a Tony for Edward Albee's *Seascape.* He then starred in *Dracula,* winning the rarely bestowed Delia Austrian Medal of the Drama League of New York. On Broadway, Frank also appeared in *Amadeus, Design for Living, Sherlock's Last Case,* and as William Shakespeare in William Gibson's *A Cry of Players,* for which he won the Vernon Rice Award as best actor of the year. His *Leonardo* on television was nominated for an Emmy, and his films include *Diary of a Mad Housewife* and *Dracula.*

Judith Ivey began her career at the Goodman Theatre in Chicago. She performed with regional companies including Washington's Arena Stage, and the American Shakespeare Festival in Stratford, Connecticut. She established her reputation off-Broadway, at places like the Public Theater, the Manhattan Theatre Club, and La Mama, and made her Broadway debut in *Bedroom Farce* by Alan Ayckbourn. Her Broadway credits include *Precious Sons* and her Tony- and Drama Desk Award–winning performances in *Steaming* and *Hurlyburly.* She's been seen in such films as *The Lonely Guy, Hello Again, Harry and Son, The Woman in Red, Compromising Positions,* and *Brighton Beach Memoirs.* Judith handles a wide range of accents with ease. Her Brooklyn Jewish accent gave authenticity to Aunt Blanche in *Brighton Beach Memoirs,* and her Cockney accent for Josie in *Steaming* made everyone think she was British. Her television appearances include her own series, *Down Home,* and the remake of the 1958 film *The Long Hot Summer.* At one point Judith thought of leaving the stage for veterinary medicine (she keeps many pets) but she is now firmly ensconced in the career of her choice. "I feel like Cinderella and I hope the ball goes on forever."

When I saw Frank Langella as Prospero in the Roundabout Theater's production of *The Tempest,* he moved with a catlike grace that has become one of his trademarks. Even when reciting Shakespeare, his voice was a velvet purr. Frank's partner for our session was Judith Ivey, whose own unique sassiness has contributed to memorable performances in *Steaming* and *Hurlyburly.* At the time of our meeting, she had recently given birth to a baby girl.

Both Frank and Judith established reputations for being serious actors by working off-Broadway for almost eight years. I asked them if that experience helped when it came time to take on Broadway roles.

"Any experience you have on the stage helps you for the next experience on the stage," said Frank. "It didn't really matter to me if it was off-Broadway. I did regional theater for twelve or fourteen years. By the time I made my Broadway debut, which was in 1975, I had already done eleven or twelve plays in New York, so I felt as if I were working at home in my own community theater. The Broadway theater didn't scare me because I felt I was a New Yorker and part of it. All the plays I did in New York and all the theaters I worked in around the country helped immensely."

Is it easier to avoid being typecast off-Broadway because of the greater variety of roles available?

"It's hard for me to answer that," said Judith, "because I've slipped through the cracks when it comes to being typecast, fortunately. I've played a variety of roles on Broadway that are just as different from the roles I've played off-Broadway. Typecasting has a lot more to do with the actor's choices than where you play it. I've been offered roles on Broadway that

I turned down because I felt they were simply a repeat of what I had done before. It has much more to do with your own choices rather than what the community says to you."

Are there more serious plays being done off-Broadway than before?

"No," said Frank. "I don't think so. There is less of everything in the theater these days. I worked off-Broadway from 1963 to 1969 before I started making some movies. There was so much work at the time that we were handing scripts off to each other, saying, 'I can't audition for this.' There wasn't the sense of financial pressure off-Broadway that there is now. I can remember constantly reading for plays and going to auditions and hearing about a play being done at this theater and that theater. I was lucky enough to open three or four theaters. I was in the first shows of the American Place and the Bouwerie Lane and the activity was phenomenal. There was a great deal of work. Not as many actors as now, but enough for there to be healthy competition. Nowadays the off-Broadway projects are very much like the Broadway ones. You hear about them way in advance. You hear about the financing of them. You hear that they really want Sean Penn. Way, way, way, far in advance, you'll hear that a wonderful, sweet little off-Broadway play is being done *if they only can get Sean Penn for it.* It wasn't like that then. A script arrived and they held auditions or, if you knew the director, you were asked to come in. There was a sense that it was beginning within that family. Now, because of the economics, they have to go see if Michael Fox will take a minute off."

"My off-Broadway was from 1978 until now," said Judith, "and showcase theater began because off-Broadway was beginning to become this thing where they needed Sean Penn to make it happen. Showcase theater meant that you were paid carfare. That was competitive. Now, even Sean Penn's doing showcase theater. Because of the diminishing numbers of projects, there's less and less, and unfortunately, the financial stress is making it less creative and much more formula. They have to make a lot more money than back when I was starting out."

"Also the critics have changed," added Frank. "Since the critics changed, the theater has changed. I don't know which came first, but because the nature of the critical community in New York is so lethal and so cruel and so vindictive, it sends people away who don't wish to get on the horse again. So it gets harder and harder. I've produced and directed now in the last five years and it gets harder and harder to get people to come to do a play in New York because they simply don't wish to spend that much time working and have somebody dismiss them with a pen stroke. You *can* dismiss somebody intelligently and constructively with a pen stroke, but it doesn't happen that way now. So that's changed the atmosphere, too."

Does having played Cyrano help when it comes to playing roles like Leslie the Lizard in Edward Albee's *Seascape*?

"Just acting helps you," Frank said. "I've been doing it since I was very, very young and no amount of classes, not even any amount of watching helps. Just going to work every day is the best teacher. Sure, I've done Cyrano twice and that helped me play a lizard, and that's helping me play Prospero now, but it's all in the bag. And you don't know it's helping you at the time. Some of the things that have helped me the most are the plays that *didn't* succeed, or the characters I just never quite got. So the next time I was working on a part, I would sort of remember where I had let myself down in a former role and I'd resolve not to do it again. I'd try harder the next time."

Judith's experience with classical parts was followed by her role as a balloon dancer in *Hurlyburly*. Is there something in the technique of a classical role that helps with a more contemporary part?

"Juliet's a little more difficult," said Judith, "getting it across the footlights. I think they go hand in hand. Each one takes you to the next step, as Frank says. It doesn't matter that one is classical. Once I did a lot of Noël Coward. Then, stepping into David Rabe, it was almost like being in a foreign country. So in some ways they don't help you, they can't be compared. Two completely different countries . . . [but] that makes it exciting."

Frank said, "I went from *Amadeus,* which was a Peter Shaffer play, to Arthur Miller's *After the Fall,* to Noël Coward's *Design for Living,* to *Hurlyburly,* and then to *Passion* by Peter Nichols, and they were five very separate styles of acting. Every one, I hope, made the next one a little bit better. I asked to be in *Hurlyburly*. I saw Judith in it and I saw Bill Hurt in it. When I saw it I thought, 'God, no one ever thinks of me in a pair of torn jeans and an old T-shirt. I really want to do that.' So I called Mike Nichols, who directed it, and I asked if I could be in it and he said no. But I kept asking, and finally I was able to play that part. I wanted to see if I could take most of my classical training and lose it, but keep it, too—because in order to do David Rabe, you must be classically trained. He's not a moment-to-moment writer. He's a great, fabulous, epic writer, and *you need* all that energy and breath control that you have learned from classic work. You need it in David's work as well."

Does that mean that some contemporary playwrights require a classical training?

"Yes. David Mamet does, too," said Frank. "David Mamet is deceptive. It isn't just line by line. It requires a tremendous sense of training to do him as well."

Frank was having a sold-out success with *The Tempest* at the time of our series. I asked him why he thought Shakespeare had such longevity.

"Because he writes universal truths about the human condition," said Frank. "For me it's that simple. In this particular play, he writes profound truths about what it is to become a man, what it is to become a *mensch,* what it is to finally take responsibility for your life, which is what I think Prospero is about. I find that every night I work on it, I'm in the presence of someone who just understood humanity as well as any great writer can. That's why I think he survives. He's timeless. The things he writes about are as true today as they were when he wrote about them."

The Tempest is sometimes considered Caliban's play and sometimes Prospero's play. In this case the director was Jude Kelly, a woman who runs her own theater in England. Was there a new approach to this production of *The Tempest*?

"A psychological approach rather than a political approach or a sociological one," explained Frank. "Just how to take Prospero on this journey. How to do a play about a man who has lived alone with his child for twelve years. He has really, in a sense, walked away from the world and is blaming everybody else, which we all tend to do. And he decides in the course of the evening that in order for him to re-take his place in the world, he must forgive. It's a very simple story, isn't it? A very simple theme, but very difficult to make come across.

"So Jude wanted to approach the play from the fact that Prospero wants desperately to re-enter the world and doesn't quite know how, and through the forgiving of his enemies, he once again finds his own self, his own heart. We stayed very much away from grandiose political themes and stentorian acting and shouting and screaming. We tried to play it purely for his heart."

"They did *The Tempest* when I was in college," said Judith. "It's so great to hear what it's really about, because in college they updated it and made [the characters] into space people and did this weird interpretation so I never fully understood what *The Tempest* was about."

"We auditioned about three hundred actors for the play and it was amazing," Frank recalled. "Every single actor had a *Tempest* story like, 'Well, I was once in a production where the Ariel was blue and green' or 'I was in a production where the Caliban was played by six actors.' Everybody seems to mess with *The Tempest,* and [they] just do it for all kinds of crazy reasons. I was very happy when Jude said, 'I think the play should be done on an island and I think it should be done from Prospero's psychological point of view.' "

Frank continued. "I did a play called *Passion* a few years ago on Broadway, and we were not getting it. It was going to be a disaster as opposed to what it was, which was sort of a semi-success. About the third week of rehearsals I went to the playwright and I said, 'We're not getting this, are we?' And he said, 'No, you're not getting it at all.' And I said, 'Will you do me a favor? Will you read the play out loud to us?' And it was as if I was giving him a glass of water in the desert. He said, 'Yes, yes, yes, I will.' But I couldn't get the rest of the company to agree, because they were afraid that he might do something which would get in the way of their imagination. So I went around and I said, 'This is the man who wrote it. This is the man who understands it. This is the man who knows what it's about and we don't. We're missing the point.'

"I went and bought a lot of Danish and made a lot of coffee and they all came to my house and the playwright Peter Nichols sat down and read *Passion* from beginning to end and it was the most extraordinary experience. Suddenly every actor went, 'Oh my God, so that's what that means!' Then I would see them going off in rehearsals and saying to the playwright, 'Give me a line reading.'

"If you're sure enough about your own sense of what you want to do as an actor, all of that is grist for the mill, anything the writer says, or the director says, or another actor says, or the janitor. I like to hear everybody's opinion and then, out of all of them, I choose what I feel strongly about. We are lucky when a playwright's alive. Wouldn't it be great if I had Shakespeare, because I still don't know how to do certain things in *The Tempest.* I'm not sure I've got the playwright's heart in my hand when I do a speech, and if he were alive I could say to him, 'What did you mean?' It would help me a lot."

Are there other playwrights besides Shakespeare who leave a lot to the imagination?

"David Rabe does," said Frank.

"To the imagination of everybody," Judith added.

In Tennessee Williams's introduction to *The Glass Menagerie,* he says it's a memory play, and therefore it can be presented with unusual freedom. What about Chekhov, Beckett, and Pinter. Do they also tie the actor down less?

"Chekhov's my very favorite playwright to perform," said Frank. "I'm prejudiced in favor of Chekhov. He doesn't tie you down at all. No, I don't think stage directions are there to tie you down. They are just there for guideposts, and you can either pick them up or not. Any information is valuable. Nothing gets in your way really unless you let it."

How does the actor in Shakespeare deliver the poetry without interrupting the acting?

"In the conversations I have had," said Judith, "the British actor embraces the poetry and the American actor embraces the acting, and I agree with that. But what really makes it work when I have seen it work, is when it's a meeting of those two: where the poetry comes out of the emotion that they have tapped into and feeds it so that it becomes alive, and sometimes you hear it as poetry and sometimes you are caught up in the emotion. I went to Stratford, Ontario, in Canada this summer and saw plays there and it was wonderful to be inundated with Shakespeare and this theory was true in the wonderful performances. There were people who had found what the truth of the moment was, but didn't relinquish the poetry, because many times the American actor unfortunately hasn't been trained well enough to embrace the poetry and many times the British actor has only been fed the poetry and not embraced the heart of it. As Mike Nichols would say, 'The event doesn't happen.' The story isn't told because it's lopsided. One muscle is being used and not the other. I think the best performance is the combination of the two."

"This is only my second Shakespeare play," said Frank, "but what I am discovering in attacking it every night is that if you pour all of your emotion into the poetry simultaneously, you get the best performance out of yourself. You don't try and act around it. You don't try to *avoid* the poetry. When you try to have a powerful emotion and then use the language over it or on the side of it or past it, it doesn't work.

"I have three incredibly famous speeches, and they are powerful and wonderful and they work best inside me. I have no idea how they work outside. They work best inside me when I pour my feeling into the words. If I say, 'Our revels now are ended,' with my full heart as opposed to having a full heart and then saying," (he spoke softly) " 'Our revels now are ended,' it doesn't work as well. But when the words and my heart are together, it's very much what Judith said. It's really thrilling in Shakespeare more than almost any other playwright, because he's so economical and so powerfully structured that if your breath and your thought and your heart are all going at the same time, you have that thing that keeps you an actor. It doesn't happen every night, but when it does it's thrilling."

Does the actor have to arrange his breathing and phrasing to fit the verse?

"Yes," said Frank. "It's as much an exercise in breath control to act Shakespeare as [it's an exercise of] any other part of yourself. You have to make decisions. You have to say, 'I'm going to get myself here and then take a breath,' because if you find yourself caught short, if you haven't thought it out, you'll murder the meter and you'll lose confidence in delivery. Breath is a very important element in Shakespeare. Not false breath or stentorian acting, saying, 'I can say all that in a line.' I don't mean that. I mean you have to think it out because you'll look at a page of Shakespeare and think, 'Where the hell is the verb?' You have to find the verb. It's in there somewhere, and that requires a lot of breath."

"That's true of David Rabe," Judith said. "I had a long speech where you wouldn't get the laugh if you would breathe in the wrong place, because then you broke up the rhythm and the audience heard it. So when you would miss it and breathe in the wrong place, by God that laugh was gone."

"I lost a laugh in *Hurlyburly* that I had got consistently for two months," said Frank, "and I called Mike Nichols and I said, 'Would you stop in and take a look and see why I've lost this laugh,' and he said, 'I don't have to stop in, why don't we just do it on the phone.' So he went and got the script and I got my script. Mike said, 'I'll be Phil and you be Eddie.' He read the lead-in line and then I read the next line. He said, 'Oh, you're not getting the laugh because you're not taking a breath here and then emphasizing the last word, you're emphasizing the first word.' And sure enough, I went back in my mind and when I had gotten the laugh, it was *that* technical. You don't get the laugh if you go da *da* ta da as opposed to da da ta *da.* So that night I went in and I got the laugh back and I sent Mike flowers. Mike's brilliant that way. What is the cliché? Life is easy, comedy is hard."

It seems that certain playwrights require a specific technique. Is David Rabe one of them?

"I think so," said Frank.

"Noël Coward," added Judith.

"Noël Coward does, too," agreed Frank. "Immense technique. Judith and I tend to work with playwrights who require it. We have both been very lucky."

"I did Arthur Miller's movie *Everybody Wins,*" Judith said, "and I would sit and read the script. Let's face it, most movies don't have great scripts, or great language, but you really had to work on the script of *Everybody Wins* or it would not work. There was a meter to it and a beat."

"I'm very lucky," Frank said, "because I've gotten to be Noël Coward characters and David Rabe characters and Arthur Miller characters and for the most part in my career I haven't had to do a lot of 'Don't move or I'll shoot' stuff or 'Get down quick!' Should I say 'Get down *quick*' or should I say 'Get *down* quick'? I haven't had to do a lot of that stuff and Judith hasn't either. It doesn't mean that there is a Rabe style or a Shakespeare style at all. Just be honest to the character in that play at that time."

Did the actor in Shakespeare's time feel the emotions when he acted?

"I bet he did," said Frank. "We don't know about it, but

how can you be human and not feel emotions? They were human beings. Jude Kelly, before she went back to England, used to stand up at the matinees, because we have mostly young people who have never seen Shakespeare before, and she would say, 'I just want to remind you that this play was written by an ordinary man, like you and me, who sat down with a pen.' Shakespeare was just a guy who said, 'This might get a laugh' or 'I bet this will give them some tears,' and then he handed it to his favorite actors who were known for doing certain things, and he wrote set pieces for them. There is no way that actor couldn't say, 'Look what Bill wrote me!' and not also say, 'I can't wait to get out and do that!' or 'Am I going to get them with that!' It's impossible. We are now much too reverent with Shakespeare. It's why there are so many bad Shakespearean actors around. People think they have to impose upon it something other than the truth of what the man was trying to say."

Frank played the young Shakespeare in William Gibson's *A Cry of Players.*

"It was a play that Bill Gibson wrote about the young Will Shakespeare," explained Frank. "Anne Bancroft played Anne Hathaway. It was at Lincoln Center in 1967. Shakespeare was a young man trying to get away from his older wife and kids because he wanted to go off and find his muse. That's a universal story. Everyone was very angry with Bill Gibson. They thought, 'Will Shakespeare shouldn't be written about that way,' as if he wasn't a young vital boy who wanted to go off and do his thing."

Shakespeare was an actor as well as a playwright. Sam Shepard, Harold Pinter, and Noël Coward were also actors. Is there a relationship between acting and playwriting?

Frank nodded. "I just think if you are creative, you are creative, and if you let yourself go, you can probably find all sorts of things you can do other than the thing you think you can do."

Are the essential elements of creativity the same in all the arts? If you can act does that mean you can also paint or write?

"I'd kill to play the violin," Frank said.

"I was a painter long before I ever began acting," said Judith. "But obviously expressing myself artistically was my bent rather than mathematics. I don't know a lot of actors who are even good at mathematics. They tend to be good at another artistic thing. It's what your soul says."

"I have begun to write recently, in the last couple of years," Frank said, "and I find that it's something I respond to very, very dramatically. I cannot paint. I've tried. And I can't play a musical instrument. But when I sit down to express myself in words on paper, I find it's a lot easier, often easier than acting for me. Whatever the thing is that you find yourself going to, you should encourage yourself to do."

I asked Frank if he started thinking about becoming a playwright because he had been called upon to come up with lines in rehearsals or tryouts of new plays.

"No," said Frank, "but look at the playwrights I've worked with. They are all brilliant. I can't imagine Peter Nichols saying, 'Give me a line there, Frank.' I just can't. That would happen more in television, where they have to make it up as they go along anyway."

The actor sometimes has *more* insight into his role because he is looking at the play specifically from his character's point of view. Sometimes in tryouts the actor says, "I can't say that as the character. I wouldn't say that." What happens when an actor is speaking a line in a new play that isn't appropriate?

"It doesn't come up when you work with really wonderful writers," said Frank, "because they have created the person before you. I may be a bit stronger on playwrights than a lot of actors are. They are really my gods. I never had actor idols. I always had writer idols. I feel lucky they are alive, so when I work on an Albee play or a Miller play I can call them on the phone and say, 'I'm not making sense of this speech. This is really how I say it.' I never say the speech is wrong, because I always feel there must be a way into it. Ninety-nine-point-nine percent of the time Edward or Arthur or somebody would say, 'What I feel about that is' or 'You are missing this rhythm,' and I would say, 'Oh, of course,' and it would become clear to me. But they are all excellent playwrights who are very considerate men who don't just dash a line off because it's time for dinner. They really have thought it out and I respect that. If I really can't make it work, then I might have the courage to say, 'Maybe the line is structured wrong. Can we try it out loud another way?' But most of the time the playwright will fix it for me."

"I have found that many times Judy gets in the way if I'm

doing that," added Judith. "I usually accept whatever is there. I'm horrible at improvisation so I have to rely on the script, and I trust that there is a reason for it to be there. I remember when I did *Precious Sons,* I felt I was being terribly defensive and protective of my character because she was the only female in the play. About halfway through rehearsals I woke up to that. I loved her so much and I felt sorry for her, and I knew she was the bad guy but I wanted everybody to understand why she was doing what she was doing. There were certain lines that I would resist. That taught me that most of the time, it's *me* getting in the way. It's not that the line is wrong or inconsistent or 'Oh, she would never say that.' Judy would never *let* her say that."

"That's a very profound statement she just made about actors," said Frank. "It really is. Often you don't want to show a particular side of yourself, even through a character, so you keep fighting the playwright, saying what you said earlier, 'My character would never do this.' Maybe Judy was thinking, 'I don't want to be presented this way' or 'I don't wish to show that side of myself,' so you fight the playwright.

"A friend of mine was in a movie that was immensely successful a couple of years ago, and she's a theater actress and she rang me from the set, saying, 'I'm amazed. This is a brilliantly written script, absolutely brilliant from the beginning to the end. And,' she said, 'the actors in it are forcing the writer to keep rearranging and rewriting it to fit their mouths because they are not skilled in his particular language and they are decimating it.' Finally, the writer won out, but what Judy said is really true. If you are not on top of yourself every minute, you might find yourself twisting a character or a writer around your finger to suit whatever it is *you* might want to project about yourself in that role. I'm always on guard about why I want to take a part, because I think, 'What is it I want to hide?' So I have to keep fighting those two things."

Speaking of actors writing, Frank wrote an article for *The New York Times* that caused a stir in the theatrical community. It was called "The Demon Seesaw Actors Ride" and it was creative writing about the business of acting. What is the "demon seesaw actors ride?"

"There are so many of them that we all ride," said Frank. "I pulled it out of the book I'm writing because I had read too many b.s. interviews with actors in the *Times* and other newspapers and seen one too many on television. I'm very tired of the press and journalists misrepresenting actors or actors misrepresenting themselves, so I wanted to write what I believe the truth of an actor's life to be.

"I started it by writing about a man who is very well-known and whose career had just crumbled. I met him in a restaurant and his hands were shaking very badly and I identified completely with the tremble. I went home that night and began to write about it because I knew that something in his tremble was awaking something in me and was true of all actors. I began to remember what each actor had told me about fear. And I began to record actors' fears and terrors. What happens with actors is that either you read interviews that are terribly soupy and overall [everybody's] one big happy family, or you read a lot of aggrandizement. An actor's life, just like anybody's, is fraught with pain and terror and feeling and all sorts of things. Camus said that actors should never hold themselves apart from society. They should jump into the center of society and be neither higher nor lower than any common man. I believe that, too. That's why I started to write it."

In the article, Frank writes, "Why do actors live the lives we do? Whether we are newcomers, superstars, an enduring light, a flash in the pan, a has-been or a comeback king, from low self-esteem to insufferable arrogance, we are the seesaw kids, kids who hold on tight and wait, wait for the call, the audition, the part, the review, and then we do it again." Frank writes about an actress he knew and how he spotted her at six o'clock in the morning by the pool drinking and she said, "I hate revealing myself and I despise myself for wanting to be liked." Does an actor have to reveal himself in order to act?

"You have to reveal yourself artfully," said Frank. "You don't have to go out onstage and reveal Frank Langella because that wouldn't be art and it wouldn't be talent. It would just be coming out and displaying your neuroses, which would be a stupid thing to do. You act *in spite* of your neuroses, you don't act *because* of them. That actress was very moving because she had a very difficult time, as a lot of actors do, going on and wishing to continue to open herself.

"If you have a part that requires a tremendous understanding of pain, you know as you get older you have to go deeper to get that pain. And if you are honest with yourself, you also have to uncover things most people spend a lifetime protecting themselves against. If you have any respect for your craft, you think, 'I have to play this part and I have to go there to be honest in playing it and I'm not certain I want to go there eight times a week.' Someone else wrote that the actor travels in one night a distance that the ordinary man takes a lifetime to go. As Prospero from eight o'clock to eleven, I have to travel this extraordinary emotional path. It's why so many actors drink."

"And then you have to go back and be that person who spends all that time covering that up," said Judith. "To use Camus, if you do put yourself back into the stream of things, and not remove yourself, and you get on the subway and you go to the dry cleaners, and you don't have somebody else doing everything for you, then you've got all that pain of normal living. Buck up and be strong. Come on, straighten yourself and go back and be a normal person! Otherwise, we'd be riding the subway weeping all the time. That to me is the hardest part about being an actor, the seesaw of going back and forth."

The other complaint of Frank's actress in the article was that she couldn't stand being an actress anymore because of wanting to be liked. Is that a motive for actors when they take up a career?

"That was her specific demon," Frank said, "but I do think that it's more prevalent than most actors would like to admit. I think the reason that Sally Field took such flak is because she said the truth, not because she was saying something false. Everybody got uncomfortable because she said, 'You like me, you really like me.' Well, what the hell is so wrong with wanting to be liked? She just admitted it, and in an industry where people pretend to be cool and distant and aloof, basically what she was saying is what every actor really feels, which is: 'Like what I do.' It's such a miserably difficult profession. Why get up there on the stage if you want to be hated? It doesn't make any sense.

"Of course you want to be liked. When asked what it took to be a great star, Bette Davis, my favorite movie actor other than Gable, said, 'It takes the courage to be hated.' If someone like Bette Davis, who didn't seem to give a damn what people thought of her, thought it required courage to be hated, then she obviously wanted to be liked, too. It took courage for her to be hated. Yes, it's at the bottom line of every actor's need."

Does the film actor have to reveal more of himself than the stage actor?

"You have to reveal more of your body, not your heart," said Frank.

"I don't know. I had to reveal quite a bit onstage," said Judith (who had appeared totally nude in the play *Steaming*).

"You certainly did," said Frank, grinning, "and I saw it all." Then he added, "I'm not a very successful movie actor. I hope in the second half of my career to get better at being as free in front of a camera as I can be in front of an audience. Film acting is a particular skill which I admire greatly because there is a kind of nakedness and simplicity about film work that is breathtaking when it's right. The camera *does* lie. It's not true that the camera doesn't lie. But when an actor is able to open his heart and soul and let the lens catch it, it's among the most thrilling events you can see, right up there with thrilling acting in the theater.

"Most of movie acting is toss-offable, but when there is somebody who really can do it . . . last night I watched Clark Gable in *San Francisco*. This is a great movie actor. This is a man who was quite capable of walking up to Jeanette MacDonald and having a four-minute love scene in which he spoke his heart and mind and soul and you believed it. Try to get a modern actor today to speak that wonderful, flowery, romantic language. Some of the greatest movie actors are the great behaviorists, people who already have personalities that are so extraordinarily individual that you then see a whole group of people trying to copy them."

The director Frank Perry calls Judith Ivey "a character star." Is it more difficult for a woman to be a character star than for Dustin Hoffman or Al Pacino?

"I think so," said Judith, "partly because you're supposed to stay attractive. There's a double standard on how you're supposed to look. When I did *Brighton Beach Memoirs,* I gained twenty pounds for the role and they also padded me. That was a character role in that movie. It was 1985 when I shot that. I lost all that weight [but] I'm *still* proving to people that I'm not over forty. Robert De Niro gained a hell of a lot of weight to do *Raging Bull,* and everyone thought it was an *artistic* choice. Our hearts were in the same place. I think there is a double standard. Judy Ivey was all of a sudden a woman over forty and overweight and Robert De Niro is an artist. It's harder in that sense.

"I also have to laugh when they ask, 'Are you a leading lady or a character actress?' because I want to know [what] the leading ladies are *playing*. They should be characters as well and should be approached as characters. It's frustrating because I was trained that way, so I don't know how to do it any other way.

"It is changing. Leading ladies are becoming more interesting, but they don't write very many of them. Most of the films that are done are still about men. It's *their* story. There are very few women and there's a handful of actresses who get to do them, and they pretty them up. I thought Jane Fonda did a wonderful job as an actress in *The Dollmaker,* but she still looked like she came from gym class, and I would venture a good portion of my money that she *had* to do that, that that was not Jane Fonda's choice."

The actor has to repeat his creation every night onstage. How does the actor avoid becoming bored with his work?

"I keep reminding myself," said Frank, "that in a demanding part like Prospero, there is a thin line from the offstage to the onstage. It's a little black sliver from the dark to the light and when I step from the dark to the light, I'm not any different, I'm not a different mass of protoplasm. I'm just Frank Langella and Prospero together and I try to tell myself right before my first speech that I've never, ever done it before and that I am simply going to say the first words that come to me as the character and they will then lead me to the next. If I go onstage thinking, 'Oh I did this before' or 'This worked last night and let me try to re-create it again,' then I am in terrible shape.

"If I tell myself it's fresh and alive and new and I will discover something new in the actress's face opposite me, and I will say the line the way it comes out of me—hopefully, truthfully and viscerally—then the night flies by. My best performances are on the days when I am extremely busy and I have very little time to think about it or, when I get to the theater, I just have a few minutes to calm down and then go on. My worst performances are when I have had nothing to do all day and I come to the theater already slightly down."

"I remind myself that this audience hasn't seen this before," Judith said. "That usually does it for me, and the audience the night before maybe didn't laugh or I felt that I was phony in a dramatic moment—I'm always remembering what I did the night before and challenging myself in different moments, which invariably changes whatever happens after that moment. Usually I have to say, 'These guys haven't seen this tonight. This is going to be great!' "

Frank narrated a PBS biography of the life of Stella Adler. What kind of influence do acting teachers have on the careers of actors?

"I didn't study with Stella and I didn't know her," said Frank. "I had to give her an award at a dinner after the documentary. I introduced her and I said what I thought of her, which she liked a lot, so she rang me on the phone and she said, 'Mr. Langella. You will come for tea. You will not cancel and you will not be late!' 'So,' I thought, 'how can I resist that?' She's ninety, so I went to see her, and we became very good friends and I fell very much in love with her as a teacher and a mind.

"If you want to read a book about acting that is the best book I have ever read, it's Stella's book, *Techniques of Acting*. She says acting is heart, mind, and spirit. And she does believe that an actor must have size and dimension and great grandeur absolutely rooted in truth. She's often misunderstood. People think, 'Oh, she's this old dame from another era.' She's not. She's as modern a teacher of acting as Judith is as modern an actress. She's absolutely of the moment. She's a brilliant teacher. I had a teacher in college named Sawyer Falk when I was at Syracuse University and he had a great effect on me. I still remember things he told me, but I didn't have any teachers after that."

"I went to Illinois State University," said Judith, "in a professional acting program as opposed to a teaching program. There was a professor that cast me in his plays quite a bit. I never took a class with him—but I did so many plays with him—and it's his nature to teach, so he completely influenced me. Anytime I walk out on a stage, I'm waiting to hear him in the back saying, 'I can't hear you!' "

Judith has an amazing ability with accents. Where does that come from?

"That came from moving a lot," said Judith. "I moved from

the southern part of our country to the northern part and there's a big difference in the way we talk. I was made fun of because I had a southern drawl, and I learned how to get rid of it. I also learned how to make fun of the Yankee talk. Then I became facile at changing, and I started being cast in British plays. I found out it's just like our country, you can't just do a general British dialect. You have to know where in Britain you're from to do it correctly."

Should actors take voice lessons because of the special demands of the stage?

"I didn't take lessons," said Judith.

"I grew up in Bayonne, New Jersey," said Frank, "and until I was about seventeen I tawked like this, and I said, 'Maaah, I want some cawfee' and 'You better cawl nawoo!' Then I saw John Gielgud in something and he became my vocal idol. I thought, 'This is the most beautiful voice I've ever heard.' So I took all my money and I went into Times Square and I bought all the John Gielgud records I could find and I went into the attic and I taught myself to speak this way. Except I'm better now, because when I was nineteen in New Jersey I was saying, 'Ooh that this tooo tooo solid flesh . . .' and my friends would say, 'Ey, Frankie, what you doing, you tawk like this!'

"Years later I got to work with Sir John and I got to know him. He's famous for these honest statements he makes about people, like he once said to Helen Hayes, 'Oh we don't want to have bad actresses like Helen Hayes. Oh, not you, Helen, the *other* Helen.' So I walked up to him and I said, 'Oh, Sir John, I'm very happy to meet you. For a long time I sounded like you and I emulated your sound.' And he looked at me and said, 'Well, you're quite over it, dear boy.' "

C H A P T E R E L E V E N

MAUREEN STAPLETON
AND
BEATRICE STRAIGHT

"What are you doing slobbering all over the Virgin?"

© MARTHA SWOPE

Maureen Stapleton in "The Little Foxes"

Beatrice Straight in "All My Sons"

© MARTHA SWOPE

Maureen Stapleton was born in Troy, New York, on June 21, 1925. She attended Saint Mary's School and Catholic Central High School, planning even then to be an actress. "I'd been preparing my family for it since I was ten," Maureen once said. She studied acting with Herbert Berghof and then later at the Actors Studio. After a stint in summer stock, Maureen landed a small part in Guthrie McClintic's production of *The Playboy of the Western World.* Her big break came when she was only twenty-five. After reading eight times for Tennessee Williams, the very Irish-looking Maureen was chosen to play Serafina, the Sicilian widow in *The Rose Tattoo.* During her career Maureen has won two Tony awards (for *The Rose Tattoo* and *The Gingerbread Lady*), one Oscar (for *Reds*), and an Emmy (for *Among the Paths to Eden*). Her numerous stage appearances include *The Glass Menagerie, Plaza Suite,* and *Toys in the Attic.* Her film roles span a wide range, from *Bye Bye Birdie* to *Airport,* from *Nuts* to Woody Allen's *Interiors.* Among Maureen's many television credits are the specials *Queen of the Stardust Ballroom* and *The Gathering.*

Beatrice Straight is the granddaughter of William E. Whitney, and a cousin to Gloria Vanderbilt and Jock and Sonny Whitney. In 1946, at an early point in her career, she said, "Call me stagestruck Annie, but don't call me a socialite." Along with Michael Chekhov, Beatrice founded the Chekhov Studio, which led to the launching of her professional career. She was a founding member of Theater Inc. and was responsible for the first visit of the Old Vic company to the United States. She won a Tony for her role as Elizabeth Proctor in Arthur Miller's *The Crucible,* and she won an Oscar for her role as William Holden's wife in the film *Network.* Beatrice's stage roles include Blanche in *A Streetcar Named Desire,* Lady Macbeth in *Macbeth,* Gertrude in *Hamlet,* and Mrs. Alving in *Ghosts.* She has appeared in such films as *The Formula* and *The Promise,* and with Audrey Hepburn in *The Nun's Story* and *Bloodlines.* She has also performed in approximately forty television specials. Beatrice was married to the late Peter Cookson, whom she met when they appeared together in *The Heiress.*

I first got to know Maureen Stapleton on the train from Los Angeles to New York back in the sixties. I very quickly learned that Maureen refuses to fly. She is willing to take chances on stage and screen, but not in an airplane. I had left my coproducer for *The Impossible Years!* in Hollywood to search for our star, while I returned by train with my two young sons. During our three-day journey, Maureen taught my sons poker and regaled us with tales of her adventures on boats and trains as well as in the theater. She made no attempt to censor herself. The honesty and truth she communicates on the stage is also part of her personal charm.

My other guest for the evening was Beatrice Straight, who, in addition to her career as an actress, was the cofounder of the Michael Chekhov Studio. Michael Chekhov had worked with Stanislavski at the Moscow Art Theater, but he had broken away and founded his own acting school after disagreeing with some of Stanislavski's precepts.

Like Maureen, Beatrice has a wonderfully expressive face. She made her entrance onto the New School's stage with great style, possessing the regal bearing of a woman familiar with playing royalty.

I told Maureen that when I watched her onstage, I was amazed she could still convince me she was someone else, since I knew her personally. I asked Maureen and Beatrice if they had a difficult time as audience members, losing themselves in the illusion.

"No," said Beatrice. "That's the great thing, I love going to the theater, except when I get bored. It's the same magic. When we are off the stage, we are just as good an audience as everybody else. The magic is there. There's something very special."

What happens if the actors onstage are friends or colleagues? Is it harder to believe them?

Maureen said, "We all have our lists of people we love to see. It doesn't matter if I know them. They still do it and it's still magic."

"I love to go and see people I know," added Beatrice. "It's great fun to see people we know are wonderful and see them do different things."

To understand how the actor makes us believe she is somebody else, we need to know what she does. Some of our guests have said they weren't sure, but there are some things we have discovered that everyone agrees on. One of them is that the actor must have a specific goal to pursue in each scene. When Maureen played Serafina in *The Rose Tattoo,* did a strong playwright like Tennessee Williams indicate what to do in each scene? Who makes the choice?

"It's usually in the script," said Maureen. "The script dictates your choice, but it's collaborative. You and the other actors and the director. I was in a play called *Toys in the Attic,* and Arthur Penn was the director. Anne Revere and I were sisters, and Jason Robards was our brother. The character I played came home after she had been fired from her job. So I came in and Anne asked me something and I cried. I cried *buckets.* You get fired, and it seemed logical to cry. Arthur Penn said, 'She would never cry there.' I could have given him eight thousand reasons for why I cried! He said, 'She is angry. It is cold, hard *anger.*' I didn't know how to do it, so I said, 'Please, Arthur, show it to me because I have to get there by another route. Let me try to imitate you.' I saw what he meant and I saw that he was right. So I just tried to imitate the way he did it till it became a normal reaction for me. That's what the director does. Of course, you have to trust him."

What happens when the actor *doesn't* trust the director?

"You have to trust and like the guy and know that he's good," said Maureen. "Then you go along. Even if he makes a mistake it's okay. But if you know that he's no good, you have to protect yourself. Robert Preston told me years ago, 'What you do is you tune him out. You listen and you smile and you nod, "Oh yes, yes, I see, I get it, okay." And you tune him out.' But you don't tune out anybody that is good. If the director isn't really up to it, very often I go to the other actor and say, 'I'm in trouble here, help me work on this.' "

"I remember doing an adaptation of Racine's *Phèdra* for off-Broadway," Beatrice said, "and the director was from the Comédie-Française and he could not speak English. He would say, '*Plus vite! Plus vite!* (Faster! Faster!)' And that offended me so much, that we should do it faster. The French way is very different from our American way of working. In the end it worked out. I guess I was the only one who understood French."

How do actors learn to make their own choices?

"I was very lucky," said Beatrice, "because I had a wonderful teacher, Michael Chekhov, who was Anton Chekhov's nephew from the Moscow Art Theater. He had believed in Stanislavski, except Stanislavski always said, 'Find your own feelings and then do it.' Chekhov believed that would limit you. You couldn't play a lot of parts. So he developed a technique which was called 'psychological gesture,' which could awaken feelings that you had never had.

"We were always taught to find the objective of the character. What was the character going after? When you first analyzed the part, you would try to find out what the objective of the character was and, if it was well written, generally the beginning and the end would be in contrast. You had to find out what the character was doing in the beginning and then how it had changed in the end.

"All of his technique was very helpful in beginning to work on a part. The director didn't know that that's what you were doing. If you were lucky and had a good director, he would tell you a lot of things, too. Many directors are more general about a play and how they want the play done, [and they're] not so good at telling actors. So Michael Chekhov's training was very useful to me.

"He was an absolutely wonderful man. He started the second Moscow Art Theater with Stanislavski's blessing. Then he was playing poker with a man who said, 'Escape tonight because they're going to arrest you.' Chekhov was blessed by Stanislavski, but he believed in spiritual things and Russia did not at that time. So he escaped to Germany and played there and then went to Paris, [where] Georgette Boner, a wonderful Swiss woman, backed him. He did productions there with the company and then they came to New York.

"I was a very young girl and I was studying with [Maria] Ouspenskaya and I went to see him one night and he was unbelievable. He was amazing as an actor. He was a short little man with a stub nose and a funny voice. You would see him do parts and you couldn't believe it was the same man. *Completely different.* His whole being was different on the stage. He was also very nice.

"I said, 'Do you want to go to England and start a school?' because my family was in England. He said yes, and six months later he spoke beautiful English. He taught us there.

"I was just in Moscow a month ago. I was invited there because now Chekhov is considered their greatest actor. It was very exciting because they were honoring Stanislavski and there were three hundred people there from every country. The translators were going crazy. People got up and spoke. Instead of a speech, I made people do a few exercises, which they loved. There's a wonderful feeling in Russia now and Moscow is such a beautiful city. I hadn't realized how much space there is. There's going to be a Chekhov network. I taught three workshops and a lot of people said they wanted to come to America to study. So I think it's a tremendous moment. The people themselves are being freed and the young people were wonderful. This is what theater does. Theater is a wonderful medium for exchange. You don't have to really know the language. If the acting is right, you can feel it and be moved."

How did the Michael Chekhov Studio start in this country?

"He said he would go to England," said Beatrice, "and then I brought him back to America and we had a studio. He went to California to do films, and then he passed on. But he's keeping a good eye on us. He says, 'Behave yourself!' "

In Michael Chekhov's book *To the Actor* he says it's the job of the creative artist to interpret, not to copy.

"I think what he says is true," said Beatrice, "because depending on what size and shape and everything else you are, two different people playing the same part would be very different. Each person has their own personal feeling. One loves certain actors because they suddenly bring something so different to a part. You can see the same play three times and then suddenly it comes alive because of the actor you are watching."

"Years ago," Maureen said, "when I was young, people said *Hedda Gabler* was a great play, but I didn't get it. I thought, what *is* this? Finally, once at school, I saw Kim Stanley do the first act, and I thought, 'Oh, *that's* what it's about!' I never could have done it or imitated what she did, but she knew what it was about. She was brilliant! It depends on how much you trust the director and the writer. It all comes down to common sense."

Reveries suit Maureen; there's an urgency to the way her eyes become slightly distracted as she fixes on some moment from the past with her entire being. She continued. "The first big part I ever had was in Tennessee Williams's *The Rose Tattoo.* We opened and did very well, and Tennessee went away on a vacation. During his absence, I found what I thought was a brilliant acting moment. In the third act, the woman I play finds out her late husband had been unfaithful, and her whole religious mania goes berserk, and she blows out the vigil light in front of the Virgin, and runs out of the shrine where she has kept her husband's ashes. One night, after I blew out the light, I *hugged* the statue and I was crying and crying. Other actors told me it was a great moment and how much they loved it.

"Tennessee came back and saw the show. He had invited me out to dinner afterwards, and while I was getting ready, I was waiting and waiting for him to tell me how wonderful the moment was. As we were going out the door, he said, 'Oh Maureen, what are you doing slobbering all over the Virgin?' I was shocked. I said, '*Slobbering* over the Virgin?' He said, 'Yeah. What are you doing? Just blow out the candles and get out of there!' I said, 'It doesn't take long, just a quick hug and a couple of tears and out.' He said, 'No, no, no, she would never do that.' So that was the end of my great acting moment.

"I saw Julie Harris do a great thing once as Saint Joan. The play was *The Lark* and I remember going to opening night. They bring Saint Joan out of the cellar where she has been kept for three days. They bring her up and she is being interrogated, and at some point, I don't know how she did it, I couldn't imitate her, but in the middle of answering her questions, Julie yawned. You suddenly felt how tired this girl was. I started to cry, and the rest of the entire play I cried from just that one Goddamn yawn. She just blew me away."

"That's a wonderful thing," Beatrice said, "when an actor does something that seems so out of key and yet is so deep."

"You know how brave you have to be to do that?" said Maureen.

Emotional memory is a device used by actors to get in touch with their feelings from a past incident, and it is usually associated with the Method and with Stanislavski. In his later years, Stanislavski abandoned emotional memory because he began to realize that as you grow older, your memory of what happened earlier changes.

"I didn't understand emotional memory," said Maureen. "Maybe I just saw the wrong examples of it, but it used to drive me nuts."

Michael Chekhov studied with Stanislavski. Where did he stand on this?

"Emotional memory was one of the reasons why Chekhov broke free," explained Beatrice, "because he said that it limits you. If you can only do what you remember emotionally in the part, then how can you murder somebody, or express certain anger, or have a wonderful love affair? It limits you. You can't play tragedy or comedy, so that's why he did psychological gesture."

What is psychological gesture?

"It's doing things physically which will awaken your feelings," said Beatrice. "It can awaken really enormous emotions. If you can find the psychological gesture, you'll probably play parts that you would never dream of playing."

When Maureen played Serafina delle Rose in *The Rose Tattoo* she was twenty-five. If it's the artist's job to interpret, how does an actor bring depth-of-life experience to a part when she hasn't lived?

"David, I was born old," explained Maureen.

Do actors have to experience more than the rest of us, in order to act, or do they learn to imagine things they have never experienced?

"A lot of people spend their lives just imagining things they've never experienced," Beatrice said. "That's the whole point. We have to have wonderful imaginations."

Ellen Terry used to say that actors had to have the three

I's in order to act: Imagination, Industry, and Intelligence. Of the three, she said imagination was the most important. What are some of the other qualifications needed to become an actor?

Maureen leaned forward. "Like anything, you have to *want* to be [an actor] deeply enough. If you want to be a doctor deeply enough, you can become a doctor. It's up to the person. You have to *want* it. Then you find out how to get it. Wanting comes first."

"I was in a play when I was seven years old," Beatrice recalled, "and I had to be pulled off the stage. Everybody had gone, and I was still looking out at the audience. It started that early. Some people can't do it because they feel they shouldn't and others are born with it and are that crazy."

"Crazy is *way* up there," agreed Maureen. "Wanting and crazy."

How much are actors born with and how much can they learn? Talent versus technique.

"They're not versus," said Maureen. "There has to be a framework or a technique or whatever you want to call it because it's not a one-shot. You have to be able to do your magic tricks *every night,* so you have to set it up. That's what they call technique. It doesn't matter how you do it, just as long as you *can* do it. What works for me might not work for you or vice versa. You find the thing that will enable you to do it over and over and over again and try to keep it fresh. I have a girlfriend who says, 'I just like opening night. I don't want to ever do it again.' "

"And when you don't feel well, you have to leave all of that behind," said Beatrice.

Does too much technique get in the way of feeling?

"Actors are generally emotional people, not intellectual," said Beatrice, "so I don't think one gets stuck in the technique so much. Technique is useful when you're not feeling well or the feeling is gone or something. Technique is then useful to cover up or to help you through a scene. You can fall back on it, but on the whole, when you are doing a play it's already part of you."

"Common sense dictates a lot too," said Maureen.

"But the technique has helped you get there," said Beatrice.

What ability does the actor need to keep her performance fresh?

"You get nervous every night," said Beatrice. "That keeps you young in spirit."

"It's a different audience every night," added Maureen. "You can't say on Thursday, 'Gee, you should have caught me on Monday. I was really terrific.' "

"A lot of actors specialize in certain things," said Beatrice. "They can be wonderful at comedy, but find it impossible to do tragedy. I wish I could do comedy, but I have never been able to. I have no sense of comic timing. Other people can do both wonderfully."

"Comedy has to be in the writing," Maureen stated. "Tennessee is very funny. There are a lot of funny things. If it's there, it's the writer's gift."

"Of course we were very lucky when we started in the theater," said Beatrice. "It was so much easier and the whole attitude was so different. The theater meant something. People would go to the theater because they weren't watching television at home. It hadn't started in those early days. The wonderful thing was the tickets were four and five dollars. It's so disgraceful now that they're thirty and forty dollars. People could go to the theater. Young people went. I feel so badly because nowadays people can't go. And then when they do go, they say, 'Why the hell did I pay fifty dollars?' That's the trouble.

"We started the first nonprofit theater in New York with Dick Aldrich, who was the husband of Gertrude Lawrence. We were a bunch of three or four young people including Dick, and we decided to do *Pygmalion* with Gertrude Lawrence. I had three sets by the best scenic designer and we did it on Broadway and it cost thirty thousand dollars. That show now would cost a million and a half at least. And we brought the Old Vic over from England for its first visit to America. I had been to see them and we raised one hundred thousand to bring them over and it was all made back, so we gave it back to all the backers. In those days it was possible. Everybody could go to the theater. I feel so sorry now for young people."

Beatrice's company discovered some talented young actresses.

"You gave me my first job!" exclaimed Maureen.

"Maureen and Julie Harris were our two apprentices," Beatrice said proudly.

With delight, Maureen recalled, "Julie was a walk-on in *Oedipus*!"

"It was an exciting time," agreed Beatrice.

At that time, Beatrice won the Tony for her performance in *The Crucible.*

She nodded. "*The Crucible* was exciting because it had something to say. I had to leave because I was supposed to be a virgin and I was pregnant. Then we were all blacklisted because Arthur Miller had written the play. It was such a shock. That was the time when everyone was afraid of Russia. We were blacklisted just for having acted in that play."

We have heard a lot about the importance of the actor's ability to concentrate on what he is doing. When Maureen played Birdie in the Elizabeth Taylor revival of *The Little Foxes,* Austin Pendleton, the director, said of Maureen's performance, "She has that gift of just being there, to a degree that a lot of extremely talented actors do not. She is unusually oriented to a place, to a room, and to her relationship to the people in it. She works very hard. She has enormous concentration." How does an actor learn to concentrate like that?

"That comes with working," said Maureen.

In film an actor needs to concentrate for only minutes at a time compared to two hours for a play. How did Elizabeth Taylor manage the adjustment from film work to concentrating on the stage in *The Little Foxes*?

"Working with her was a great joy," said Maureen. "She's a great lady. It was wonderful to see her in rehearsal get better and better and better and better, because it's a very difficult thing when you're trying to work and it's an event, like a circus. It took her a while. It was rough. We opened in Fort Lauderdale and we played Washington and then New York. She got better and better. She was absolutely open to the director and everybody. It was wonderful to see. A few people had their knives out for her."

"It was very brave of her," said Beatrice.

"It sure was," agreed Maureen. "She had never worked in the theater before."

Do actors use the same skills to act in film as they do in the theater?

"If you did as much in film as in the theater, they wouldn't use it," said Beatrice. "It would be overdoing it. It's very hard. If you are lucky to get a director like Sidney Lumet, they will wait and let you do it, and then you can have that emotional thing. But mostly, especially now with the pressure of time in film and television, you have to come very well prepared if you want to do anything. Even then, they skip from one scene to another, so if you want to have a sense of the whole thing, you have to work very hard on your own."

Maureen worked with Woody Allen on *Interiors.* He has a reputation as a director for letting actors do their own thing.

"I guess I got along fine with him," said Maureen. "He's not shy. That was a mistake I made years ago with Wally Cox. I would drag him to parties and all kinds of things and he said to me once, 'You've made a great mistake about me. You think I'm shy. I'm not shy. I'm antisocial.' I had never met anybody who was antisocial before. I didn't know what it meant. And that's Woody. He's darling and he's sweet and he's antisocial. But he has an infallible ear when it's not right. He's not very talkative but you get the point that it's not right. But not a lot of talk. He even has another guy yell 'Cut!' "

The *Variety* film critic wrote about Beatrice's performance in *Network:* "Her range of responses, complementing William Holden's, constitute one of those outstanding memories of a lifetime." It was extraordinary, because in a period of four minutes Beatrice seemed to experience an intense range of human emotions. How did that come about?

"First of all, the script was very good," said Beatrice. "Secondly, William Holden was a wonderful man to work with. And then we had a director who worked with actors, so that we were not pressured in any way. "

Who decided how Beatrice would react to the William Holden character in her climactic scene in the film?

"That was all my choice," said Beatrice. "I was allowed to do what I felt like. We are lucky that we did theater before film because the theater gives you a background and a training and a sustaining feeling. It's much harder for young people just going into film."

"The first couple of films I did, I couldn't believe I ever learned three acts of a play," said Maureen. "I didn't know the technique or how to pace myself with a film. I would be ready, and go out the door. That was on Monday. I didn't come out of the door till Thursday. It took a long time, because each thing has its own technique. You have to be in tip-top physical condition, because your energy has to be always more than you need. You have to have more."

"The wonderful thing," said Beatrice, "is that even if you are feeling sick, when you are on the stage, somehow for those two and a half hours, you feel something happen. And then you can go and throw up right afterwards."

"Because your concentration is so strong," added Maureen. "It's wonderful because some actors give you so much."

"I took over for Wendy Hiller when she left the tour of *The Heiress,*" Beatrice recalled, "and I played with Basil Rathbone and opposite a young leading man named Peter Cookson. We toured for six months, and Peter and I were falling in love more and more. Basil would get mad and say, 'You are showing too much feeling!' Every night Basil would forget a different line in a different place, so Peter and I would have to be ready to prompt him. We had to watch that we didn't change the characters because we were falling in love with each other. At the end of the tour we got divorced from who we were with and got married."

In theater, the actor spends two hours living as the character in the imaginary circumstances of the play. She has time to develop the character's feelings. In film it's different. When Maureen walks into the courtroom in the film *Nuts,* for example, it's her first appearance in the film. She has to come in already extremely emotionally upset. How is that accomplished?

"It's like anything," said Maureen. "The more often you do it, the more often you become accustomed to the technique of film, the more you'll be able to pace yourself for it. The first few times, I was just lost. Gradually you find a way. Some people read between setups, some people play cards. I find playing cards or doing crossword puzzles helps. I can't sleep, because then I get too groggy. If I do the lines too often, I'll draw a blank there. For me it's cards or crossword puzzles, so that I'm awake and able to concentrate."

How does an actor in film get into the character after waiting around for five hours?

"You damn well have to," said Beatrice.

"That comes in the preparation before," said Maureen. "You do a lot of your own homework. You learn to prime yourself so you'll be ready when they say, 'We're ready!' Because when the lights are ready, you better be ready."

In film, the actor doesn't have a chance to experience the growth of her character the way she does in theater. Sometimes it's even shot backwards. Do actors ever *prefer* working in the movies?

"I prefer the money," Maureen said, laughing. "But for satisfaction, of an emotional or personal kind, I prefer the give-and-take of the theater. In movies, you just have the director, who you rely on *totally.* I never know where the camera is, or what part they are using, or what part they are cutting."

When an actor takes on a role a third entity is created, a unique combination of what the actor brings to the playwright's composition. To make this happen, the actor needs to find a middle ground where her own personality merges with the character. I asked Maureen and Beatrice if they prefer roles where they can immediately identify with the character, or if they like to play parts where it takes longer to find the handle?

"You start with yourself," said Maureen. "I was never an Italian seamstress. I knew one but that didn't help me for *The Rose Tattoo.* I keep coming back to Tennessee. It's in there, in the script. As the great sage Milton Berle once said, 'If it ain't on the page, it ain't on the stage.' "

"I love playing different kinds of parts," added Beatrice. "That's why Tennessee's wonderful. I enjoy doing Phèdre and Lady Macbeth, who are certainly not like Blanche. It's exciting to do different kinds of parts. I don't like doing anything like myself."

When actors play roles that are far away from themselves they need to do more research. How much research was necessary for Emma Goldman?

"I read her autobiography," said Maureen. "That was heavy furniture. They were a humorless bunch of bastards. I read that book and there were all different groups: anarchists, communists, socialists, and everybody had their own little store. But the minute there was a revolution, they were all together. She had a beau who got a gun and went to Philadelphia. How he got into Frick's office I don't know. He was going to assassinate Frick. He shot him five times. He stabbed him eight times, and he didn't kill him. So he was in prison for fifteen years, and when he got out he wrote a tome on penal systems in America, which was very good.

"Emma sent it to Jack London, who was a friend. He wrote the preface and he goes on about how fine the book is, and then he said, 'Of course, his philosophy is different from mine. He's an anarchist and I'm a socialist.' He went on about how much better his story was, and then at the very end he said, 'And besides, any guy who can't shoot straight can't think straight.' That was the only laugh I got in two thousand pages. He sent it to Emma Goldman and she never spoke to him again. She didn't use it. He was out. I thought, 'Good grief, lady, at least laugh!' That was all I read because there's just so much you can do. In the movies you rely on the director totally."

Actors are often offered parts that are similar to roles they've been successful in. Should actors look for roles that are different from those they've already attempted?

"No," said Maureen. "When I first came to New York, I was in a class and there was a girl in that class who wanted to play Saint Joan so bad she was like *possessed.* Wackoed out. I thought, 'My God, if she doesn't play Saint Joan, I want to leave town. I don't want to be around.' I also thought, 'It's going to be so tough to get a job anyway, *any* job, that you don't need to give yourself the extra added handicap of saying, "I've got to play Saint Joan," or, "I will never be happy unless I play this." ' I don't think you should do that to yourself. Be happy with what you've got. Take what you can get."

Actors get to know what they are capable of by playing a wide variety of characters. Does that mean an actor should take any role that comes along?

"I have a very artistic standard," said Maureen. "If I don't throw up, then I do it."

Every character is unique, like every human being, so each new role helps an actor expand her emotional range. I asked Maureen if she found it rewarding to play Burt Reynolds's wacky aunt on television?

"It was a job," said Maureen. "It was a nice script. One thing about television is that it goes fast. You don't have all that time that you do in movies, where you sit around for five hours and wait till the setup. Television is quicker. I like to keep going and not sit for four or five or six hours. It really dissipates your energy."

As actors grow into their roles during rehearsals and (if they're lucky) during a long run, they often discover aspects of the character they didn't know were there. I asked Maureen and Beatrice if they had any favorite roles.

"You can't have favorites," said Maureen. "You love each role you come to and you do the best you can. It's like if you have had a lot of husbands, and you're still wishing you had husband number two and you are on husband number eight. You can't do that. The next thing has to be brand-new and that's it. You'd never really be happy with what you were doing if you wished it were something else."

An actor needs to listen and react to the other actors she is working with in order to bring her character to life. How do actors do this when they're in a play with someone they don't like personally?

"That rarely happens," said Maureen. "I guess I've been lucky. There were two times. I couldn't *stand* him. I couldn't staaaaaand him! You just find things, if you have to like him. You find things to like. Maybe his necktie. Whatever will help you."

When actors work a lot in the theater they often have to find other ways to make a living. Younger, less well-known or struggling actors often wait on tables or tend bar. But even established talent often find it necessary to resort to other means. I asked Maureen and Beatrice if they feel compromised when they have to endorse products on television.

"I never felt there was anything demeaning about making a living," said Maureen. "It's a job."

"But I certainly wouldn't do a commercial of something I didn't believe in," added Beatrice.

"How deeply do you have to believe in shredded wheat?" asked Maureen.

CHAPTER TWELVE

STOCKARD CHANNING
AND
F. MURRAY ABRAHAM

"It's more fun when you help."

Stockard Channing in "Six Degrees of Separation"

F. Murray Abraham in "The Golem"

STOCKARD CHANNING was discovered when she was a freshman at Radcliffe by Timothy Mayer, who cast her in a production of *The Threepenny Opera.* In New York, Stockard landed a part in the chorus of John Guare's musical adaptation of *The Two Gentlemen of Verona* and played the lead in the touring company. She went on to perform in *They're Playing Our Song, The Rink, The Golden Age, The Lady and the Clarinet, The Homecoming, Absurd Person Singular, The House of Blue Leaves* (for which she earned a Tony nomination), *Six Degrees of Separation, Four Baboons Adoring the Sun,* and *Love Letters.* Stockard won the Drama Desk Award as Best Actress for *Woman in Mind* and a Tony for her portrayal of Sheila in *A Day in the Death of Joe Egg.* Film audiences first saw her in *The Fortune* with Warren Beatty and Jack Nicholson. Major roles followed in such films as *Grease, The Cheap Detective, Meet the Applegates,* and *Married to It.* On television, Stockard has appeared in *Table Settings, Not My Kid, The Room Upstairs,* and *Tidy Endings.* She received two Emmy nominations, for the miniseries *Echoes in the Darkness* and HBO's *Perfect Witness.*

F. MURRAY ABRAHAM began his career as the Fig Leaf in the Fruit of the Loom underwear ads. He eventually quit commercials for more serious acting. "If you can't take pride in your work, you can't have pride in yourself . . . I was a sickly child with a thick Mexican accent. I made myself what I am." Murray's first lead on Broadway was in Isaac Bashevis Singer's *Teibele and Her Demon.* He also appeared in *The Man in the Glass Booth, Legend, The Ritz, Sexual Perversity in Chicago, Bad Habits, 6 Rms Riv Vu, Uncle Vanya, The Seagull, The Caretaker, Little Murders,* and *Cyrano.* At the Public Theater, he played Malvolio in *Twelfth Night* and a rabbi in *The Golem.* His film credits include *The Sunshine Boys, The Prisoner of Second Avenue, All the President's Men, The Name of the Rose, Serpico, Scarface,* and *Bonfire of the Vanities.* Murray played the coveted role of Salieri in the film *Amadeus* and earned the Oscar. On television, he's costarred in the miniseries *Marco Polo,* and he was seen as Professor Leopold Nettles in Havel's *Largo Desolato* on public television's "Great Performances." Murray is a professor of theater at Brooklyn College, and in 1990, New Jersey's Rider College awarded him an honorary doctorate of arts.

One of those transcendent moments in the theater happened for me when I watched Stockard Channing in John Guare's *Six Degrees of Separation.* She played Ouisa, the wife of an affluent art dealer. One night, she and her husband let into their house a young black man named Paul, who claims to be the son of Sidney Poitier. Ouisa believes in Paul, and trusts in him. The encounter jolts her and sends her through new doors opening into other worlds. Then Ouisa discovers that Paul's identity has been a hoax. At the end of the play the lights fade to a single spotlight on her face, and it's an intimate, breathtaking moment when we feel we've shared her journey.

I had a similar sensation watching F. Murray Abraham as Salieri in *Amadeus.* Although this was a film, his performance drew me in so completely that I felt I had experienced the events of the drama with him. In my session with Stockard and Murray, their performances in these two roles were always on my mind.

John Guare's *Six Degrees of Separation* has some very powerful insights about life in New York, and life in general, and at the same time it's funny and moving and we care about the characters. But it almost seems to be a kind of play different from anything we have ever seen before. It's fast-moving like a farce. There are times when the characters speak directly to the audience. And there are places where the actors sigh and laugh in unison, which makes it seem choreographed. I asked Stockard if this makes it harder for her to concentrate on her role, compared to a more conventional play.

"I am now a great believer in a certain kind of discipline,"

Stockard said, "which I don't think I had access to when I was younger. Jerry Zaks, our director, is a very organized, controlled, structured human being. Oddly enough, the last time we worked together, in *House of Blue Leaves,* we used to struggle a lot with each other. When I came into this piece and I saw the kind of piece that it was, that it was seventeen people in an hour and a half on the stage, I realized after about two days that I had to surrender to him.

"I think of this piece not as a collaboration but as an act of cooperation. There is a very specific difference between those two words, because everybody involved in the production, the designers and all the actors, had to trust each other that eventually we would end up at the same point. Consequently, we just drilled. We didn't sit there and talk about my character Ouisa's background or how Flan and Ouisa got married and all that sort of stuff. There was no place or time for that. We sort of, by an act of will, became a company. We found the colors in this piece.

"When I first read it, I knew it was extraordinary, but I didn't have any understanding of the emotional reverberations it would have. I was just trying to find out what the events were. I realized I had to do it backwards, compared to how I might have done otherwise. We had to see the forest before we saw the trees. We just had to drill and drill. We got into run-throughs very early on, almost learning stuff by rote, and then the life started to happen. We also had all the technical things done very early on, a week earlier than usual. We had dress rehearsals for a full week after we had our techs, before any audience saw it. We felt like we were in a piece of sculpture. You understood how you stood in the light, the costume you were wearing, the color, how your face looked. All that started contributing to an emotional life, which is totally opposite from the process. It's a very unusual piece that way. You're absolutely right. It had to be approached in a very different manner from traditional theater pieces."

Murray said, "What Stockard touched on is the key to the theater, and the key to any art process, which is faith."

"Faith and discipline," added Stockard.

"Stockard said she trusted that at one point they would all come out at the same place," continued Murray. "But what if they hadn't? You can't even think in those terms. You have to devote yourself and give yourself completely to the process."

"I went to Jerry the second day of rehearsal," said Stockard, "and, as I said, we had worked together very well three or four years before, but I was constantly saying, 'Now wait a minute, wait a minute,' and Jerry doesn't like that very much by his own admission. So we had—not a stormy time, but one of those 'What's-she-going-to-say-now?' kind of times.

"On the second day of rehearsal I said, 'Can I talk to you?' and I said, 'Now look, I want to tell you that I am totally surrendering myself to you. Whatever you do and say for me to do, I'll do it and we'll talk about it afterwards.' I realized that this piece requires that we get on with it. And he looked at me and said, 'Yeah, right.' " (Stockard gave the line a sarcastic twist.) "And about two days later, he realized I wasn't kidding. A lot of people took their lead from me because of what I had done. We all were like a ballet corps. Jerry was genuinely grateful.

"And then we had the most amazingly precise, free, wonderful discussions when we were in dress rehearsals and previews. Even to this day we can talk about moments. It was fabulous. The precision of it became liberating. And it didn't lose one instance of emotion, because when we got in front of an audience, we were ready for them to tell us what they understood and what they saw. We weren't presenting them with a result. We said this is the story we are telling and *they informed us,* and we were ready for it. That's a very interesting way to go about this."

When an actor takes on a new role, he usually has some concept of what the character's going to be like. Then the director appears with his own concepts. How does the actor reconcile his own concept of his part with that of the director?

"What we talked about was a discovery of the piece through the process," said Murray. "If you have a director and she insists that you do things her way, you're not going to discover a damn thing. It's as bad as an actor coming to a part and *insisting* on doing it his way. The reason you're doing the play is to *discover* the play. If you already know what the play is going to be, there really isn't any reason to do it."

"What I really like to do," said Stockard, "is to sit down [with the cast] and read a play aloud, top to bottom, rather than read it to myself alone. It gives me a sense of the flow of the play. And, frankly, I think it gives a director some sense of first impulses, and then from an equal level we can discuss it. Because, let's face it, someone could look at a piece of material and just start off with a really firm conviction in left field, and it would be pretty hard to disabuse an actor of a notion that's that strong, depending on the personality, and the communication between the people. I think it's always better to start from a level of cooperation and equality so that you can discuss. Clearly, if you have totally different visions of the piece, you probably shouldn't be working together. I do agree with Murray. You've got to explore. Otherwise, why rehearse?"

One of the amazing things in Murray's performance as Salieri in *Amadeus* is the way he was able to express his conflicting feelings toward Mozart. There's a scene where Mozart's wife brings Salieri a copy of Mozart's latest work and as he looks at it, we see a whole series of different reactions as he realizes it's Mozart's first draft with no mistakes. In a scene like that, when an actor runs the gamut of emotions, from envy and admiration to jealousy and hatred, is he able to forget all the technical things that he needs to know, such as the fact that he needs to be standing on his mark?

"You're looking at a fifty-one-year-old man," said Murray. "I've been around for a while. That's my job. I don't want to put it down but I should know how to do that by this time. I'm not belittling the performance. I'm very proud of my work. But that's what I should be able to do. You hire a carpenter to pound a nail. I act. You got some acting? I'm your man!! I mean it. I really think a great deal of my talent, it's God-given, and I've worked on it very hard, but there's a lot of talent around, I gotta tell you.

"Good fortune has a lot to do with our lives. Stockard and I are not old friends. We know each other. We may behave as though we know each other as old friends. It's because we know each other's work. We could, I believe, pick up a script of a play we've never read before and probably do it very easily, as easily as we're sitting side by side. We respect each other's talent. You can't sell the material short, and you can't give too much credit to the material if you have a piece of work that's very light.

"If it's a half-hour comedy on television, which I don't put down, you can't bring the same kind of weight as you do to a piece of Shakespeare or Molière. It doesn't work. It doesn't sustain the weight. With a piece of work like *Amadeus,* the fact is it's such a well-written piece of work. It's just so *good.* It's tasty." (Murray licked his chops.) "If you can't, as an actor, with as many years of experience as I have, make that work, you better pack it in."

In *Amadeus,* Salieri accuses himself of having killed Mozart and we learn of his obsessive belief that God punished him by making Mozart, instead of Salieri, immortal. We find out all about the motive of Salieri at the beginning of the film. We also find out how the story ends. Did this create a special acting problem?

"No," said Murray, "because we filmed it in sequence. I approach all of my roles in film as I do onstage. It's the only way I know how to do it. When I go into a film I know the whole thing beforehand. I never understand these actors who show up from day to day and learn the lines as they go along. But they can do it and I respect it. It's almost like a mystery to me.

"I'm starting a film in L.A. next week and I already have most of it memorized. I have to do that, because sometimes we will shoot my death before I even start to live. With Salieri, I learned the whole thing. It's such a marvelous piece of work you could have picked it up anywhere out of sequence. You could have picked the sixth day of shooting and shot it first and I would have been okay, because that's my job.

"They come to you and they say," (Murray stepped into character, playing a shark of a producer), " 'All right, Stockard baby, here we go, baby. We got three weeks, baby, and you're going to be great! And what we're going to do is we're going to shoot this and this and this. So you learn this first. You learn this last. Don't worry about it. You get this on the weekend. We're okay.' [Then] they come and say, 'The set burned down. Sorry, Stockard baby, you got to do the last scene first.' You say, 'But I didn't learn it.' 'You better learn it because it's *time.* We gotta do it *now*!' "

"I totally agree," said Stockard. "I actually diagram things out. I diagram my wardrobe, my wardrobe changes, everything else to the point where I surprise people with my knowledge. I'm compulsive that way. It means that you go through a script and you're in ten or twelve scenes, and I write out the page numbers. I write out the date, the time passage, what I'm wearing, time of day, anything I know about it, so when I get to it I have a sense of what I'm wearing, why I've been wearing it, if it's hot out, all that sort of stuff. And it's often information that other people haven't been dealing with. It grounds me. I learn the whole scene. I learn the other actor's lines as well as my own. The way you would in a play. I have to know as much information as a director would and sometimes a little more because he's got the whole film in his head. I'm a control freak."

Murray became pensive. "I like Fred MacMurray. I think he was a wonderful actor and he was mostly a terrific bad guy. Remember him in *Double Indemnity*? Oh, what a snake! In *The Caine Mutiny*, in *The Apartment*, what an s.o.b.! He made his big money in "My Three Sons." In "My Three Sons," speaking of diagramming, he would shoot all of his scenes in the first two weeks. His contract was for many, many millions of dollars. Every scene that took place in the kitchen, he shot. He didn't need any other actors. He had all of his wardrobe in the other room. He'd come in and say, 'Hello, dear,' and he'd sit down. Then they'd say, 'Okay, that's it,' and he'd go and change clothes for the next one and come into the kitchen and he'd say, 'Hello, Chip,' and sit down. Then he'd change again. 'Hello, Mike. Oh, you did?' And he'd sit down."

"Are you making this up?" asked Stockard, with a laugh.

"This is God's truth!" said Murray. "Then, when the kitchen stuff was done they'd do all the living room stuff, get all the living room stuff done. The point is *what happens* to an actor who works that way in films and television? . . . You go out to California to make a living and, by the way, that's where the work is. It's dying here in New York in terms of commercials and a lot of movies. That's how I used to make my living, commercials. It's not happening anymore. They're all going to Florida, Chicago, Arizona, and Los Angeles. They're going out there because they gotta make a living.

"What happens is you get plugged into certain places. And they begin to expect certain performances from you. This is F. Murray Abraham. Because of his face, because of what he does, he's a killer. He does killer parts. They don't want to see you *create* anything. They don't want any surprises. They want you to come in for your two weeks, or month, and do exactly what it is you did on the last film.

"So what happens is, because you don't have any time to work on it, you only have time to learn the lines. You get the script now, shoot tomorrow, and you begin to do *the same thing* because it's safe. Because you don't have to worry about the character. Because all you have to do is say the words, collect the money, and go home. And this is the biggest danger of the electronic medium. It happens to our politicians too, doesn't it? They begin to sound like some kind of dummies who are talking. And it doesn't make any difference what comes out of their mouths, because what they *do* and what they say have no relationship."

Even when the scenes are isolated and shot out of sequence, an actor in film still has to find a way to bring truth to his work. Is there a different kind of concentration required for the film actor, as opposed to the stage actor?

"My image of making movies," said Stockard, "is being underwater in one of those big tank suits. You are really at the technical mercy of everything around you, the crew, the makeup person, the hair person. People come and they touch you up. You have no idea *what* you look like. You break down the scene. You do this ten million times. You have to surrender to the fact that you are underwater. You feel and you move slowly, and you're very encumbered. If you let that get to you, it can drive you nuts. You have to find a way to still live inside that big cumbersome suit.

"On the stage, it's sometimes like jumping off a mountaintop, with all the dangers involved. It's up to you in that sense. Once you're out there with an audience, it's never dull, and if it starts getting dull, you know you're in trouble. It's like sending a satellite beam out. You bounce there, and they bounce there, and it comes back to you. You don't say, 'This is what I want you to think, this is what I want you to feel.' You go 'Pht!' and they see it, and something else comes back, and there is this weird thing that goes on, but it's of air. It's light. It's a totally different kind of media. They're very different."

"It's difficult to explain to anyone who hasn't done it," said Murray, "but it's as if you were to try to ask someone in your family who's from the old country, or who's quite a bit older than you are, how do they make a certain dish? How do they make a certain food? You know they can never tell you exactly how to do it, but they always do it, don't they? And it's always good. It's always a little different, but it's always good. And they don't seem to be working on it! They're talking and answering the phone and they throw some of this in and they do this and they say, 'Go away,' and they give a little to the kids. It's the same thing with our work. I really mean it. It's all those ingredients we put in. You can't think only about the cooking. Because it's not just the cooking! It's the life. The cooking *is* the life. That's why the kitchen's the center of the household, isn't it? It's where you feed everyone. People come in, they go out, there's a lot of action.

"It's the same thing with the theater. The difference with the theater is we could stop right now, and we could have a good time. We could say, 'Let's do this again. Let's ask that question again.' I do that. I don't mind stopping the show! A lot of actors don't like it when I do that but I don't care. If a cat walks across the stage, what am I to do? Pretend the cat doesn't exist? I don't. I'm going to play with the cat for a while. The point is, in the movies all the things that Stockard has said are true. You know that. You're aware of that. It's the lights and the camera and the makeup. It's true! It's very difficult.

"What you have to do is find the truth, because that's the essential element that is the middle of all art. It's the middle of acting, whether it's for the camera or on the stage. It's the middle of painting. It's the middle of dance. It's the center of our lives. It's the truth. And once you get a piece of that truth, as in the wonderful script for *Amadeus* by Peter Shaffer, or this wonderful play by John Guare, once you capture the truth in your own terms, nothing can happen that will bother you. Anything can go on, and you will still maintain the truth."

"That's absolutely true," agreed Stockard. "How you get there can vary from person to person. Everybody you listen to on the stage will have different ways of getting there. It's the goal, it's not the getting there, in this case. When you hit the true note, it's like the center of the racket. It goes 'Ping!' And it cannot be denied, and that's important."

"Stockard mentioned something about working with Jerry Zaks," said Murray, "and questioning and questioning and then at one point deciding, 'Jerry, I will go all the way.' What she didn't mention (and I don't know this, I'm guessing), what she implied was, 'I'm going to go with you, but if it doesn't pay off I'm going to rip your head off.' "

Murray and Stockard laughed. "I was talking about the early process of just shuffling through this material," explained Stockard, "which was *Six Degrees.* It's interesting how it has a form on the stage now, but it was never read aloud until the first day of rehearsal. John never had readings of it. It's amazing. You had to get to the point of how it was going to look, as I said, after a certain point, when we all had our *language* down and had a way of communicating with each other, and had this trust that was built not by talk but by *action.* It's about people believing each other, that you are going to surrender. Oh yes, [Jerry Zaks] knew that if I really didn't like something, I would bark. You didn't have to bark then. You just said, 'What do you think? Oh, fine.' And then we had all the adjustments and changes and we were all in the same gear.

"I think of doing a play like show jumping, if you've ever gone to a horse show or seen it on television. You watch horses with riders take jumps. It's often *excruciating* because they go, 'Ahh!' and then they slow down, and then they go, 'Ohh!' and then they slow down. As an audience, I find that amazing to watch. It's the same thing that happens in theater when it works. If you can get an audience to go, 'Ahh!' with you, and breathe with you. But first we all have to be making the same thing. So it's about trust. It's about cooperation and faith. At a certain point, if people trust each other, if one person says, 'You know, I don't think this is working,' another can say, 'You know, you're right.' Then you're all in it together."

When an actor is performing onstage and is totally absorbed in his character, can he at the same time influence the audience to respond to what he is doing?

"It's a very dangerous game," said Murray. "It's legitimate and it's something you always feel you want to do, but once you start trying to manipulate the audience, you fall into the trap of following *them.* Because once you try to make them do something, what happens when they start to do it? You try to get them to do more, right? And they start laughing and carrying you along with them. What happens to the play? What happens to the character? Because I've done it, and I'll probably do it again.

"What happens with the audience is they'll laugh and let you think you're doing a good job of manipulation, but at one point they will stop because the belief ends at a certain point. You have to trust that the character in the play will carry them along with you. The manipulation is part of your talent, part of the reason that you're an actor. It will happen without your trying to be like a puppeteer. That's a very dangerous game. And you'll do it, but you'll find out that you'll get hurt in the end.

"I'll tell you why. Because they want the same thing you do. They want a *great* experience. They want to come away from this thinking, 'This was the reason I came to the theater. This is the reason I'm an audience. To have the experience of a lifetime.' Even if it's a little tiny play. That's why I'm in the theater! I want to experience this thing that has *never happened before,* and because of the nature of the theater, *it will never happen again.* That's not true of movies. The movie happens again and again, the same way. But with a play, it's the only time it's ever going to happen. If you start manipulating that kind of thing, it suddenly is not the experience of you and me. It's me pulling you. It's not honest.

"It's a very serious point because we've been talking about it from the actor's standpoint. This is the difference from an audience viewpoint. What is it that you can distinguish between the wonderful rapture you have when you go to a movie and the rapture you have when you go to a play? Can you identify it? It would be very helpful if you could. Is there a difference? If you're at a movie and you're having a wonderful time or if you're having a terrible time, whatever kind of time you're having, you can get up and leave! You can say, 'Okay, I'll come back for the next showing.' The immediacy is not there. The thing that the play needs, the movie doesn't need, which is you. The movie's there, whether you're there or not! *I need you at the theater.* I feel like Uncle Sam. I NEED YOU! COME TO THE THEATER!! What we need is a theater that only charges seven dollars!"

"I have to say one thing," said Stockard. "You can manipulate people with images and music and shifting things in film for the sadness, the poignancy of stuff. But I don't think there's *anything* like an audience sitting in a theater, watching the stage and [the actors] are making you laugh and your brain is exploding because you're suddenly getting it. You're surrounded by these people and you're watching someone do it. That man or that woman's brain on that stage is saying a thing in such a way that it's directly communicating to everybody in an audience. It is the most *thrilling* thing imaginable . . . Whether it's timing or focus or whatever, there is nothing like that. The fact that it's not being manipulated by lighting, by camerawork or editing, is an extraordinary, original experience. It's the primary source. It may falter a lot but it is the primary source."

Shakespeare doesn't say anything about the characters in his plays, except what they say about each other in the script. In *Six Degrees,* all John Guare says is, "I think that Ouisa is attractive."

"He wrote that after Stockard got the part," said Murray.

"Thank you, Murray," Stockard whispered.

"It's true!" said Murray. "I know John. He lives around the corner from me."

Stockard said, "I read this play and I had a day or two to make up my mind. I said, 'I don't know what to say or what to do.' Two directors I know read the play and loved it, but they each said, 'Who is this woman?' I said, 'I don't know.' But it's a very specific woman, and we just patched her together like bits of clay, with patience. There's another thing you need: patience. Because when I was younger I used to think (and still it's nice if it happens) that you walk in and you read the thing aloud, and you get a little hook, and it's there and you know who you are. This is not the case with this particular play at all, because the character is only part of the whole theatrical experience, extremely abstract in many ways, and as you say choreographed. [I] didn't say, 'Well, I know who I am and I'll just take this home with me like this.' You couldn't do that. You had to serve the play, serve the moment, serve the rhythm and the tone of the overall piece, because that was the task for Jerry, to find the very specific tone for that play."

"I know a lot of actors who cross out stage directions before they even read them," said Murray. "They have their assistants or their lovers or friends cross them out. They don't want to get what the playwright thinks."

Stockard grinned. "That can get you in trouble. If there's a direction like, 'He kills his mother.' "

Murray agreed. "*That* kind of direction is rather important. But Shakespeare doesn't have any, and what he accomplishes is he insists that you find it yourself, so there is no real definitive anything in Shakespeare. The idea of saying someone is attractive is interesting, isn't it? Do you want to describe what that is? Aside from Miss Channing, of course. It's a very broad description."

In theater an actor lives through a specific time period in the life of his character. In film, do actors get less of a feeling of having lived through a role because of the fragmented nature of the work?

"I've been doing a lot of film work lately," said Murray, "but my training is the stage. I came to the theater when I was about seventeen. It was either the theater or prison. The connection I have with the theater is visceral. It's really from my blood. I really *need* the theater, and I function very comfortably on the stage. The connection I have with you now is one that I need, because it reminds me of the art form, of the nature of the theater. You can't find that in film, because there are too many people and things between the actor and the final receptor, the audience. There are just too many. What I do in front of a camera *has nothing to do with what is going to come out!* Because of the lighting, because of the sound, because they may put in another voice, and because finally, they may change the lines!

"I've traveled in places, in Budapest, for example, and people come up and chatter to me in Hungarian, and I don't understand Hungarian. But the film's been dubbed in another language. They *insist* that I know how to speak Hungarian! It's not even my voice! 'You're putting on a voice!' 'No, I'm not. This is my voice.' 'No, it's not.' My point is, when you see something in the movies or on television, there's no way you can be sure that *I,* the actor, am doing what you are seeing! There are too many tricks. Colorization. Suddenly we have a different color. We have a different voice. We can accomplish things on the screen that are not possible by the actor.

"The thing about the stage is, what you see is what you get. Unfortunately we have a lot of amplification now. But, my point is, it's *primitive.* The connection between you and me is as old as the cave people. You have come together here, to see us, in the flesh, exchange views, exchange ideas, exchange feelings. There is something extraordinarily primitive about this communication! It transcends all of the descriptions and definitions. It's like you are coming here to find out something else, aside from the words, aside from what it is that the writer is saying. *It's a communication beyond language.* It's like a reassurance of your lives, our lives, of something else that is primitive that goes beyond politicians, that goes beyond everything that's been happening in your life today, before, and what's coming tomorrow. It's like you want to find out *something* for yourselves, whatever that thing is. I'm not about to second-guess it. That's what's missing so much in the theater today. I get very hot about this.

"Oddly enough, in the live theater, not movies, the theaters are getting bigger! We are looking at 2500- and 3000-seat houses. And the movie theaters are getting smaller! They're like cineplexes. You're in a big living room. You're listening to the sound next door and the sound next door and the sound up here. Movies are supposed to be big. It's supposed to be two or three thousand seats. With a big picture and big sound amplification. It's *reversing* somehow. You have come to the theater to hear the natural voice, and look what you're listening to! There's something that we have to get back to. I would like to see smaller theaters. I would like to see plays that talk to you and me. The difference between the theater and the electronic media is simply blood. It's something very basic and very primitive. That's what I think we are here for."

Both Murray and Stockard have acquired reputations for their ability to play a great *variety* of parts. Were these roles chosen on purpose or did they just come along in a certain sequence?

"I am not yet in a position to demand whatever I want to do," said Murray. "There are many things I've refused to do because they were repetitious."

"If something comes along," said Stockard, "and it's fun and interesting and I feel I can do something that's going to stretch me without making a fool of myself or it's going to activate something I haven't dealt with, I'll do it. I don't think either Murray or I are personality actors. Although I find that people sometimes think that I am unless they've seen a couple hunks of the work. I deal with a lot of people projecting stuff on me because they see one thing I've done that's set in their mind."

Stockard once starred in an unsuccessful television series. I asked her what would have happened if her show had been a success.

"I'd be a rich woman today," replied Stockard. "I remember very distinctly the second year of the show and the producer of the second year was a wonderful man named Aaron Rubin and he was a contemporary of Norman Lear's. He did 'Mayberry R.F.D.' and other things and he was a great guy. We just busted our butt for this thing. We didn't have any writers, any money, we were working twenty-four hours a day. I was in New York doing *They're Playing Our Song* for a few months and I got the word that the TV show was canceled. Aaron was of a certain age. It wasn't a big shock. He was a wealthy man. But we had had to sort of get him out of retirement to do the show. Mike Ovitz got him to go see me playing Rosalind in a production of *As You Like It* directed by Tony Richardson the summer before. He had agreed to produce the show because of watching me play Rosalind.

"It was like a family breaking up when the show was canceled. And you're so exhausted. And [Rubin] came from the core of TV. He said, 'This could be a blessing in disguise.' I certainly didn't feel like it at the moment because I felt very tossed about. But I knew what he meant because he knew that, as much as I'd worked very, very hard, I *did* feel very crowded by the sameness and the routine of television. I don't put it down. You want to be good at what you're doing and I think the worst thing in the world, worse than not having a job, is getting the wrong job. That's true for an actor as well as anybody, because if you don't do your best work in something, you end up with a bad reputation. So I think that I was pretty lucky in a way."

Some of my guests have said the actor is only half-alive without the audience. Does this mean the actor is not fulfilled in film, where there is no audience?

"There's always somebody there," Stockard said. "First of all, you act with the other actor. In the movie I just did [*Married to It*], there are three separate stories of three marriages. The person playing my husband was Beau Bridges, a wonderful man, a wonderful actor, a lovely person, and we just had our rhythm that we would play before they would roll the cameras. We would improvise. We would play with each other to try to get some of that energy on the screen. That became our performance. In movies you make the tapestry. That's all we do. We make the cloth, they cut it. But you have got to make a great cloth. It could be bolts of incredibly complicated, embroidered fabric or not. Murray is right. They cut it up any way they want. But you as a human being have to give yourself the gift of the process with the other actor and the moment, and try to be as alive as you can, and give it your best shot. It's very different from acting on the stage."

"It's really a good question," said Murray. "I had never couched it in those specific terms. How do you act if there is no audience?"

Stockard said, "Mike Nichols told me when we worked on *The Fortune,* very early on in my career, he said, 'You have got to keep the sound of the audience laughing in your head.' It's absolutely right. You keep that in your head. In rehearsal you don't have an audience. For comedy, especially, you are constantly checking in, 'Did you get it, did you get it?' For the other, I don't know . . ."

"I think the answer is that you must take it back to the stage," suggested Murray. "You have to go back to check yourself out. This is the only place you can really know. I do quite a lot of work in Hollywood. I have a good time, but there's a different language in L.A., which I find difficult to adjust to because I want to believe everything they say. And they say, 'That was great!' Well, it ain't! It can't always be great. Great to them is the lighting was right. The sound was right, and you were in the middle of the camera."

The actor in a play knows how the story will turn out. In *Six Degrees,* Stockard's character, Ouisa, goes through a major transition in a period of ninety minutes. In beginning a performance, how does the actor avoid thinking about where her character is going to end up?

"It's like singing a song," said Stockard. "I like to sing. Lyric and music combine and you stay in the moment in that song. One of the key problems of acting is anticipation, and it's one of the basic problems we all have to struggle with. One of the gifts of being on a stage and doing a performance like this every night is that every time you return to a moment, you can be in it and then be out of it. You don't muddy the colors. It's like Seurat. It's like pointillism. You do *blue.* Then you do *green.* You don't think about the purple coming up if you are really listening in the moment. It's all about *not* anticipating and being *in* the moment. It's a basic acting thing. It's the most difficult thing to do. When you can do it over and over again, a weird patterning appears in one's body."

Both Stockard and Murray are extremely successful at becoming unrecognizable in the roles they play. Murray, as the older Salieri, seemed far removed even from the younger Salieri, and it wasn't just the makeup. He spoke and he breathed differently. And when Stockard played the minister's wife in *Woman in Mind,* some of her own friends didn't recognize her. Is there a specific moment when the conception for a character comes together in the actor's mind?

"Again, I think of it like putting the bits of clay on the armature," said Stockard. "I do operate a lot off of external stuff, but it's stuff that is immediately perceived by the external world, namely things like voices, accents, looks, body posture, things like that. I was able to find the right voice for the woman in *Woman in Mind;* she was a very specific suburban London vicar's wife. The class thing was very important. It was important that she herself did not have a certain education. She had a husband who had an education. She had no money. She wasn't poor.

"I try to make the character fit the setting of the play and illuminate the situation of the play. How she was dressed, down to the hemline on my particular leg, what that looked like . . . the color of the wig . . . We found that if this beret was here, and there was any color on my mouth, I looked too young. Once we got that set, I could do the emotional interaction with the other actors. I am one of these people who has to find that frame. I do that in rehearsal and once I've got it, I'm pretty okay at holding to it, but that's what I need."

"This idea of the voice is not just a term with me," added Murray. "I am very attuned to the voice, and once I find that sound, it seems to me to connect with the truth. I believe everything that Stockard has said, but it's just finding that thing that will work. It could be one thing, that's all you need. It's like cooking. 'It needs something. What is that? No. That's not right.' And sometimes the dinner never comes out. But what we are talking about is the attempt, taking a shot, giving it a try. That's another thing that separates the theater from the movies: You never know what's going to happen. Anything can happen. It's like the curtain goes up and you say, 'Here we go! We are in this together.' You give it a try."

"That's another important function," Stockard said. "The function of the audience. I think that audiences have to surrender themselves to the fact of being active participants. They are not just going to lie there and go, 'All right, do it to me.' It's more fun when *you* help. Even with a play like *Six Degrees,* which is a wonderful play and a fantastic production, and we are in a rhythm of playing, there still will be people, you can feel them say, 'Ohh, what? We have to go to the theater tonight? You have tickets for what? It costs what? You paid *what* for them?'

"Sometimes there are people who say, 'Let's play ball,' and they just go wild. And then there are other audiences, and we have ways, we have our ways, we have our means for getting you guys to come along. But, believe me, we sort of go, 'Oh come on, come on,' because they don't want to play. *The theater is about play!* We play. You guys play, and everybody comes out the better for it at the end. I'm not talking about giggly play approval. I'm talking about engagement. Murray's absolutely right about unamplified sound. If we were sitting here without these mikes, you guys would sit forward a little more. It's like an animal response. If it's unamplified, there is a different response in the audience. We're not amplified at the Beaumont and you feel that leaning forward. And that's a house with over twelve hundred seats, which traditionally has been a difficult thing. But if you have got it going, and that current is going between an actor and an audience, the audience itself learns to be present."

"In a movie," said Murray, "the film can be running if there is nobody in the house. That doesn't happen in the theater. If there is no one in the house, it doesn't make any difference if we do the performance. It's not a performance. It's a rehearsal. We need someone out there."

It's easy to see how the audience participates in a comedy. Laughter tells the actor that the audience is with her. But what about a serious play? Can an actor tell if it's the right kind of silence?

"It's wonderful," said Stockard. "They become like one being. It's as if you're having a conversation with somebody. And it's true, sometimes they're coughing, they shift, whatever. Silence is one of the loudest things you can feel on a stage. It's louder than any roar of laughter I've ever felt. It's almost more gratifying."

At the end of the session I asked Stockard about the moving and insightful moment when the spotlight catches her face at the end of *Six Degrees.* I wondered whether there was a specific image she wanted to project.

"Apropos of our earlier discussion of this play," said Stockard, "and the fact that there are no stage directions, there also are no indications of production design. The last line of the play is 'The Kandinsky is painted on both sides.' There is no indication of this moment in the script that I read. (I don't know if it's in the published script or not.) It's very difficult to describe something like that because it's so much a product of the culmination of the entire evening, of everything everybody's experienced. I frankly can take very little credit for that moment, because if we've done our job right something very mysterious—now there's a word—happens, and I don't want to give a name to it.

"It would help revive the theater if ritual and mystery and all those things that are the sources of the theater are returned to us in some form on the stage. I wish I could tell you more about that moment. I just know it was one of the most thrilling things when I did it, because I realized that silent communication can exist. I don't make hand gestures or anything. It is just a tribute to communication between twelve hundred and fifty-three human beings."

CHAPTER THIRTEEN

JIM DALE
AND
ELAINE STRITCH

"Once you learn how to fake sincerity, you've got it made."

© MARTHA SWOPE

Jim Dale in "Barnum!"

Elaine Stritch in "Company"

© MARTHA SWOPE

Jim Dale left his hometown of Rothwell, Northamptonshire, England, to join a traveling vaudeville troupe, with whom he toured the music halls of England's Midlands for two years as a comic tumbler. He often did dangerous stunts. "Sometimes I could feel the blood running down my knees. It was sad, perhaps . . . I guess it's wanting to be loved, really—that's the answer any clown will give you—wanting to make people laugh or cry." After working as a pop singer and a star of the *Carry On* films, Jim made his West End debut in *The Wayward Way,* a musical version of *The Drunkard.* Jim made his American debut as Petruchio in the National Theatre's production of *The Taming of the Shrew.* He won the Tony for *Barnum.* His other Broadway credits include *Scapino, A Day in the Death of Joe Egg* (earning nominations for the Tony and Drama Desk awards and winning the Outer Critics Circle Best Actor Award), and *Me and My Girl.* Jim also starred in the Roundabout Theatre Company's revival of *Privates on Parade.* In addition to his acting career, Jim has been a rock singer, hosted a TV show, and written the lyrics to songs like "Georgy Girl," which won him an Oscar nomination.

Elaine Stritch comes from Detroit, Michigan, the youngest of three daughters of an executive of the B. F. Goodrich rubber company. Elaine's interest in theater dates from the age of four when her father took her to meet the Ziegfeld Follies comedian Bobby Clark. Before entering show business, she had to complete twelve years at a Roman Catholic school for girls and the Duchesne Residence Finishing School. According to Elaine, "All that crap about extending the pinkie finger while sipping tea is a myth. Convent schools are breeding grounds for great broads and occasionally one-of-the-boys. Convent schools teach you to play against everything, which is what I'm still doing." Elaine made her Broadway debut in *Loco,* and then played Melba Snyder, a wisecracking columnist, in the revival of *Pal Joey.* Among her other Broadway credits are *Made in Heaven, The Little Foxes, Angel, Bus Stop, Goldilocks,* Noël Coward's musical *Sail Away, Who's Afraid of Virginia Woolf?,* and *Company.* Elaine's films include *A Farewell to Arms, Who Killed Teddy Bear, Cadillac Man,* and Woody Allen's *September.* Edward G. Robinson once said, "If Elaine Stritch wasn't born on the stage, she should have been."

Jim Dale was trained in all the techniques of a classical clown, and clowns are what first attracted me to show business. A few weeks before he was due to appear in our series, I went to see Jim, who was starring at the time in *Me and My Girl.* In his dressing room before the performance, he was trying out some passes with a new sword. He was dressed casually, and he spoke about the energy he receives from the audience when he's onstage. We talked right up until five minutes before the matinee performance was scheduled to begin, and Jim hadn't even started to put on his makeup! On his intercom, I could hear the audience buzzing to each other, and the orchestra begin to tune up. I thought about the eleven hundred people waiting on the other side of the stage, and I marveled at how relaxed Jim was. Since there was no indication he wanted me to leave, I excused myself and said I would see him after the performance. A few minutes later, Jim made his entrance, in costume and in character, singing, dancing, and acting with consummate skill.

Along with Jim, my guest for the evening was Elaine Stritch. Elaine is one of those actors we feel we know personally. She somehow seems to represent our point of view, with her sly sense of humor and her knack for understatement. Elaine may have a star's personality, but when you talk to her you get the feeling there's more to her life than show business. She is a striking woman, long-legged, with an exuberant smile and a salty, instantly identifiable laugh. Jim and Elaine knew each other and had worked together.

In our session, I pointed out that both Jim and Elaine had made their reputations with comedic acting, and both had been impressed by comics at an early age.

"In 1942 I lived in the middle of England and there was very little theater there," said Jim, "so a trip to London was an event, and my father took me to see Lupino Lane in *Me and My Girl.* It's the first show I ever saw. We sat in the second balcony, and I sat in the aisle, because I wanted a view of the whole stage. When you come from a very small town, and you've only heard maybe three or four hundred people cheering at a football game, there's quite a difference between that and two thousand people laughing very loud. The hair *does* tend to go up on the back of your neck. I couldn't believe that one little man onstage, dressed in a cloak, was responsible for giving so much happiness to all those people. I said to my father, 'I want to be like him.' The very next day my father arranged for ballet dancing and tap dancing, and I [took] ten lessons a week for six years.

"I can't remember what Lupino Lane did, but I do know that he was terribly funny, and I can remember bits of shtick. We have incorporated them [into *Me and My Girl*], along with other bits that he wrote in a small book called *How to Be a Comedian.* I have it in the dressing room. Hundreds of little drawings on how to do backflips, how to do splits, and this became my bible for a number of years. Once having learned the shtick, you can't forget it. The unfortunate thing about vaudeville, variety, and these wonderful shtick merchants is that when they die, the shtick seems to die with them. I think we should televise and capture all this wonderful visual comedy and put it in the archives, so that in a hundred years' time another young kid will be watching *Me and My Girl,* and will see something there that encourages him to come into the business. The shtick belongs to all of us. We steal it from each other. We tend to die because we are not captured on screen. We only exist in the theater in people's memories, and once their memories go, we no longer exist."

Someone once said, "Actors are forever carving statues in snow." They were referring of course to stage actors, and not those in film or television. How does an actor take pride in his work when it's so short-lived?

"It's one of the frightening things that happened to me when I began to be asked to do movies," said Elaine. "It was like being frightened to death all over again, because one of the advantages of acting onstage, if you are a little bit insecure about the theater, is you never have to see yourself. However, it's fun to see yourself after you've done a movie and it's *good.* I'm telling you, it is so exciting! You can't believe that you are doing that, like the movie stars you saw as a kid, who were up there on the screen having dinner, and yelling and fighting and driving in cars. I can't get over the fact that I'm up there doing those things. And when it's good, it's so terrific because you're sitting at home with a drink and your dinner, and you're working up there and it's over and you can enjoy it. That's one of the joys of motion pictures. But I do agree with Jim. When you revive a play or a musical, and they say, 'What was the choreography for that song? What was the dance?' A new choreographer can do it, but how wonderful it would be to be able to go someplace and see fifty years from now what Michael Bennett did in *Chorus Line*."

The fact that the stage actor's creation disappears makes it unique among the arts. Musicians' performances are captured on recordings, and even though something is lost by not having the experience in person, most of the creative work comes across. Not so for the actor. Film and television cannot re-create what happens in a theater between actor and audience. And yet the only means for an actor's work to be preserved is through the medium of film and television. I wanted to explore this further by discussing the different techniques actors use in film. I introduced the question by referring to Jim as a star of the *Carry On* films.

"I hate the word *star,*" said Jim.

"*Why* do you hate the word *star*?" Elaine asked.

"I hate the word *star* because I'm just an actor," said Jim. "We are just working. In the *Carry On*s, we were just a group of comics who had great fun for eight weeks. We weren't stars. We were there to have fun and enjoy each other. The difference between acting onstage and in film is that onstage you know that the whole audience is going to be able to look at any part of that stage at any time, including you and you and you, and the ground and the ceiling. Whereas in film, the director tells you what to look at. That's the problem! That's the problem when you yourself are doing something that is not going to be in the film. Suppose you're just listening? If it was on the stage, then the audience could flicker their eyes around and watch you listening. There was a famous lady in England, Dame Sybil Thorndike, who was the best listener the theater world has ever known. You didn't look at the people who were talking when she was on the stage. You watched her listening. In a film, she wouldn't be in the scene. The camera would be on the people talking.

"That's the joy of the theater. The audience can see you from your toe to the top of your head. You're not acting just with the top of your head. In the car I was talking with David and we were talking about soap opera. It's acting from your neck upwards. Can you imagine the whole cast are little midgets? They've all got big heads and little bodies. You'll never know. I love the fact that on the stage you can control what you are doing with the full length of your body, whereas in film it's the director's medium."

Elaine created the role of the proprietor of the hash shop in *Bus Stop* on the stage, and she also created Diane, Mia Farrow's hard-drinking, hard-living mother in Woody Allen's film *September*. Is film acting entirely different from acting in the theater?

"I think these things are different for each individual actor," said Elaine, "and I just cannot afford emotionally to complicate it for myself. I see no difference. I know there is a difference, but for me, I see no difference in acting on the stage or television or film except for volume. One of the problems is that you have an enormous amount of energy and you walk on a stage and things start to happen. In film you can't get up like that . . ." Elaine got up to demonstrate, and got tangled in the wire of her microphone. "You can't get up like that here, either . . . You can't say," (Elaine spoke very rapidly) " 'What did you say?' because it's too quick, or at least it used to be. Bette Davis had a good deal to do with changing everybody's mind about that. She influenced the technique of cameras moving faster and having it look real, because nobody was going to slow her down. When she walked across the room it was unbelievable and it was very attention-getting. They did that her way, but even today in movies, you have to move a little bit slower.

"For me, it's just the concentration of what the character is about, and what I'm supposed to be feeling and doing and saying. If I let myself think beyond that, I get scared. If I let myself think in a grander scale, and say, 'All right, now I have to behave this way, this is a movie and that was a television series and this is on the stage,' I'd rather not get into it. It really is like politics or religion to me. I just get scared to death to discuss it. I'm afraid it will go away. Back to the snow."

"We also have another problem," Jim said. "Onstage you can be surprised by something that happens very quickly; a bit of shtick, somebody walks on the stage, and before you know it, he's done a forward somersault and crashed on his back. It surprised you and it got a round of applause, or it gets a reaction the way it's meant to do. If this were to happen on television, the director would have to cut to a wide shot, which immediately gives the game away that something is going to happen. That's the problem. You lose the spontaneity. He's got to give you a wide shot, or you're not going to see the whole movement of that piece of shtick! This is why it's terribly, terribly difficult to convert stage shtick into television film. This was a joy in the old days with the silent films. They managed to get over it mainly because they did give a wide angle through most of the film. It was lovely. Most of those old films are just wide angle, and you can see everything that is going on."

Every character an actor plays has a background and a history. The character's life does not begin when the actor makes his entrance. An actor has to create his character's biography, a story that brings his character up to the point when he first appears. Is this harder to do in the theater?

"The background that you have to go into, and the exploration that you do, and the questions that you ask, are all the same," Jim said. "The way you develop the character is the same. Whatever method suits you, it's your method. Because I have been trained in the English theater I start work from the outside, if it's a stage production, because I know the audience is going to see me from my toe to the top of my head. I want to see what sort of character is going to be out there. As Larry Olivier said, 'You buy your shoes first.' Buy the shoes for the character. Get used to that. Then, once you see the character in your mind's eye, you get inside him and start working there. Everything on that stage, every movement he makes is a character movement. It's the body's language you have to create as well.

"Whatever works for you is your way of making it work. It's your method. We all have different methods. It doesn't matter. It's wonderful."

Does every technique have a label?

"Hers or mine," said Jim. "That's the label. You can't say it's the Stanislavski or it's this or that. It's *my* way. I've listened, and I've studied, and I've watched, and this is the way I seem to get my satisfaction."

"I tried to get away with murder for a few years," added Elaine. "I think one of the main things was that I would put on a label if someone asked me about acting. I know I can act. I wouldn't still be here if I couldn't. I think I'd have sense enough to get out. I have developed an enormous amount of discipline over the span of my career, and I think it's the most important thing I have for my work. That means discipline of emotion, as well as getting up early in the morning and studying your lines. It's not all as dull as that, but I'm talking about discipline in every way. I think it's the best book of rules for being good at anything, not just acting."

Nobody has written a serious history of acting. We have essays and some books by actors, critics, poets, and philosophers that describe acting in particular periods of history. In sixteenth-century Italy an actor-manager named Leone Di Somi wrote a dialogue on the subject. In it he said, "We cannot frame any rules for this profession. Truly it must be born in the individual." Is acting an inherited talent?

"No," said Jim. "My father played a piano, but no better than a pub pianist. I became a comedian in music hall, which is a little different than vaudeville. Up till the age of sixteen, I had been in amateur talent contests, working in front of an audience and failing miserably. I wasn't a very good comic, but there was such an urge for me to get up there and make people laugh. I would do *anything* to make them laugh. I didn't take acting lessons because I was in variety. This meant stand-up comedy, and in those days it wasn't the sort of comedy that you see at the clubs or on television. I was only sixteen and I had to have a very innocent type of act.

"I think that what developed was a rapport with the audience, of getting to know who the audience was, and finally working with the *Carry On* team. We knew our audiences, so we had something in common. We learned from watching each other. Nothing better. To watch a good actor is far better than reading about how to be a good actor.

"My father, who was a steel foundry worker, had no idea what the theater was about, but he said something to me when I was nine. He said, 'I think you should learn how to move.' That, to me, is the secret of theater, learning how to move. So I studied ballet and tap and ballroom dancing and judo and comedy and eccentric dancing for years . . . I was aiming for the comedic side of theater. I was not interested in Shakespeare until I was thirty-two."

I asked Elaine if she also wanted to make people laugh when she started out.

"I didn't have a choice," Elaine said. "I just did. I was a little frightened about that, because sometimes that can get out of hand. You want people to stop laughing at you and take you seriously. The grass is always greener on the other side. One of the most important things about learning to act is the same principle as learning to live. We learn to live right by experiences of living wrong, or living too right, or not so right. So we grow up, and we develop as better human beings every day.

"I have gotten all the lessons that you could possibly want, from just getting up every morning and going to bed at night. That's the way it's been with me. It's very hard for me to separate life from acting. I think, because of that, I have suffered more as an actress. Because if it doesn't turn out as real as life is, I'm not satisfied. That's almost impossible . . . Jim told me a funny line backstage, but we can't remember who said it . . ."

" 'Once you learn how to fake sincerity, you've got it made,' " said Jim.

"In order to be able to laugh at a line like that," said Elaine, "you have to be able to sincerely or realistically reproduce life, which is an extraordinary, extraordinary experience. It's extraordinary to forget about yourself for a while! Incidentally, it's terrific therapy.

"I am quite serious. *Who's Afraid of Virginia Woolf?* was a great turn for me because I had been doing a lot of comedy and musicals. I'm so pleased that I *can* do dramatic stuff because it's good for me to do that. It's good for anybody to do a variety of things. When I finished doing *Virginia Woolf,* everybody would ask, 'Aren't you tired? Aren't you exhausted?' I never felt that good in my whole life! (But you can't get up every morning and do the script of *Virginia Woolf* in your living room and expect to feel good by dinner time.)

It was such a *catharsis* of emotion, and such an unloading, even though it wasn't my life. It was somebody else's life. It left me spent.

"Have you ever had a real bang-up evening (this is a silly thing to ask) where you stay up and you drink and you laugh and you scream and you holler? We've all done that and I used to have the experience of going to work the next day, like a matinee. It's a big joke in the theater about 'Don't go out the day before a matinee.' But when you're young, nothing fazes you. I remember being so relaxed in the theater when I had been up late, because you're so tired, you're so spent, that you don't care. You just don't care! You go out on the stage and you're wonderful." Elaine shook her head and groaned a warning, "For all the young people: That does not last. It happens for about two years and then you have to go to bed."

"One thing that we always tend to forget," said Jim, "is that we are talking about ourselves acting, but there are people who are responsible for the whole production. The people called the directors. There are many actors who have never worked with a good director, but it's only when you've worked with a good director that you realize the input that he can give you.

"There is a poet in England named Christopher Logue. Christopher wrote a poem which I have on my dressing-room wall. My wife had it knitted into a sweater, so you can all read it as I walk towards you, and if you miss the last lines, you look back and I've got it on the back as well. His poem was so simple: 'Come to the edge. / We might fall. / Come to the edge. / It's too high! / COME TO THE EDGE! / And they came, / And he pushed, / And they flew.' That's what can happen when you put yourself in the hands of somebody you can trust. You have to trust somebody in this business, and it's usually the director."

"I agree with Jim—wholeheartedly," said Elaine, punching out each syllable of the word. "You never know you can fly until you get the right kind of guy or dame to tell you what to do. I don't care how clever you are."

Just as actors have different methods of acting, directors have different ways of working with actors. Elaine was directed by Woody Allen in *September.*

"He never said anything to me." Elaine's flinty voice

sounded perplexed. "He didn't tell me how to do it. He *reacted* to how I did it *wrong*. And it made me laugh, and I was so eager to please him, because he scared me. All those emotions are going on and it makes you come alive. There are so many different kinds of directors. I can't even talk about them. It's too scary."

Jim recalled, "Tony Richardson in a film once said to me," (Jim's voice became very nasal and very British) " 'I want you to go into that corner, Jimmy, think about thith theene, come awut, and do thomthing maavelous!' I said, 'Right!' " (Jim got up and went to a corner of the stage.) "So I went into the corner, and I thought, 'I wonder how long to stand here.' I said, 'Right.' He said, 'You ready?' I said, 'Yes,' and I did the scene. At the end of the scene he said, 'Cut! Not quite maavelous enough.' That was the direction I got from him. Real helpful. Real helpful."

When it comes to creating the character, most of the work takes place between the actor and the director. In theater, who contributes most to the concept for a character, the actor or the director?

"Don't forget," said Jim, "when you're playing a major role in a play you don't meet the director for the first time at the first reading. You've met him and you've discussed why you should even be in the play, why he wants you in the play. All of this comes together during the many meetings you have with him. And you, of course, *do* have some idea of the character. The director doesn't have a concrete character that he wants you to copy and [he doesn't say], 'This is the way you should do it.' The director watches the way you are going when you're rehearsing. He watches that direction. A clever director will let you go in that direction until you yourself say, 'Hey, this is not the real way, is it?' Then he'll say, 'Why don't you try it this way?' In other words, a good director doesn't grab you and force you into a mold of what *he* thinks it should be. He allows you to find your way into that mold."

Jim has a history of doing acrobatics onstage: First there were his stunts in *Scapino* and *Barnum*. In *Me and My Girl*, two people hold Jim in one of the dance numbers, and then they drop him on his knees. I had never seen that before. There was also a period, early in his career, when he did a trick of walking backward to the lip of the stage, and then standing there teetering.

"I stopped doing that the night I missed the edge and cracked a rib," said Jim.

What makes an actor attempt such a stunt?

"Money!" Elaine volunteered.

Jim explained, "When you are working in ensemble, when all of you are on that stage and you have rehearsed everything, it's not professional to go out there and say, 'I am now going to do something different and funny that will make my colleagues onstage laugh,' or 'It will get a bigger laugh in the audience.' That's being the most selfish actor there is. However, if you are onstage on your own, and it's a comedy, and there are moments when the director allows you to do a little bit of clowning if you think of it, that's okay. It didn't disturb anyone else's performance, which is my big concern. If you have the small laugh in the show, there should be nobody on that stage who's ever allowed to take that little laugh away from you. That's your moment. That's your spotlight. It's wrong for a star to come out there clowning away and ignore the fact that you have a certain moment, because that's all a play or a musical is. It's ten, twenty thousand moments, all put together very carefully, and one of them might be yours."

Jim took over for Robert Lindsay in *Me and My Girl.* Since some of Jim's performance depends on shtick, I asked him if the show had to be redirected.

"I've been in *Me and My Girl* seventeen months," Jim said. "If one originates a show, you can be there from the first day of rehearsal, and you and the director talk over various moves and various shtick, and you may do a piece of choreography that takes you to that side of the stage, and from that the scene develops. However, when you take over from somebody, the choreography of the show has already been determined by the director, and by the previous performer, and there are forty people on that stage. So far be it from me to go into that show, and insist on all the choreography being changed just to accommodate me.

"They say you follow in someone's footsteps. It's like a dancer. He may be doing the same dance steps as another dancer, but what he is doing with his body, and above those footsteps, is purely him. Nureyev is doing the same steps as Baryshnikov, but the performance above those footsteps is very individual. The same applies when you take over. You are given certain basic movements that you have to do on that stage, but what you *can* do in those movements, and in the space and time that you have, can be your own. You have to develop your own, or it's called doing an impression of Robert Lindsay. He's a super performer, and I wouldn't want to do an impression of him, and I wouldn't want anybody to do an impression of me."

A musical is different from a play in the way it evolves. When Noël Coward's *Sail Away* was on the road, two roles were combined to make it a vehicle for Elaine.

"There was the old format of a musical comedy," said Elaine. "There was the leading lady (who was very, very beautiful, and very dramatic, and emotional, and romantic), and the leading man. And then there was the soubrette, and then a kind of funny guy, and those two paired off in the end. And the elegant leading man and leading lady paired off. So what happened was extraordinary . . .

"One night we were in Boston, and Mr. Coward sent for me. He wanted to see me in his hotel room and it frightened me to death. No, not for that reason, God knows! . . . That's a laugh that could grow, isn't it? . . . He wanted to talk to me about taking over the [leading lady] part, merging the leading lady and the comedienne into one part! I was flabbergasted. It was an interesting turn of events in musical comedy because it was the beginning of the funny lady. It was Merman. Merman finally accomplished that. Merman was the funny lady, and she also got the guy in the end. It was a great big step for me. I was thrilled with it, because it gave me a chance to be vulnerable. It gave me a chance to be pretty and romantic, and have a fellow look at me, which is sometimes the reason I have given for being in the theater: You don't have to look like Elizabeth Taylor to get the guy in the end.

"In motion pictures, forget it. You have to be so beautiful to get married in the movies! I mean really beautiful. If anybody is the least bit unattractive, they are a maid, or somebody's best friend with curlers in her hair. It's true! It's getting a little bit better. I think Barbra Streisand had a great deal to do with it. I think she's great looking, but she is not what we have been used to looking at, in terms of [leading ladies who] fall in love. Suddenly she does look like a lot of people that you see in New York. We never had that. How many Jean Harlows do you see on Forty-fifth Street?

"I don't think I'm bad looking. I think I'm a nice-looking girl. But I'm only beginning to get movies since I've left my fifties. This interests me, because I get wonderful, exciting character parts, but I could never experience having a romantic part in a movie."

Jim said, "Elaine finds it wonderful to look at herself on film and say, 'Hey I did a good job!' I can't think of one film in twenty-two that I can sit back and look at, and really have that feeling that she did. I'm always so icky picky, that that was wrong and that was wrong, too much."

With a sly grin, Elaine said, "I'm just so thrilled I got away with it! It isn't that I think that it's terrific. I was talking today with a guy who works at Twentieth Century–Fox in the publicity department. I have a movie [*Cocoon: The Return*] coming out (that I thought you'd never ask me about) and I haven't seen it. I'm terrified. I cannot begin to tell you.

"He didn't say anything. He said," (Elaine affected a rather guarded look) " 'Oh, have you seen the movie, Elaine?' (so, you know, Twentieth Century–Fox) and I said, 'No. No, I haven't.' I said, 'Did you enjoy it?' " Elaine motioned for a response, like an orchestra conductor asking for more tone from the violin section. "I was just *dying* for him to say, 'You were great!' And he didn't say that. I said, 'How should I feel about the movie, Dennis?' Because he wasn't giving me *anything*. He wouldn't say anything to me! Finally I said, 'Look, I'm frightened to go to the screening, so give me a little confidence.' And then he did. But I had to *drag* it out of him. My point is, how hard it is to watch yourself. It's one of the hardest things in the whole world. And when it's good, I just can't get over how thrilled I am."

I asked Jim and Elaine if they attend screenings of their films to see how audiences react.

"I've never gone to a theater to see one of my films," said Elaine. "I've always wanted to do that, but that scares me too."

"I'm recognized by people with big bags under their eyes," said Jim, "who are insomniacs because my films go on about four in the morning. 'Oh you're the guy I saw . . .' I have films on cassette at home. I *never* put them on. It's nice to know that they're there but I don't sit and watch the films that I've been in. That's happened, it's gone now. Let's get on with something else."

"But you see it once," said Elaine.

"I've even walked out of a film," said Jim. "I'd only seen half of it."

"Now, Jim," said Elaine skeptically.

"I actually had to walk out," said Jim. "I was so ashamed of the film. This is why. The director said, 'I want you to play this scene, the camera's way back there and I've got a wide-angle lens. So I thought, 'Great. This is almost stage acting. He wants it big.' He said, 'Yes, please. The bigger the better.' When I saw the film, he had lied. He had not had a wide-angle lens. He had had a zoom lens and I was in closeup. And I was playing as if it was thirty feet away and the expressions on my face were grotesque and overdone for that distance. That was not right."

"Where is that director today?" asked Elaine.

"I think he must have changed his name," said Jim. "I haven't heard from him since. But that's wrong. That doesn't help me at all. That's cheating a bit. If you want me to do a subdued performance, tell me. If you want it big, tell me. But don't fake it like that. And the results were not very good because he did this with everybody on the film and the film went straight down the drain. Best place for it."

Elaine said, "Going to see yourself in a film is very much like an opening night, [when] you go through the performance. You get through it and you never want it to be like that again, because you want to be *conscious* of what you're doing. Opening nights I never remember at all. I never remember them. I'm on a level of adrenaline that I can't remember."

Jim said, "We always have the knowledge that if we do a bad performance before the opening night or even *on* opening night, then we've got another six months or more to start correcting and altering and changing. That's the problem with film. Once it's on film, that's it. On to the next one, good or bad, it can't be helped."

Do actors ever want to walk out on one of their own stage performances?

"Yes," said Jim. "It was called *Sancho Panza.* It was on at the National Theatre. It was for children and it lasted four-and-a-half hours and all the kids were asleep. Terrible show."

"That's happened," added Elaine. "An actress did that in New York."

If the pay was the same for a favorite role on stage or screen, which would be the medium of choice?

"Oh God what a question!" said Elaine.

"On the stage," Jim said.

Then Elaine asked, "How long would it run?"

"Not for a year-and-a-half," continued Jim. "Not as long as that. But for maybe six to nine months."

Why theater as opposed to film?

"It seems as though I picked the theater," said Jim. "Well, the theater's picked me. I've been over here from England fourteen years and [I've done] one television show, with Elaine. That's the only situation comedy show that I thought was worth doing. 'The Ellen Burstyn Show.' It was a giggle. I haven't made a film in ten years and it doesn't seem to have stopped my career. I've concentrated on (hopefully) good theater. The things I've turned down haven't gone on to become hits on Broadway. I've been very selective.

"When plays don't come your way, then you have to instigate them. *Joe Egg* was an example, and in the new year I will do Peter Nichols's play *Privates on Parade,* which I did many years ago. I've always tried to concentrate on quality stuff and I've been very, very happy so far."

"I'd like to do it on the stage and then have them make a movie out of it," said Elaine. "I just can't answer that question. I guess if I was shoved up against the wall, I'd probably like to make a film. That's newer to me, so it is so challenging. I'd like to prove more of myself in film than I would on the stage, because I've been on the stage for so long and in so many different things."

"When you have a reputation as a stage actor," said Jim, "and you get a film sent to you, the first time that happens, you go through the roof, you think, 'That's marvelous, that's wonderful,' forgetting that there's a long list of film actors who are well-known to the audience. They give it to this film actor first and if he turns it down, they give it to the next one, and by the time it gets to you, it means that everybody who is anybody in the *film* world has turned it down, and they're now coming 'round to people in the *theater*."

"*Who* are you talking about?" asked Elaine, somewhat indignantly.

"I'm talking about films like *The Return of the Return of the Return of the Living Dead,*" said Jim. "Junk films. One cannot expect a film to come along out of the blue with a big starring role for *you.*"

"Shirley MacLaine is a super super super star," Elaine said. "And *she* financed her last movie. How about that? No wonder she's touring all over the place and doing publicity. It's her money! It's extraordinary that that would happen. My hat's off to her. That's really wanting to act. Imagine how much money it takes.

"The honest-to-God truthful answer is it really doesn't [usually] happen that way. It would be nice if it did. It may for some actresses. It certainly does for Meryl Streep, who's just magical. She can do anything she wants to do. So she says, 'I'm going to go for that now.' She's the boss. She's running it because her movies make money. But for an actress like me, I may hit a stride in my life where I may have that wonderful feeling of saying, 'I'd like to do that,' but it isn't the way it happens. The script is sent to you and you're thrilled to death. And unless you really don't like it, you do it. You're just thrilled to find a part that's right.

"I must say that I have turned down things because I can't do it. In *Cocoon: The Return,* I play a tough, jazzy broad who runs a motel in Florida. That's a little bit of a stretch for me. When I first got the script there was some kind of rough language in it. There was an expression which I don't particularly like: 'If you had any balls you wouldn't act that way.' I don't like that expression. I don't like it because I don't like to think of men that way. I just *hate* it. That's how emotional I am about that! So I said to the director, 'I'd like to play this part, but some of this stuff's got to go. I can't. I can't! I CAN'T!! I don't want to be difficult, God knows, but I can't say that!' So I'm getting all excited saying, 'I can't,' and he says, 'So we'll cut it.' So all the dramatic acting was for nothing! I could've just cut it.

"So I got on the set and Jack Gilford and I are doing the scene in a nightclub and I rehearsed it with him once and I went to my trailer and I said, 'I gotta say that. It's no good if I don't say that.' So you know what I did? I said, 'How can I soften this?' It's very difficult to soften *balls.* It's either there or it isn't there. So I came up with something and the director let me say it. I said, 'And if you had any, if you'll pardon my French, balls,' and it was an expression that a tough gal like that might say because she doesn't want to be too crude so she says something jazzy like, 'If you'll pardon my French,' which doesn't make any sense at all and it's kind of fun. The interesting part of the story is that what I objected to was something that had to be, or the scene didn't have any importance to it. There are some scripts that are sent to you that you *just cannot do* because you wouldn't know what to do when you got there because you don't understand the script, and you don't understand the part. That will happen."

"I was sent a script once not to even play the role, but to do the voice-over of the animated character," said Jim. "I read the script and I said I can't do it. I can't do it and I won't do it. I think it's rubbish. It was called *Howard the Duck.* Remember that? I didn't even have to be in it and I turned that down."

Jim did play Dr. Terminus, a live-action character in the partly animated Disney musical *Pete's Dragon.*

"That was a film with Mickey Rooney," explained Jim. "It was just a joy to work with people like him and Red Buttons. How often in your life do you get a chance to do that? We had great fun."

When I talked to Jim in his dressing room, before he went on in *Me and My Girl,* he told me about the energy he receives from the audience. In film there is no live audience. Where does that energy come from?

"The crew," Elaine said. "It's *extraordinary.* I can turn twelve guys into the Music Box Theatre. What's the difference? If I were up here, and there was just this first row," (Elaine counted ten people in the first row of the auditorium) "I would be doing *exactly* what I'm doing now, I promise you. As long as one person, and even sometimes when *nobody* is watching, you can deliver. Just give me a few people in a room, and even when you have to do an emotional scene in a movie, and everybody's quiet, you feel so wonderful that all these people care about you, and you say, 'I've got to be good. The director wants me to be good and the cameraman wants me to be good and my dresser wants me to be good and the makeup woman wants me to look right,' and you deliver."

"When you do a good scene," added Jim, "there's nothing nicer than to hear rounds of applause and you look up and there are a couple of electricians who have been leaning over on the spotlights watching. It makes you feel as if that was a royal command performance. Something comes back because it's just a camera there, and it's great to have those lovely people behind you. They really are lovely. The crew of most of the films I have worked on have been a great joy to work with. I've seen them there with handkerchiefs stuffed in their mouths, because the director got fed up because they kept bursting into laughter. It's wonderful to have a crowd like that around you."

Does that mean that in film the actor does not perform for the camera?

"I tend to be able to see what I'm doing," Jim said. "I like to think I'm out there watching it all the time, monitoring it. That gives me some sort of security."

In addition to the energy that actors receive from the audience, do audiences influence the performance of the actor?

"Absolutely," said Jim. "If you have a marvelous audience it tends to make you want to give more. And if they're a rotten audience you give more. So it's Catch-22. You can't win. That's why the sweat's always flying when I'm up there."

Can the film-crew audience influence the actor's performance in the same way as an audience in a theater?

"No, they can't," said Elaine. "They can make you feel awful at the end of the day but they can't influence it."

Jim said, "But they can also give you a big round of applause when, after forty-seven takes, the director says, 'Okay. We'll keep that one.' "

"That's like a curtain call," said Elaine.

"To an empty house," added Jim.

Jim once made an analogy between the actor's relationship to the audience and fishing.

"When you have a lovely audience," explained Jim, "and you're feeling good yourself, and you don't have a migraine, and everybody onstage is being absolutely wonderful, it's as if you've got hundreds of fishing lines out there and they've been bobbing about and suddenly that one gets hooked and another one, and there's another laugh, and that one, and gradually the bobbing goes on and you feel as if you've got all the audience on the end of this line, and it's a very slender line and it might break any minute and you don't intend it to. It's a wonderful feeling. It's called *playing* with the audience. You're playing with them and they're enjoying it. You're reeling them in and letting them go out again, but you've caught them. You've got them. It's a nice feeling."

Our conversations took place on the stage of the New School's auditorium, which was originally used as a theater. Several of our guests had studied acting at the New School and Elaine was one of these alumni. I asked her what it was like.

"It's thrilling to even be asked about it," said Elaine. "This was our theater. We used to do plays in here. It's a far cry from the Actors Studio, I can tell you that. It's just so wonderful. It's a beautiful theater where young students were able to do full productions of wonderful plays under the guidance of Erwin Piscator and Stella Adler and Herbert Berghof. It was just wonderful. It was an awfully lucky break to fall into this place, coming from Birmingham, Michigan, and suddenly finding myself in Greenwich Village in the theater, studying to be an actress with this kind of atmosphere.

"I read for a lot of parts but I didn't get them. I was so scared and I couldn't move. And I'm a good mover, but I couldn't get it out. I was too frightened. Every time I was cast in a glamorous part or a young girl in love or anything like that, I couldn't do it, and Piscator knew it. So he said that maybe one day I'd be able to do it.

"However, there was a call for auditions for Feste in *Twelfth Night* and I figured maybe if I could do somersaults and that kind of thing, maybe I wouldn't be so embarrassed about being a woman. So I got it! I got the part of Feste! That was the first thing I did on the stage. It was wonderful. Piscator was so marvelous with young actors who were frightened. I can't tell you how frightened we all were!

"I remember Piscator would get up on the stage. (Some actors would say, 'Oh my God. I can't stand that.' Well, that's too bad.) When you're seventeen and you're frightened and he gets up" (Elaine stood up) "and [he] says, 'Why can't you do zis? Why can't you do zis? Zis is very easy!' " (Elaine bent over and picked up her pocket book) " 'You *pick* up ze bag,' " (Elaine bent her arm back, ready to throw the pocket book) " 'und you throw it!' And you got so involved with this darling man with the accent telling you how to do *everything*. The excitement of it took the onus off of you and you weren't the only fool up there. Your director was also a fool. It's easier in groups. The director is so important. You're lost without him."

Jim is an English actor who works in America. I asked him what he felt the difference was between English and American audiences.

"There are certain actors," said Jim, "who have made it in England who come to America and die a death and go rushing back to England. I think it's about half and half. It all depends what you're doing over here. The Americans, thank God, have a great love of the Brits. Due to television they've been able to understand us a lot more. That was the problem. [Then there was] the advent of 'Monty Python's Flying Circus,' etc.

"I was down in Tennessee and we had the hillbillies come down with their dogs and their long rifles and when they saw we were making a film there, one came up to me and he said," (Jim yelled at the top of his voice with an American accent) " 'DO YOU KNOW BENNY HILL?' I thought, 'My God, if *they* can understand Benny Hill, then I've no problems.'

"There is a difference in certain types of comedy. Our stand-up comics don't seem to register over here for various reasons, the same as a lot of your stand-up comics would not register in England. There is a different type of humor there. We have a very crude humor in England and we're born with it."

Jim looked up with a boyishly mischievous grin. "When as kids we go to the seaside on a holiday, we buy a postcard which you would call a dirty postcard. Dirty French postcards. This one that I remember buying for my grandmother was of a guy wading in the water with an old-fashioned swimming costume on with a huge belly and he was looking down and there was writing at the bottom and the writing said in parenthesis, 'I haven't seen my little Willie all day.' That is crude English humor. A four-year-old will laugh at that and Granny will laugh at it too.

"And then we have the whole gamut of crude material there. We can find a dirty meaning to any sentence. In *Me and My Girl*, this woman says, 'Do you know my daughter May?' I say, 'Really? Thanks for the tip.' We get absolute *silence* on that joke. And I say to the actress, 'Let's try it the number two-hundred-and-eighty-third way.' We have tried it every conceivable way. 'Do you know my daughter May?'

'No, but thanks for the tip.' In England, that would bring the house down. Here they're not expecting something as quick and as crude as that, but gradually you're coming 'round to our way of thinking." Jim smiled and winked, like a vaudevillian on a roll, unable to resist one more chestnut. "Infamy, infamy. They've all got it infamy."

CHAPTER FOURTEEN

SWOOSIE KURTZ AND ANNE MEARA

"Onstage I relax. Real life makes me nervous."

© MARTHA SWOPE

Swoosie Kurtz in "The Fifth of July"

Anne Meara in "Romeo and Juliet"

© MARTHA SWOPE

Swoosie Kurtz was born in Omaha, Nebraska, the only child of an Olympic diver and the most decorated of World War II bomber pilots. Because her father's profession required that the family relocate frequently, Swoosie attended seventeen schools before enrolling in Hollywood High School. Her high school drama teacher encouraged her to give up ambitions to be a writer or a ballerina and suggested she take up an acting career. Swoosie went to London to study at the Academy of Music and Dramatic Arts. She landed her first role in New York in Paul Zindel's Pulitzer Prize–winning *The Effect of Gamma Rays on Man-in-the-Moon Marigolds*. She followed this with major roles in *Ah, Wilderness!*, *Tartuffe*, Wendy Wasserstein's *Uncommon Women and Others, The Fifth of July*, and the Lincoln Center production of *The House of Blue Leaves*, for which she won the Tony. In film, Swoosie has played Paul Newman's wife in *Slap Shot*, a prostitute in *The World According to Garp*, and Goldie Hawn's sister in *Wildcats*. She was nominated for two Emmies for her TV role of Laurie opposite Tony Randall in the series "Love, Sidney." Her other television credits include *Guilty Conscience* with Anthony Hopkins and the weekly sitcom "Sisters."

Anne Meara is the only child of a devoutly Catholic Long Island lawyer, her mother having died when Anne was six. After finishing high school, Anne studied with Uta Hagen. She met her husband, Jerry Stiller, in a theatrical agent's office after they had both been turned down for a new play. They decided to collaborate on an improvisational comedy routine and became, among other characters, Hershey Horowitz and Mary Elizabeth Doyle. They worked for years in clubs and on television and once in a while they were able to work in New York or summer stock theater. Together Anne and Jerry won awards for their radio and television commercials. Anne appeared with Zero Mostel in *Ulysses in Nighttown*, and in many roles with the New York Shakespeare Festival. She created the role of Bunny in *The House of Blue Leaves*, starred in Harvey Fierstein's *Spookhouse*, played an eighty-three-year-old grandmother in *Bosoms and Neglect*, and a homeless bag lady in *Eastern Standard*. In film, Anne has been featured in *Fame, The Boys from Brazil, Lovers and Other Strangers*, and *Awakenings*. On television she starred in "Kate McShane" and has played recurring roles on "Rhoda," "Archie Bunker's Place," and "ALF."

Being friends, Swoosie Kurtz and Anne Meara said they would like to appear together in our series. Because they are both so good at submerging themselves in the parts they play, I was unprepared for their natural beauty. I asked them if it was a deliberate choice, to play older, eccentric, and neurotic characters.

Anne quipped, "I saw Swoosie in *House of Blue Leaves* as Bananas. If that wasn't typecasting . . ."

Swoosie laughed. "I find it more fun to play people that are far away from me. This is what I find difficult about doing television, because they usually cast you as yourself. Movies do that to a great extent, too, so it's not as much fun. I became an actress to play people *other* than myself, and to take on a whole different set of circumstances, somebody else's life, somebody else's problems, somebody else's eccentricities. I enjoy that. The further away it is for me, the more I enjoy it."

Swoosie once said she liked to tap those parts of herself that we "civilians" (Swoosie's word for the rest of us) keep covered up. Does that mean that being an actress calls for taking on unique challenges?

"Yes," said Swoosie. "We get paid to expose those emotions and eccentricities that as civilians we all have to keep masked."

Both Anne and Swoosie could get jobs playing people they resemble physically and temperamentally, but they continue to pick roles far away from themselves.

"I don't feel that far away from any of them," said Anne. "I guess it's because the circumstances of the life of the character are different, but the well you draw on to create that character is within yourself."

"There is a kind of freedom in being somebody who is not like you at all," added Swoosie. "It's very liberating for me. The series ["Love, Sidney"] I did on television, basically playing myself, and soap operas, are what I call behavior, as opposed to acting. A lot of people are capable of doing that. That is why there are so many young actors on soaps who don't really know how to act. There is a difference between behavior and creating a character."

The actor uses her technique to create a character. We have learned there is a basic difference between American and English acting technique. Why would a nice American girl go to England to learn to act?

Swoosie smiled. "I often ask myself that question. I think it took me ten years longer to get going than if I had gone to Yale, which my mother wanted me to do. And she was absolutely right. I came back knowing nobody and nobody knew me. I was always a great Anglophile. For me, technique is not a dirty word. Technique enables you to feel, or look like you are feeling, the things you want to feel at the moment when you are required to feel them, when you may not feel like feeling them."

"That sounds like Beckett," Anne deadpanned. "Boy, are you deep."

The English stress externals, such as voice and body movement, whereas the American actor is told to get in touch with her feelings. Do actors trained in England have a problem adjusting to American actors when they have to act with them?

"No, not at all," said Swoosie. "That stereotype might be true at the Royal Academy of Dramatic Art. At the London Academy of Music and Dramatic Art, where I was, there was a terrific balance between internal and external, between technique and subtext. There was lots of subtext going on. It was great. I had no problem at all. On the other hand, I do have a problem with Stanislavski when it comes to the Method versus technique."

"Which method?" interrupted Anne. "That's already old hat. The Method is really *a* technique, by which you achieve certain results. There is bastardization of it and misuse."

"It's the misuse that worries me," said Swoosie. "People

taking acting classes are being told, 'You must sit there and wait until you feel what you would feel if you lost your father, or your dog was run over, or you lost a child or whatever. Just wait until you churn that feeling up within you, and then you can say the lines or do the part.' I don't think you can sit around waiting for that to happen. A great illustration of this is something that happened when I was at LAMDA. It's not an illustration of English technique, but a great example of technique versus going ahead and 'having a go,' or, as they say, 'Let's just plunge in and try it rather than sitting around waiting till we feel like it.'

"We were in the second week of rehearsal for a Chekhov play, and one actress was supposed to be having an incredible fight with her husband. She finally goes up to him and she hits him, in the text. [The actress] had never done it. Every time she came to it, she couldn't do it and she would say, 'This is where I hit him.' Finally, the director said, 'Is there a problem with this moment? You can't seem to build up to it. Are we ever going to see you hit him? We open next week.' The actress said, 'I just never feel that I have gotten to that point where I can actually hit him.'

"The director said, 'May I ask you to do something just as an experiment, totally technically? Don't worry about it, don't think about it, don't feel anything. Nothing is required of you, except saying those lines, and when the text says for you to hit him, I want you to go over and hit him as hard as you can. Hit him on the shoulder or something so it won't hurt. Just really haul off as a purely physical act and let him have it.'

"So she did it, and by the mere act of doing it she got herself to the point of being angry enough to hit him. And she never had a problem with it from there on. It was outside-in, the physical act bringing you to the emotional point. If she had sat around waiting to get angry enough to hit him, we would still be there."

At the time of her appearance with us, Anne was playing the bag lady, Mae Logan, in the Manhattan Theatre Club production of the play *Eastern Standard.* On her very first entrance, Anne's character is in a rage. How does an actor get into a state of rage before making an entrance?

"Anger is the easiest emotion to reach," said Anne. "Really, it is . . ." Then she interrupted herself with an edgy sigh. "I don't know the answer to any of these questions, David. It's so depressing. I fight my stage fright, I work it through, I go to family therapy. I mean, we all hang by a thread in this world. I don't have the answers.

"I love doing the part. I'm starting to enjoy myself. As some people in my family would say, 'It's nothing you wouldn't hear at home.' Mae Logan is very angry. She's an abandoned child in her late fifties. She's a street person, and she's in need of medication. For me it's easy to get angry. If you can't get angry, then you shouldn't do this part," (Anne's voice began to rise) "you should do some other parts. You could play ingenues or the leading lady, the good guys!

"I have trouble with anger in a destructive way. I can be in touch with those feelings and channel them creatively, and hopefully help service the play. That's a good thing, to be able to do that."

It seems actors are allowed to express emotions that the rest of us are taught to avoid. We are told to *avoid* scenes with family or friends, to *avoid* being emotional. As I said this, I felt my own voice rise with emotion.

"I know!" Anne said. "That makes me angry! There now, we have it," she said, pointing to me. "You can play my part in drag! See, it's easy. Just think about all the things people told you not to do and you can play Mae Logan."

I asked Anne how she prepared for the role of Mae.

"I talked to one bag lady when I was doing *Romeo and Juliet*," said Anne. "I would take the subway down to the Public Theater from the West Side. There are a lot of street people, homeless people, dangerous people, mentally ill people, some fakers, beggars, whatever. It's like a whole Victor Hugo bunch of people. And then there's also children. I mean there are *people*. They are all there . . . You are aware of it. I don't walk around with a notepad, saying, 'Oh, she went like that.'

"I think I really go about it by remembering what I think Mae's life was and what I can relate to, feelings of abandonment that we all have experienced, whether we try to be good little soldiers about it or not. And then I deal with those feelings."

The *New York Times* critic Frank Rich had been very complimentary toward Anne's performance in *Eastern Standard*, and I began to ask her about something he had written when she interrupted loudly, "I don't want to hear . . . I beg you. I don't want to hear, and if I knew you were going to quote a review, I wouldn't have come! I really can't listen to the good, and I *don't* listen to the bad. I beg you, or I'll burst into tears and go home."

It seemed as if Anne was about to walk off the stage. She was able to reach anger easily, just as she had said. My guests had agreed to talk with me about how theater works, but there were no ground rules. It was hard to know where to draw the line with my inquiry. To reassure Anne we would stay off the subject that bothered her, I said that we would eliminate any questions about whether critics affect the actor's performance.

"They do!" said Anne. "I'm telling you, the critics *do* affect your performance. At least I feel they do."

"That's why we don't read them," said Swoosie.

"I'm writing in *The New York Times,*" suggested Anne. "I'm Frances Rich or Clivette Barnes. 'The stage is translucent when Swoosie Kurtz walks down stage left to the French doors, holds that champagne and says the immortal line, "Here's to you, my son!" The audience wept!' Wednesday night Swoosie gets to that moment and she says, 'What did Clivette Barnes and Frances Rich say? . . . It was translucent? Transcendent? Oh shit, I'll *never* be that again! How am I ever going to be translucent?' "

"It is, after all, an opinion," said Swoosie. "I also find that critics don't know a lot about acting. They may know more about playwriting, I'm not sure. But I don't think they really know about acting."

Brooks Atkinson, a former critic of *The New York Times*, had the idea that the job of the critic was not just to give his own reactions but to also report how the audience reacted. So he functioned partly as a reporter.

"Stark Young, *Immortal Shadows*," said Anne. "Did you ever read that? It's a book of criticism of the theater. He was a devoted critic of the theater and the actors of his time and he seemed to follow them from one performance to another. He would say of John Barrymore, for example, 'You're capable of so much more. Remember when you did such and such? Don't get seduced by the . . .' There was a continuity in his work."

"So it's about the body of your work," said Swoosie.

"Critics are important," said Anne. "There's economic reasons someone wants to shell out a lot of money for a seat. So before they make the commitment to spend the money for the night and the dinner and the babysitter, they're going to read the review and make their determination [based] on it rather than have the luxury of spending the money and making their own decision. So I think economics may govern that quite understandably. I think it might be good to have two critics in each paper simultaneously review a play and have them be from different age groups and different ethnic groups."

In an interview for the *Times*, Swoosie was asked, "You always seem to play these neurotic people. Are you afraid of getting typecast?" At the time Swoosie said, "Why don't you take a look at the neurotic people that I played, and see how much alike they are. They are so wildly different."

"That's what we talk about in acting: choices," said Swoosie. "The fascinating thing is choices. I've been to see a couple of plays lately where they weren't terrible or anything. The way the director handled it was not terrible, and you can't say it was bad. I came away saying, 'He made the wrong choices.' "

If the words are written by the playwright, and the director takes charge of staging the play, what kind of choices are left to the actor?

"The how-to," Anne answered. "The playwright knows the what. The actor's job is to get not what, but how. There can be many valid routes to how."

In John Guare's *House of Blue Leaves*, Bananas is the wife and Bunny is the girlfriend. Anne created the role of Bunny. Swoosie played Bananas in the highly successful revival at Lincoln Center. For the part of Bananas, we are given certain details like her age, and the fact that she has a child, etc. That's the first thing the actor has to deal with, the facts. Then there are the physical actions, such as throwing rice, and making hamburgers out of Brillo pads. We are also told that Bananas has been crying for six months in her nightgown. These are all details provided by the playwright. Where does the actor get a chance to make a choice?

"Well," said Swoosie, "you could say to yourself (and this is one of the traps in that part) that this woman has been in her nightgown for six months, she's never left the house, she's been crying for six months. We find out at the end of Act One she went up on the roof in her nightgown, when there was a blizzard outside. This is not a happy person. This must be a person who feels very sorry for herself. And you could play it self-pityingly, if you didn't have a great director like Jerry Zaks.

"At the first rehearsal, I came out and my first line was, 'Is it morning? Is it light yet?' I came out like this pathetic little creature, sort of frail, and saying those lines weakly, and Jerry said, 'Look, Swoos, you're just an ordinary, very happy housewife in Queens with a lovely marriage, and it's morning, and your husband is a zookeeper and you love animals. Just come out and say, "Good morning, is it light, I didn't know anybody was up," that's all. Don't play the character, play the situation.'

"There were other traps which could be death for that part and the play. Bananas is looking at her husband and [his mistress] Bunny, and the two of them are talking about how they are going away, and nobody is paying any attention to her, the wife. The action John Guare has written in the script is, 'Bananas throws rice at them.' There are many different ways to do that. That's where the choice comes in.

"In the early previews, when we first got in front of an audience, I was throwing it at them from behind—pow!—which is the obvious choice. They were sitting on the sofa. Jerry Zaks came up to me after we had done it that way a couple of times and he said, 'Swoos, it's wrong. I don't want the audience to be worried about you in that way, that early in the play. So try it a different way tomorrow night.'

"I thought about it and thought about it and then I thought, 'Rice! Celebratory! It's a wedding. They're going away together!' It was what we call playing against it, in acting, and it worked like a dream. There was a big laugh. At that point in the play, we weren't going for a laugh. It would have been fine if they hadn't laughed, but it was a moment of worry, so we found the right choice, through trying different things. That's a choice."

So there was no feeling on Swoosie the actor's part to see Bananas as angry and hurt by her husband's infidelity?

"That was my original instinct about it," she said. "Bananas can't deal with things directly, so she's going to throw rice at them like a little kid would, and that's how I started playing it. But choice by choice, moment by moment, I worked away from all of those moments, from being angry, from being self-pitying, and into the more 'up' choices. Jerry kept telling me, 'Make the positive choice.' "

Anne said, "The paradox is, of course, that it was heart-rending."

In important moments in a play, does the actor know what the audience is feeling?

"How it affects you may not be how it affects this lady or that lady or that gentleman," said Anne. "It would be to the audience's detriment for me to start focusing on anything but what I am doing onstage. If I, for one nanosecond, allowed myself to think how you're digging what I'm doing, I'm in deep trouble. I have to be focused totally on my fellow actor and my intention. Of course I'm *aware* of the audience. I'm not really wacky. But for me at that time to be concerned with anything other than my task at hand would be self-defeating."

The greatest directors are in a sense non-directors. They seem to provide an atmosphere where the actors get to initiate things.

"I don't agree with that," said Swoosie. "I hate non-directors. What you say about creating an atmosphere is crucial. That's wonderful, an atmosphere in which you can work and create. But, unlike a lot of actors, I love to be directed within an inch of my life. I want to be told what to do only if he or she is good. I want to be told every little step, where to turn, etc. Then I'll make it my own. But I *love* to be directed. I love to be given notes. I just love to absorb all of that. I don't like those directors who actors talk about, 'Oh, I loved so and so. He just really left us alone.' That fills me with terror! It's like, 'Here's a boat. Go off in the wilderness with no oars and no map.' He's gotta be out there for a reason and I like a real structure."

"The atmosphere must be created," said Anne. "I don't want to be directed within an inch of my life but I certainly want someone who can show me an insight and a specific or a trigger that will open something up."

When I saw Anne in *Eastern Standard*, there was a moment when I started to believe she *was* the character. I also began to care what happened to Mae. It was the point when she went from the incredible anger that she has, to winning over the waitress. That's the moment when she got me. I don't know about the rest of the audience, but she got me, and it was a moving moment.

"My need, quite physically," said Anne, "is to stay in that restaurant, and I realize at one point that this waitress can be my ally. But I'm just intellectualizing because I'm sitting here in front of people. This isn't what I really go through when I'm up there. I'm trying to sound intelligent because we're in a school."

We have talked about the fact that both Anne and Swoosie enjoy playing people different from themselves. What about the *similarities* of these characters to their personalities? For example, Swoosie said in an interview that the problem of understanding what Bananas wants is something she came to in rehearsal. Swoosie decided that one of the things Bananas dislikes is change. She wants to go back to a period of time when everything was happy with her marriage. "She hates change," Swoosie said, "just like me." Speaking about portraying the nurse in *Romeo and Juliet*, Anne once said, "She's loving, caring, silly, and not too bright, not far away from me." It seems actors look for similarities in the characters they play and seek traits that remind them of themselves. Does the actor bring herself to these characters, or does she have to search for new depths in order to find these qualities?

"I don't know," said Anne. "This is where I'm not so good at these talks. To tell you the truth . . ."

Afraid I was about to lose Anne again, I reassured her that I loved her performance.

"Well, there's *that* seduction, too," Anne said. "Actors do like that. It's better than a kick in the face with a wet fish . . . I know it's a slow process. I know that I'm fine in rehearsals, until the first audience comes, and then I'm gripped with deep panic and deep fear which I can't even joke about. But I've gotten through that. It's a personal problem. You're not my therapist. Why should I bore you? Very real, very real and very scary. At one point I realized I just have to do the job. I don't have to be perfect. Perfect is dead. There is nothing more to do when something's perfect.

"My job is to do the job. I love being in this play. I told you that in the car coming down. For the amount of time on the stage, it's the smallest part in the show. It's a beautifully written play by a talented young man. My character is an integral force in this play, and I feel very good about being part of the ensemble. In the beginning it was something else. I don't know what it was. Anything I am doing in a play impinges on my life, and each affects the other. And in this last case, it has been for the good.

"I have such respect for actors and the cast I am with. These kids are devoted, consummate actors. Everyone has their own hoodoo. There is no other word. Everyone does their own hoodoo before they go on. People chant 'om.' People go through rituals. Barbara Garrick and I go through our first-act scene when they call fifteen minutes. When I'm sitting on the stage, before I'm visible at my table, as each of the guys walks on, they give me fives. If one of those things doesn't happen, I go crazed. I'll go, 'Hey, where's the hand?' like everything is going to fall apart that night if I don't get the hand. So there is a little, dare I say the word, religiosity involved. Let's say spirituality. Religion has such narrow confines . . . We're really in a business of transcendence. If I could say that without sounding too . . . " Anne waved her hand as if shooing something away. "I don't care how I sound. That's what I am saying. It's a business of transcendence.

"A part of the work is to be able to share with everyone in the audience the common bond and new things, or whatever the playwright says; to be that tool of transcendence, of feeling, of thought.

"I do feel everyone is an artist. I really know that everyone in the audience, like Swoosie and myself and you, has an artist within them. That's all. It's that simple. It's no big deal, but it's there. Whether you believe it or not, it's still there, some sort of creative self in all of us."

The actor uses her own body. She is her own instrument, unlike the painter and the pianist. Are there more significant differences between the actor and other artists?

"I'll tell you the problem an actor has," said Anne. "An actor needs *you* to show up. If I acted Mae Logan alone, in my apartment, or alone in this auditorium, they'd really come from Bellevue and take me. But if only two or three of you showed up to watch me do it, that's a validation there. So an actor is interpreting the playwright's message, with the consent of the director and the playwright.

"The term is to *give* a performance. You're giving something, and that's what it is. Someone's got to be there to receive it, whereas you can paint a masterpiece in a garret or a Long Island house. You can compose. I don't know how musicians feel. Don't they like people to hear their music when they're playing?"

Anne is living proof that the arts are related. In addition to her acting career, she has written material for herself and her husband and, recently, she wrote a play.

"I've written a full-length play that I want to rewrite," said Anne, "because I feel differently now than at the time I wrote it. I think I have a very good ear for the people I write about. I co-wrote a movie of the week. Mainly the purpose was to write a good part for myself and give myself the best lines—which I did. It's a dog-eat-dog world, you know. I'm very flattered when you say writer, because I hope someday soon to talk more about it, but I haven't put it out there enough yet, really. Except commercials. I'm proud of those. Jerry and I write those.

"We wrote our own nightclub routine. Whenever we did nightclub sketches on television, on 'The Ed Sullivan Show,' that was terror! That was cottonmouth. I remember facing upstage. We were doing something where Jerry was playing Walter Flonkheit, I was a screaming harridan at the door, Regina Margaret Mulcahy, or I was Mrs. Santa Claus. Live television. Live from New York! It was scary. That's a presentational form. In a nightclub, when you do a sketch, the immediate objective is to go over. To go over well. And if it's comedy, to have them laugh. It's tough. I don't do that anymore. It's scary stuff but you learn a lot."

In nightclub work the actor has to break through the fourth wall and deal directly with the audience. Was it hard to make that transition?

"In the beginning, Jerry and I didn't," said Anne. "We couldn't talk to the people. We'd say, 'Good evening, ladies and gentlemen. We'd like to show you a girl and a boy saying good night at the door.' Then we'd do the sketch. But we didn't admit them [in] really or *tummel* as they say. We didn't say, 'Hi, I'm Jerry and I'm Jewish, she's Irish,' and go through that whole schmeer. That came later, when we dealt with our own backgrounds in a fairly humorous way, in an exaggerated way, but really looking at the people, which used to scare the hell out of me. I can't do it in a play. Some people come offstage and say, 'Did you see that the whole side of the house is empty?' I say, 'When did you see that?' I mean, X-ray vision. When I'm in a play I can't look out. If I look out, I'm looking out of my head."

"But," said Swoosie, turning to Anne, "you and I both had to talk to the audience in *Blue Leaves*."

"That's different," said Anne. "That's the choice of the playwright."

Swoosie had a monologue in *Blue Leaves* that began, "Can I have my song," meaning "Can I have my say . . ."

Swoosie laughed. "I never did figure out what that line meant."

In a monologue, the audience becomes the other character the actor is addressing. Is a monologue comparable to a stand-up comic dealing directly with the audience?

"It's terrifying," said Swoosie. "Normally, in a regular play, you never break the fourth wall. No matter what happens. You hear a cab honking outside or something falls, you don't acknowledge it. If something happens onstage, something spills, for example, we have to deal with it, but basically it didn't happen. We'd go on no matter what. But when you are a character looking out and speaking to people, saying, 'I really want to tell you my side of what happened. You've heard his side, now let me tell you mine . . . ,' if people don't look really happy and really entertained, you can get very depressed. One night when I thought I was really hot stuff, I looked out and there was a guy in the first row asleep. Brought me right back to earth. Okay, well I'm not such hot stuff tonight. But you mustn't get hostile. You can't get hostile."

If it's true that the actor's life affects what she does onstage, and vice versa, then where does the actor feel most comfortable?

Swoosie answered, "Onstage I relax. Real life makes me nervous."

When the actor studies a character, she learns about other people. When Anne played a bag lady, it educated her about the welfare situation in New York. I asked Swoosie if exploring the neuroses of Bananas took away some of her nervousness in real life.

"No, not really," said Swoosie, "because I didn't do any research on the part at all, which is very scary. It means somewhere in me was all of that. It's very scary. There are other parts I've played where I thought, 'I am so far from this person,' but somehow in rehearsals, together with the director, we ask the right questions and I tap the right places, and out come things I didn't know were there. It all depends on how much of an imagination you have. I am not saying I could *act* any of these situations. I would never be so presumptuous to say that, but I can *imagine* myself in any situation. Maybe we can all do that."

"In *any* situation?" asked Anne.

"Yes," responded Swoosie. "I mean, not me Swoosie, but I can imagine how it would feel to kill my children, if I had to play Medea. I'm not saying I could act it. That would take a whole other process. I can imagine what it would feel like, so I'm not sure you have to go out into the world and study those things."

"I agree," Anne said. "The actor's job is to be in touch with his own feelings, and to realize that the more in touch you are with your own feelings, the more you can share them by transmitting them through the work to other people. The more in touch you are, the more universality. The more specific your choices, strangely enough, the more people you reach."

"Yes," said Swoosie. "To answer your question, acting does help your life. It helps me because I learn an awful lot of what I know, which is very little, from the work I do, from the plays I do . . . For me to play a part, I have to love that person, which may not mean necessarily liking them. Something about the character has to break my heart. Even in a comedy. Something in me has to go, 'Oh, look at how hard she's trying, look at her trying to do that.' Something has to touch me about her. The more I do that, the less inclined I am to make fun of people, and the more inclined I am to have compassion."

Was that also true for Mae Logan?

"Yes," said Anne. "She is a very fearful, angry, frightened lady, and I have experienced those feelings. Through experiencing them I have learned compassion."

C H A P T E R F I F T E E N

ALAN ARKIN
AND
AMANDA PLUMMER

"Whether we like it or not, we are the characters we are playing up there."

Alan Arkin in "Room Service"

Amanda Plummer in "A Month in the Country"

ALAN ARKIN was born in New York City, and became the focus of attention as a performer at family gatherings. After his family moved to California, Alan studied drama at Los Angeles City College. He accepted a drama scholarship to Bennington College for women in Vermont and for two years he played all the male leads. Eventually he became a member of Second City, the improvisational theater group in Chicago, where he was able to refine his technique. Alan made his Broadway debut with the troupe in a revue called *From the Second City.* His other Broadway credits are Joseph Stein's *Enter Laughing,* for which he won the Tony, and Murray Schisgal's *Luv* with Anne Jackson and Eli Wallach. Alan was nominated for two Oscars, for his screen debut in *The Russians Are Coming! The Russians Are Coming!* and for his portrayal of the deaf-mute in *The Heart Is a Lonely Hunter.* He has appeared in numerous films, including *Catch-22, The In-Laws, Wait Until Dark, Last of the Red Hot Lovers, Edward Scissorhands,* and *Glengarry Glen Ross.* Alan is a Renaissance man who, in addition to roles on stage, film, and TV, has been an author, musician, songwriter, and Obie Award–winning director in theater and film.

AMANDA PLUMMER is the daughter of actors Christopher Plummer and Tammy Grimes, but she didn't decide to be an actress until she was seventeen. For a while Amanda resisted her parents' profession and wanted to be a jockey, "but I came to a point where I wanted to be around people, and either I could join the circus or I could join acting." Amanda had little formal training. After a stint with an acting group in Middlebury College in Vermont she was accepted at the Williamstown Theatre Festival, where her repertoire included playing a fairy in *A Midsummer Night's Dream.* Then she was cast in *A Month in the Country,* which led to roles in off-Broadway productions of *A Lie of the Mind* and *The Milk Train Doesn't Stop Here Anymore.* On Broadway, Amanda was Eliza in Shaw's *Pygmalion* opposite Peter O'Toole and was nominated for a Tony for her performance. She has also appeared as Laura in the revival of *The Glass Menagerie* and Jo in *A Taste of Honey,* for which she was again nominated for the Tony. Amanda won the Tony along with the Drama Desk Award and the Outer Critics Circle Award for her portrayal of Agnes in *Agnes of God.* In film she has been seen in *The World According to Garp* and *The Fisher King,* to name a few.

When I told Alan Arkin that Amanda Plummer had agreed to be in our series, he said he would like to appear with her since he was a fan and they had never met. When Amanda heard that Alan wanted to appear with her, she was equally enthusiastic. Amanda was living in a small private house, and when I went to pick her up, she asked me to come in. She was smoking and seemed tense. She told me she had had trouble sleeping the previous night because she was nervous about her evening with us. I reassured her that all would be well. I marveled that an actress of Amanda's experience would be nervous about answering questions in front of an audience. I had seen her in so many roles where she took daring chances. Perhaps an actor takes a greater risk when she appears as herself, and when she doesn't know what the script will be in advance.

When I finished introducing Alan and Amanda there was much applause, but no one appeared. I could hear them chatting behind the curtain as if oblivious to the crowd that waited for them. After they had finally made their entrance and seated themselves, I explained that the series title, "The Magic of Theater," described what happens to the audience.

"The magic can happen to the actors, too, David," said Alan. "It can happen as much for the actors as for the audience."

"If it doesn't happen for the actors, I don't think it would happen for the audience," added Amanda.

I asked Alan and Amanda if their experience as members of an audience is different from the rest of ours because they are actors.

"The difference between us and an ordinary audience,"

said Alan, "is that when it's not good we know how to analyze why it's not, and when it's good, we lose ourselves the same as the audience."

When an actor watches someone he knows perform, does he say to himself, "I can see how he's doing it"?

"If I do, then he's not doing good work," said Alan. "I can get lost in my kid's work. Adam did some brilliant work last year on [the TV series] 'A Year in the Life,' so good that it was unsung. It was a living person you were seeing up there, so he didn't get an enormous amount of attention for it, but he was wonderful. He absolutely transported me on that occasion." Alan beamed with parental pride. "I forgot he was my son, and once in a while I would think of him as my son, but not know for a minute that he had those places in him where he was going. That was very exciting. If you can do it with your own kids, you can do it with anybody."

Is that one of the ways to judge good acting, when the actor is not noticed?

Alan nodded. "A lot of times, yes. My idea of a good movie is when you come out and you don't notice anything. I mean that literally. If you come out and you're talking about *a performance*, the movie didn't work. If you're talking about how great the writing was in this scene or that scene, the movie didn't work. It works if you come out and you can't talk about anything. That's when the movie works. Things shouldn't stick out. An actor shouldn't be saying, 'Hey ma, look how good I'm doing!' We should all be committed to *the event*. But it's not just in movies. It's in life as well. The more we are committed to the event, and not our participation in it, the more the event is going to work and be an entity. Some actors, I don't know how they do it, can manage to be very showy and very true at the same time. My son can't do that. He doesn't work that way."

In *Agnes of God*, Agnes is a young nun accused of bearing and murdering a child. Sitting across from Amanda on the New School stage, it was hard to imagine her playing this role. She sat quietly between Alan and myself, with her delicate hands folded in her lap, and her voice was soft and faint, almost like that of a child. I asked her what she did to find something in Agnes she could identify with so she could play the part.

"There are so many things," she said. "The easiest to talk

about is the amount of reading I did. I read a great deal of Jung on the subject of dementia praecox and somnambulism and twilight states. I read a great deal on that, and it seemed to fit in between the blank spaces of the words on the page, what is *not* being said by this character. I could fill in the back of her head, where you wouldn't know what she is really saying. She's saying something, she's meaning it, but there are a lot of other things going on *which add* to what is being said.

"Agnes was not altogether a direct kind of confrontational speaking woman. She had a lot of problems and secrets, and she was very manipulative. You couldn't take her on face value, nor can you do that with anyone, which is what's fascinating about doing any role. It's what is *not* being said, what gesture is made (and then how the opposite gesture could have been made), [that helps] you get a whole human being with a curiousness.

"Then, once in a while you reach a role where you are so enlightened and inspired and you are already dreamed into that character. So my own imagination didn't have to work. It was given tremendous allowance to find and fly on its own. That was very lucky, and I didn't have to work like a workhorse very much. I had to get the details down, but it was more exciting because she was already very much alive in my mind and my body."

John Pielmeyer, who wrote *Agnes of God*, was brought up as a Catholic. Did the playwright's background influence what he was trying to say in the play?

"I was not at all interested," said Amanda. "I loved him. He was a wonderful man and writer, but we actually disagreed on a few things. Not violently. So I took my route and it didn't invade his own beliefs that much. You could see his point of view from what my performance was, as well as the way I was living her."

There are different stages in approaching a role. An actor does a certain amount of preparation by herself before rehearsals, and a certain amount during rehearsals with the director.

Amanda recalled, "He said, 'Do what you are doing. It's interesting. I'm going to stay out of the way.' Then he asked me politely, 'Do you mind?' I said, 'No, I don't mind,' and as rehearsals progressed we got into questions. He was great.

Michael Lindsay-Hogg is a wonderful director and very curious, lots of questions, lots of 'I don't really know what's going on' and we'd find out together, which is the best way."

How did the actor-director relationship work in *Enter Laughing*?

"I kind of slavishly followed what I felt the director wanted for a long time," said Alan, "and it was failing. I had a kind of image of what Carl Reiner and the director wanted, and I was trying to do that and it failed and failed and I almost got fired. Then in Philadelphia I said, 'I want to do it my way one night. Can I do it my way one night?' And they said, 'Try it,' and it succeeded. The play worked, and it turned out that that was what they wanted all along. By trying to please them, I was just standing in my own way. That was a problem I had had, and I realized that it was a running problem in my life. Trying to please other people, trying to do things their way, and then having that moment of 'To hell with them, I'm not going to do it that way, I'm going to do it my way,' and it ends up being the way it was asked of me all the time."

I asked Alan what kind of a process he goes through to begin getting to know his character.

"I don't know what I do anymore," he said. "The last part I played was something which my wife wrote and which was based on me. We did it on [public television's] 'Wonderworks.' I didn't know how to do that because that was a conception she had of me, and I was completely lost. Not only was it me, but it was me about twenty years ago. I didn't have a clue where to even begin searching for that. It was a person I didn't want to be then, and I certainly don't want to be now." Alan looked out into the audience. "Forgive me, sweetheart. But she had this idea that she was giving me a gift, presenting me with this person I was twenty years ago that I no longer want to be. It was very difficult, and there was a war going on in me as to how much I wanted to indulge. It wasn't great, but it was all right."

What about the character in *Wait until Dark*?

"That was an anomaly in my career," said Alan. "I just disappeared. I went away. When I was in Chicago working in Second City, I met a whole underground society I had never met before. I was kind of naïve until then. I met a lot of criminals, I met prostitutes, I met drug addicts.

"The character [in *Wait until Dark]* was a composite figure based on several addicts I knew. What I found to be true of them was that they disappeared. They just went away. And I tried to disappear when I played that character, and not be there, to be in several other places simultaneously. And what I have found, oddly enough, about a lot of people who commit evil acts (I've listened to a lot of interviews since then) is that they talk about not being there a lot. They talk as if they weren't there. I hated playing the part as it went on. It revolted me. I'm glad I did it because I'm happy to find that I was revolted by things like that. I wouldn't want to do it again."

When actors do research for their characters, is it necessary to have an in-depth understanding of the historical period in which the character lives?

"I have the desire to live like [the character]," said Amanda, "and live in a part of New York City or move to Mississippi for a little while if the play takes place in Mississippi. For one play, I lived in a whore hotel for a year to communicate and make friends with people that I had not come across on such a personal level in my life."

"Every actor works completely differently," said Alan. "Just as every writer works from a different frame of reference. I was just reading a book by Hermann Hesse. I admire him greatly. In the introduction the person who compiled the book said that Hesse wrote [of] imaginary places, he wrote fairy tales because he didn't want to lock himself into a particular culture and time that he was living in. He made inventions for himself. And it clarified something about myself that I'd always worried about, because I don't take the kind of detailed notes that I felt an actor should. I like to let my imagination do a lot of the work, as long as what ends up is something truthful. Not necessarily real, but truthful.

"What ends up in Hermann Hesse's books and the things he imagines from his fantasy life are, to me, infinitely more real than a lot of the truth I see walking down the street on a daily basis. Very often attention to that kind of detail can be from people whose imagination doesn't have a lot of sweep to it. Not always. Sometimes a person can embody both. When you have a person who can embody both, boy, then you really have something. But meticulous attention to historical detail can often stultify flights of imagination."

Alan last appeared on the stage in the play *Luv*, over twenty-three years ago. That's too long for an actor of Alan's talents to be absent from the stage.

"It's too long if *that's* what I was supposed to have done with my life," Alan said, "but I don't think that's what I was supposed to have done with my life. It has nothing to do with movies or television. It has to do with something which really doesn't have to do with the theater at all.

"I found that being onstage two hours a night was a twenty-four-hour-a-day job. When I wasn't acting, I had no life of any kind. The only life I had was on the stage, and there was something in me that screamed that this is wrong. That I have no right to do this to my family, I have no right to do this to the people I love, the people who love me, and even worse, I have no right to do this to myself.

"Initially, it started in part as an idea that I wasn't going to be able to feed even the persona I was onstage, unless I had some identity to feed it with—and I felt like I had none. It began a kind of exploration into who I am that has become as important to me and as exciting to me as any character I have ever played.

"It sounds egotistical, but it's not, because when you start discovering who and what you are, it's bigger than anything you ever imagined yourself to be. And, by definition, it's generous. It's a generous exploration. The more of *you* you find, the more of you there is to give to those you love."

"I am facing the same things now, too," added Amanda. "There isn't much of a life going on." Her hand worried nervously over the hem of her miniskirt. "It is a twenty-four-hour job. I miss things, and I'm thirty-one now. I am missing a home. I want a home of my own, and it's hard to know what to do. I am just coming up to those realizations for the first time."

"Everybody has different needs at different times in their lives," Alan said, "and different ways of expressing and exploring them."

Certain aspects of the creative process are the same for all the arts. I asked Alan if his experience as an actor led to all the other creative projects in which he has become involved.

"Absolutely," he said. "Until I was thirty, there was nothing in my life of any kind except this, film and theater. From the time I was five, it was all I ever wanted to do, and I immersed myself in it to a kind of obsessive degree. Whatever success I had was at least in part due to these obsessions I had.

"My first successful employment was in Second City when I was about twenty-eight or twenty-nine. I took it because it was an abandonment of a career. I said, 'I am never going to have a career.' My first marriage fell apart, and I couldn't get arrested in New York.

"Paul Sills offered me a job in Chicago for one hundred and twenty-five bucks a week at Second City and I said, 'What the hell. Go for broke.' I had nothing here. I was sure it was just going to be a way of burying myself in something, and giving up my career. I thought it was a way of capitulating, just having someplace to go to, to earn a living. And it became the touchstone for everything else that transpired afterward. Before that time, I had had an enormous amount of very rigid and well-founded acting training. I think I was the first person who had had that at Second City. Everybody else had had a lot of training in a lot of other areas, not really a kind of rigid theatrical background."

Viola Spolin, Paul Sills's mother, has been credited with starting all the improvisational techniques and theories that we have in this country. In addition to Second City, there were the Compass Players, and then we had Elaine May and Mike Nichols, and Shelley Berman, and others. What is the difference between improvisation and acting?

"Improvisation is rehearsing in public," said Alan.

I asked Alan if there was a script when he worked at Second City.

"No," he said. "We never used a script."

If an actor on the stage knows every word that he's going to say and where he's going to stand and how loud or how soft he's going to speak and when he's going to move and what he's going to wear, what is left for him to contribute?

"If all of that is given to him, then nothing *is* left for him to contribute," said Alan. "A good director is like any kind of leadership. It's having a very clear vision of an entity in your mind, being able to share that vision with the people who work around you and then being able to adapt and change it as reality presents itself in terms of the people you have around you. Some of them may have a vision that's better than yours, and some of them won't be able to fulfill your vision. You have to adapt and change and keep that vision fluid. It means using the best and the most of everybody under you. The person who directs the way you just described is going to get not terribly good things out of his cast. Unless somebody has a voice to say, 'I have a great idea of something to wear. Can I try this?' The director says, 'Yes' or 'No, and let me tell you why.' An actor's got to feel free to bring everything of his to a performance."

But he can't bring his own words.

"No," Alan agreed. "That he can't bring."

Was the Second City training, of using one's own words, a different way into the process of learning to act?

"Right," said Alan.

Improvisation means you get up and someone in the audience says, "Let's play a scene now." Is there a different technique involved in doing that?

"Yes," said Alan, "totally different. It took me months. I was afraid I was going to get canned on a daily basis at Second City because I didn't know how to be funny. I just had no idea. I wasn't a particularly funny person. I was dour. I was kind of a depressive. I didn't have a clue, and then one day as a last resort I played a character that I loved in a scene, and it worked. I was funny! *As that character* I was funny. So for about a month I did nothing but play that specific character onstage. No matter what I did, I played that character. Then I added to that. I played another character, and another one after that until I developed a library of characters. But nobody for a long time had a clue as to who I was. And neither did I."

Do they now?

"Oh yes," said Alan, beginning to laugh. "Everybody says, 'Hey, there goes Alan.' "

When Alan played Harry Berlin in Murray Schisgal's *Luv*, one of the New York critics said, "A dog once mistook him for a fire hydrant." That basically was all the information that was given about Harry in the script. How does an actor create a character like Harry Berlin, with so little information?

"Sometimes it can be easier actually," Alan said. "The more information that is forced on you by the playwright, the more difficult it can be, because that's a very rigid mold you have to place yourself in. I was very fortunate in that I was given an abstraction by Murray. It was also easy for me because that's who I was then. Harry Berlin was very close to who I was. I had a very low opinion of myself. I was in misery most of the time, and I was just doing a comic version of who I was."

In *Agnes of God,* the playwright also left out some key background information about whether Agnes was raped. I asked Amanda if, in order to play the role, she had to make a decision about whether Agnes was, in fact, raped.

"Yes, I did," she said, "but it was *my* secret. There were shades of it in the performance, but it's never spoken in the play. There would be shades of what might have happened, but still it was up in the air. People still didn't know what really happened. In my mind and in Agnes's mind it was clear, I knew she knew. She knew it all the time, but it was under so many levels of denial."

Was there ever a discussion between the actors and the director and the playwright about that?

"No," said Amanda.

No one was ever concerned about that?

"No, not that I can remember."

I asked Alan if he felt he could be funny without playing a role.

"I think I can now," Alan said.

"You made *me* laugh," said Amanda, with a sudden, open smile.

"That's good," said Alan. "I didn't know I was there until *Catch-22.* I didn't know that *I* was onstage or on the screen. I thought it was somebody else up there. Like when I did *Catch-22;* up until that point, everything was an extreme characterization. I said to Mike Nichols, 'Who is Yossarian?' Mike said, 'He's you.' I said, 'Wait a minute, there is no such thing. There is no such person as me.' And he pushed me into just being me on film, or a facsimile of it. How would I react in this specific situation? I went to the dailies the first few days, fully believing that there would be a blank on the screen where I was, and to my amazement, there was somebody there."

There is an earnestness about Alan, an unrelenting candor that's evident in his direct, focused gaze and each carefully chosen word.

I asked Alan what is keeping him from appearing on the stage.

"What's happened to me," he said, "is that I have expiated

a lot of my demons. I don't have to deal with them anymore. It doesn't happen when I'm in a film or in a television show because it is a concentrated effort and I have no time to question it. Onstage, I find I have this desperate desire to just turn around and say, 'Hi! Hello!' I don't want to have the barriers to just saying, 'Hello, how are you? Let's talk!' I don't need any barriers. The barriers start feeling like just that. They are no longer a vehicle through which I have a voice. They have now become mostly an obstacle to having a voice.

"I suppose that would not be true if I was playing somebody that I could look up to, but most of the time in the theater you don't get to play those people.

"In the days when I would have killed anybody to play any part, I didn't feel like I had an identity, and I felt like anybody I played was in better shape than I was. So to be anybody with a fixed identity was a delight. Now that I feel some sense of identity, I don't want to play people who have less identity than I do. I already have compassion for them. If I have the opportunity of playing somebody with more consciousness than I do, I feel like that would be reaching for something. I hope this doesn't sound like heresy.

"Whether we like it or not, we are the characters we are playing up there. There is an important story I would like to tell. I did a couple of projects with Carol Burnett once, who did experiments with Kirlian photography, the Kirlian Aura. There is a lab in UCLA, where they work with Kirlian photography, which is photographing your aura. It has been going on for years, and they have had dramatic and extraordinary results. Carol Burnett went there, and they photographed her aura, which they do most easily on the hand. It's like a thumb print. Your aura is a definition of who you are, the light emanating from your hand. The electromagnetic field translates into light that comes out of your hand. That's who you are. The kind of field you project is what you are.

"They asked Carol to think of herself, without moving, as several of the different characters she played. As she did that, the light around her hand would dramatically change. And they found that when she thought of herself as one of her characters, each one of those characters had a very specific light field. What that shows you is that as you conjure up these forces in you to be another person, you become that other person, but it's also you." Alan's folded hands opened wide. "The ramifications are endless.

"Each one of us has the seeds of absolutely everything within us. Anybody who has studied acting for any length of time knows that. Sooner or later, if you identify enough with the part, you find that part in you, be it an axe murderer, be it any aberration under the sun, any elevated state under the sun you want to think of. We have the seeds of that within us. It's a question of degree. It's a question of where that graph plays out in us. If you are playing somebody who's got demonic sides, you have to throw that off every night. You have to find ways of throwing that off, and sometimes it's not so pleasant. And it's not so easy sometimes. If you are playing someone who is elevated, a saint if you will, or a great soul, then you have to reach for that constantly."

"The soul goes through a changing," said Amanda. "The actual soul that you are goes through a changed direction, and you have to follow the direction it takes you."

When an actor succeeds in immersing herself in her character, does that diminish her need to seek approval from the audience?

"That's complicated," said Amanda. "I need for that piece of work I love to be admired. It's not that I don't want to please anybody. I want people to understand. I don't want to be misunderstood." There was a sad yearning to her voice. "I don't want *my character* to be misunderstood. But I don't work towards that goal. Something comes together and you want it strong and whole enough so that people can see it clearly. They don't have to identify with it. If they do, that's wonderful. If they don't, that's wonderful. I don't do it so that they will feel it. I hope that they will."

"What you're asking falls into two parts," said Alan. "One is, 'Am I doing it the right way?' And the other is, 'Do you love me?' If you're fortunate enough to work with a great director, then you want to assimilate his ideas in order to be able to do it the right way. But then there comes a point when you've assimilated those ideas and he must leave you alone so you can digest the ideas and turn them into something that's your own, that is something more than what he has given you and greater than what you can do.

"It's like a wedding of something bigger than any of you.

Once that is accomplished, what every actor dreams of is that it starts doing itself, so that you don't think about it. And when that happens, *you don't care what an audience thinks. You don't care what you think.* It was an event. It happened. The audience can no more deny the event than they can deny a car crash that took place outside in the street. It was a reality that took place on the stage. The actor couldn't care less if they liked it or not, because what they gave them was an event. There are some performers whose constant cry is, 'Do you love me? Do you love me?' Judy Garland made a career, a wonderful career [for] there was something great about her, but every moment of her life she was saying, 'Do you love me? Do you love me?' She needed that. And people were very happy to fill that place for her."

Sometimes an actor has to portray a character with unattractive qualities. Laura in *The Glass Menagerie* is a shy girl, and to act shy, the actor has to do a lot of negative actions. We imagine that a shy person doesn't talk very much. She hides. She puts her eyes down. But Amanda found positive actions for Laura.

"A shy person can be quite outspoken and be very shy," said Amanda, "cripplingly shy, near-to-death shy. I didn't think of her as a shy person, but other people viewing her would say, 'Yes, she is a shy person.' Laura goes, 'Well, people think I'm shy. I guess that's the easiest way to explain the way I behave among people. All right, I'm shy.' Laura was a very difficult role for me. I did her very poorly."

"I can't believe that," said Alan.

"I did," repeated Amanda emphatically. "I did her very poorly, I believe. The director once brought me off the stage and sat me down in the seats and said, 'You are too close to her. Now do some acting,' or words to that effect. I couldn't do anything about it. I was so immersed in her from the moment go. I wanted to add so much to her, beyond myself. When I do a role, I want to grow. I want to learn more about who I am, since I basically am nothing, too. I like myself. This is okay. So I want to grow in these roles. I want to learn more about me, and I didn't [learn] through her. I don't know what I learned from doing that role."

What happens when an actor gets into a part where it really *is* dragging him down. I asked Alan and Amanda if they had ever tried to get out of a play.

"*Taste of Honey*," said Amanda. "Jo. My favorite play that I have ever done, and it ran for a wonderful year. I kept discovering more and more. Unbelievable. She gave me a whole new walk. Her skin." She studied her own hand as if seeing a different life emerge from within. "I could look at my hand and—Oh, it was great! Oh, what a role she was! It was my first lead role in New York City, and I wanted to listen to the director, and I listened to the director and I tried to do everything he wanted me to do. And I did, and I could do it, but I was unhappy. I knew inside I was wrong and I would have these little arguments with him. But then I would say, 'All right, I'll do it.' About a week before opening, I went to the producers and I said, 'I have to quit because I am not enjoying myself. I don't feel like I am doing this well at all. It's not what I had imagined. Or find another director.' So we directed ourselves, and then we opened."

I asked Alan if he would like to direct Amanda in something.

"I would love to," he said. "I have the feeling it would be the easiest job I ever had."

Many of the projects Alan has been involved with have a theme or a message. Alan did a TV film about toxic waste called *A Deadly Business,* and *The Heart Is a Lonely Hunter* is a film that explores both the experience of being a deaf-mute as well as a controntation between blacks and whites. Is it easier to put across a message in a film than in a play?

"It's not a question of message," said Alan. "It wasn't the fact that [*A Deadly Business*] was about industrial waste. That attracted me, but it was a very powerful story. It was a true story that affected me very deeply, and I was also very happy that it was on a platform that I care about as well.

"I feel like we're inundated with so much 'culture,' that there is a danger of culture becoming a drug instead of what it was for me when I was a kid . . . I go to the movies, I don't get moved. I get impressed a lot. I get impressed an awful lot, and I feel like that's what's supposed to happen to me now, that people are making movies in order to impress me. And I don't want to be impressed! I want to be moved. I want to be affected. I want to be wrenched, and I want to be changed.

"I want to be affected deeply, and I think we have reached the point where we get confused. We are so out of tune with being moved deeply that we think, 'The more impressed we are, the more deeply we are moved.' I can hardly go to a film anymore without watching people going for the awards. I don't see people trying to dig into themselves. I don't see people throwing caution to the winds. You don't see scenes played between actors anymore, which is frightening. You see this shot, that person has his moment, then this person has her moment, nothing but singles anymore. If you watch a movie from the thirties or the forties, you see the camera sits there and you watch the actors for five minutes. The actors have a chance to do their thing, sometimes five or six minutes.

"We saw *Adam's Rib* two weeks ago on television. They sit on Judy Holliday and Katharine Hepburn's back for six minutes in one shot! It's unheard of, it's never done anymore. People's attention span is not great enough to withstand it, number one, and, number two, the director wants an opportunity to manipulate the scene, and not let the emotion and passion of the event take its toll on us—which is what it's supposed to do. And it's not movies' fault and it's not theater's fault! It's where the culture is now. Theater and film are no more than a reflection of where a culture is now, and I think that we are in a very tentative place in our culture's history when it comes to being deeply affected by anything. It's like we have said, 'It's enough now.' " Alan tapped his head. "We want to be affected up here a little bit maybe. We want to be impressed, but we don't want to be deeply moved a lot."

Is it rare for something to work on all levels, when actor, director, and text all come together?

"I've had the experience maybe a hundred times in films," said Alan. "There've been a hundred to a hundred-and-fifty films that have just rocked me, that have changed me, that have made an enormous impression. Not just American films, but films around the world.

"I think we're living in a bad time. There's a tendency to blame Hollywood for the kind of movies that come out. Hollywood *doesn't care*. They don't care! That is the immorality! Nobody there gives a good goddamn whether it's good or bad if it makes a hundred million dollars. If [the public] wanted to see Shakespearean plays turned into films, they would happily put it out. No one's buying it. That's why they don't get made.

"They don't want to feed us junk. They don't want to feed us anything except stuff that lines the coffers. It's corporate thinking. We're not living in a country anymore. We're living in a corporation. And Hollywood is just one small example of corporate thinking.

"It has to do with dollars and cents. That's what this country is about right now. I'm not enjoying it. It's not making me happy. In the thirties and forties in this country there was play after play, film after film. They may not have been great art, but they were *moving*. There were people trying to wrench something out of themselves about dignity and about the future. Where is it? I don't see it now. I don't see films about dignity. They were commonplace in the thirties and forties. Films about dignity, about the worth of man. About self-sacrifice and the future. I don't see 'em. I think it's tragic. I think it's frightening, not about theater—about the culture we live in."

When an actor first reads the script, can he know in advance what's going to move an audience?

"I don't think it's our business," Alan said. "I don't think it's our job. I don't think it's anybody's job. I think that a lot of what's wrong with the film business is that the people who are hired to be film executives are in the crystal ball–gazing business, and there is no such thing. Nobody knows what audiences are going to like. All you can do is be passionate about what *you* like. The only thing you can ever know is what *you* like. 'I love this. This is great. This affected me deeply. I want to have something to do with this.' That's the only thing you can really know.

"The kind of films I want to do, I can't get done. It's just that simple. It's partly my fault. I am the world's worst salesman. I can't go to people and say, 'Give me millions of dollars.' I don't have that kind of ego. I'm not good at that."

In *The Russians Are Coming! The Russians Are Coming!* Alan was originally given the part of the writer, and then he wanted to play the Russian commander. Was there a hope that the film would lessen the tensions of the Cold War by showing the human side of the Russian officer?

"We felt very strongly about it," stated Alan. "We were on a mission with that movie. When *The Russians Are Coming!* was made, it was at the height of the Cold War and we were scared. We thought the movie would get banned. We thought we would get picketed. We thought that groups would come and try and stop us from shooting it. One of the great moments in my memory was the kind of sigh of relief that went around the country when that film came out. [It] said, 'Oh my God, we can mention the word "Russian" without hatred.'

"The first thing that people say when they bring up *The Russians Are Coming!* or *The In-Laws,* is 'God, it looked like you were having a good time doing that film!' And, thank God, with *The In-Laws* I can say, 'Yes, we had a wonderful time doing it.' There's a subliminal message that is carried by all of group art, music, dance, theater, film. And the subliminal message is that people can get along and do something beautiful together. There's a kind of a fear when they ask that. There's a sigh of relief when we say, 'Yes, we had a wonderful time.'

"Underneath all of the stories, underneath all of the passion, is the feeling that a group of people got together and did something beautiful that worked. And that's what we all need to see and hear when we go to the theater, when we see a symphony orchestra or group of dancers where everybody looks like they are having a good time. We can do it *together* and make it work. But if the vehicle isn't there for us to have a good time—if the vehicle of joy, a piece of writing that works, isn't there for us, it wouldn't be able to take place. The writing has to be there.

"There was a story in that frivolous comedy of *The In-Laws* that did have something to say. Underneath every insane comedy is as much truth as in any piece of tragedy. Because you laugh like hell at something, people tend to minimize its value and importance. Because it's joyous we tend to think it doesn't have as much value. You can see through that. You see that if it's joyous there is a great value in that. Yes, there's great value in joy. Probably the ultimate value is in joy."

C H A P T E R   S I X T E E N

CLAIRE BLOOM
AND
KEVIN CONWAY

"The higher the fire burns,
the greater the actor."

© MARTHA SWOPE

Claire Bloom in "A Doll's House"

Kevin Conway in "Of Mice and Men"

© MARTHA SWOPE

CLAIRE BLOOM was born in London to a father who worked in advertising and a mother who came from a well-to-do family. At an early age she saw a film of Norma Shearer as Juliet and went home and started learning the lines. Her first professional appearance was with the Oxford Repertory Theatre (she had auditioned using Juliet's "poison" speech). When the producers took over the Shakespeare season at Stratford-on-Avon, they engaged her for leading roles. Charlie Chaplin picked Claire as his co-star in the film *Limelight.* "I tested hundreds of girls," Chaplin said. "Claire has distinction, and enormous range, and underneath her sadness there is bubbling humor, so unexpected, so wistful." In addition to playing at the Old Vic, Claire's London appearances include *The Lady's Not for Burning* opposite Richard Burton, Ophelia to Paul Scofield's *Hamlet,* and Cordelia to John Gielgud's *King Lear.* On Broadway, Claire has been seen in *Rashomon, A Doll's House,* and *Vivat! Vivat Regina!* Her films range from Laurence Olivier's *Richard III* to *Look Back in Anger,* to Woody Allen's *Crimes and Misdemeanors.* On television she played Lady Marchmain in *Brideshead Revisited,* and starred in *The Ghost Writer* (based on the novel by her husband, Philip Roth).

KEVIN CONWAY was born in Harlem. "I grew up in Queens and went to a parochial school, thank God. Otherwise I probably wouldn't be here. I've been around a lot and I still never met anybody as tough as the nuns. I was on my way to being a juvenile delinquent." He saw his first play, *Stop the World—I Want to Get Off,* at age twenty-three and soon after, he started acting lessons "as a gag." Subsequently, Kevin landed a part in *The Impossible Years!* with Tom Ewell. He started to attract attention with roles like Teddy in *When You Comin' Back, Red Ryder?,* for which he won the Obie and Drama Desk awards, and as George opposite James Earl Jones in the New York Shakespeare Festival's *Of Mice and Men.* He created the part of Doctor Frederick Treves in *The Elephant Man,* taking the show from off-Broadway to full houses on Broadway. He also originated the role of Larry the Liquidator in *Other People's Money* and won the Outer Critics Circle Award for his performance. Kevin's films include *F.I.S.T., Paradise Alley, Homeboy,* and *Rambling Rose.* He's been featured on television in such films as PBS's *The Lathe of Heaven, The Deadliest Season* with Meryl Streep, and *Something about Amelia.*

Years ago, I had seen Claire Bloom as Lady Anne in Laurence Olivier's film version of *Richard III,* and I had marveled at her ability to change emotional direction at the drop of a cue. One minute she was all venom and anger, and then without warning she became vulnerable and voluntarily susceptible to danger. When I went to see Kevin Conway in the off-Broadway production of *Other People's Money*, he seemed to possess some of the same potential for mercurial emotional change. In one instant he went from the ruthless, takeover mentality of Larry the Liquidator, intent on squeezing the last dollar out of every helpless company he could find, to a softer personality capable of succumbing to the feminine charms of his legal counterpart. I decided that it would be interesting to invite Claire and Kevin for one of our sessions.

They were opposites in temperament and style. Claire had a cool grace; her mouth was taut and her voice, with its British accent, was pure silk. Kevin was a tough-talking New Yorker, with an easy smile and hands that gestured expansively whenever he spoke.

I began by describing the ways actors develop a character. Some work from the outside, starting, for example, with the character's shoes. Some begin by working from the inside, trying to deal with the character's feelings. Others concern themselves with the character's motives. Regardless of the initial approach to the role, the actor has to be sensitive to the feelings and emotions of the character he hopes to portray. I asked Claire and Kevin to discuss the nature of that sensitivity.

"Everybody is born with it," said Claire. "You then use it in your profession. You use your intuitive understanding of people or semi-understanding of yourself and your own peculiar motives. Actors use everything they can get."

"It's got to be a bit of everything to be truly successful," said Kevin. "One of the problems that a lot of actors have is that they are very good at one thing. They've got great technique and are not so good on the inner life. Great inner life, not so good on technique. You have to be well-rounded intellectually, emotionally, and technically, and nothing should escape your attention as you wander through your life in terms of little bits and pieces that you can pick up.

"One of the most successful walks I ever had was in a play I did called *When You Comin' Back, Red Ryder?* I needed the guy to look menacing without forcing it. He wasn't a crazy psycho-type guy. He *was* psycho but he couldn't give it away. I basically stole Henry Fonda's walk in a film called *Once Upon a Time in the West,* in which he had this loping kind of quality. He was the villain and it was a bit more menacing on Henry Fonda than it was on me. But it worked for me to get that feeling of the kind of controlled, unpredictable violence that this character had. It really helped making that kind of pure physical choice."

In addition to being sensitive to other people, real or fictional, the actor must have the ability to *express* what she feels. Can anyone learn to do this and become an actor?

"A lot of people think they can," said Claire. "That is your job, to express your own feelings through your own body, your own character. Where Kevin and I are different is, I probably have only played facets of myself. I've never said, 'I'm going to walk like that,' or taken something totally outside myself and been able to superimpose it on myself or make it part of myself. There are many different kinds of actors.

"The nearest I've come to that is when I played Lady Marchmain in *Brideshead Revisited.* Not only am I *not* an aristocrat—very few actors are—but I also didn't know any. I did know one and I thought, as she's the only one I know, what I'd better do [is study her]. Without her knowing it, because she's a close friend, I studied the way she spoke and her manner rather than anything specific. I certainly took that for myself and tried to digest it."

"Did you notice yourself really behaving like her?" asked Kevin.

"Yes," said Claire.

"Then maybe we're not that different," said Kevin. "I don't think everybody can be an actor. There are people who are very naturally gifted, you see them all the time on documentaries and things like that, where they point a camera at some guy and he's very entertaining and wonderful. It's like sports. There are people who are born with a great natural talent. There are people who are born with talent that they develop. There are people who are born with talent that they don't develop. And then there are people who are born with absolutely no skill whatsoever in that particular thing, but sometimes they get by anyway just by dint of hard work."

"I would hate to think that anybody could be an actor," said Claire, "because then there's no point in being one."

"Scary," said Kevin.

In 1750 an English actor and playwright named John Hill wrote a book called *The Actor: A Treatise on the Art of Playing.* In it he wrote: "Three qualities of a good actor are understanding, sensibility, and fire. The actress who has tenderness and sensibility in her nature and who easily and readily feels every passion that the author intends, is not for that reason to flatter herself that she may excel in the profession without fire. To feel the passions we are to point out to others is certainly a necessary first step but it is not all that is expected of the performer." Two hundred and fifty years ago, Hill was saying that the actor needs to feel passion in order to express passion. He calls it fire. Can an actor *learn* to be passionate?

"Of course not," said Claire. "The higher the fire burns, the greater the actor. Kean's fire must have burnt at a very high level. Bernhardt, Olivier. It's the gift you have."

"In any profession there are people who approach it with passion and people who approach it another way," said Kevin. "People can learn to tap into passion they didn't know they had. There have been people who've been taciturn in their real life and then you see them on the stage—and boom! By and large, it has to be there. It's like a lava flow. It's there and you can tap into it. I don't think you can invent or acquire it."

Maybe that's why we think what the actor does is magical.

"I don't know that it's magic," said Claire. "I think it's hard work and skill and talent, and slogging away and learning and keeping your eyes and your ears open. I don't think theater is magic. It can *create* magic but I don't think the art is magic."

When Charlie Chaplin cast Claire in *Limelight,* he praised her for her "enormous range." An example of that range occurs when we first meet her as Lady Anne in Olivier's *Richard III.* Claire is grieving over the casket of her dead husband, whom Richard has murdered. Richard enters and begins to woo her. She spits at him, but at the same time we see that part of her is attracted to him. Is this ability to show different colors at the same time something that every actor has to learn?

"How dull it would be if you were only playing one thing," Claire replied. "You would just be a dull actor. You don't learn it. It's in your everyday life. It's in everybody's life. You're not just one thing."

Kevin said, "This touches on something a lot of actors don't get much credit for—I guess with some justification—and that's intelligence. When you approach a role, if you've got any intelligence and a sense for the moments that you gotta make to make your character understandable, you're going to find as many colors, as many contradictions, as many complexities as you can, because that's what you get paid for."

"That's what draws you to a role," said Claire. "Otherwise it's a boring role and you are a boring actor and it's going to be a dull performance. You're drawn to complexity. Those are the only parts that are interesting to play."

One of Kevin's most complex characters is Laurence Garfinkle, also known as Larry the Liquidator, a man who annihilates companies in *Other People's Money.* The *New York Times* critic said that Kevin's performance drove the whole play. He wrote, "The amoral Garfinkle wastes no time on charm. Yet in Mr. Conway's portrayal, the character has a certain likability." Here again is the ability to present opposites that seems to be at the core of a successful performance. If an actor can make his performance both evil and charming at the same time, then the audience doesn't know what the actor will do next. It makes the character's behavior unpredictable. Is this the key to creating the illusion that what is happening is happening for the first time?

"That's the magic," said Kevin. "You've gotta have that. I've played a lot of villains or guys that were villains according to the script. The villain doesn't know he's a villain. Most people that do lousy things to us think they're doing the right thing. What is interesting about Garfinkle is that he, as is often true about villains, has the best lines. The villains usually have the most interesting conflict in the script.

"If you were on a desert island, who would you want to talk to: Would it be the woman that the guy is trying to tie to the railroad tracks? Or would it be the guy with the mustache and the hat? I think he might be the more interesting one to talk to. Villains have a kind of interesting life in a play, especially if the villain happens to be the leading character. But just being a villain isn't enough.

"With Garfinkle, there were a few things given by the playwright. One was that he was very fat, so I wore a body pad. He smoked cigarettes constantly. He was profane, sexist, blasphemous, a lot of things. There's a reason that people turn out the way they do and what was interesting for me was to explore what brought him to that position. We find ways to protect ourselves. One is by overeating. One is by smoking and blowing smoke at people so they'll stay away from you and there are various other schemes that we come up with. Garfinkle, for all his strength and power and seeming invincibility when it came to deals, was actually a very unhappy, lonely man. That's what made the performance more interesting."

There is a common perception that the main difference between English and American acting training is head versus heart. The English stress what are called externals—voice, language, and body movement—while American acting teachers stress what the actor should feel. Claire won a scholarship to the Guildhall School of Music and Drama and she studied privately with Eileen Thorndike, the sister of the distinguished actress Dame Sybil Thorndike. Is there such a thing as an English acting technique?

"No such thing," said Claire. "After all, our two greatest actors were poles apart, Richardson and Olivier. Ralph Richardson was all interior, and I think the greatest for my taste, but that is where my taste is. How can you act from the outside-in? There's no such thing. Our great actors are like your great actors. All great actors are the same. Vanessa Redgrave is a great actress, because everything comes from inside.

"What Kevin says is absolutely true. If you're playing someone totally different from yourself, what Kevin did with Garfinkle is what one would do. I've never played anyone that far away from myself. Olivier had a conception of what Richard would look like. Most of us do when we're playing a role, even if it's close to you, or a little further away.

"I just did a very peculiar play in London called *When We Dead Awaken,* and my character was described by Ibsen very clearly as dressed all in white like a nun, white head, with a white cashmere shawl. I tried to follow that. It helped me to have that picture. For example, playing Ibsen, I went to an exhibition of Munch, and I got a book of the work of Munch and I would look at one of his women and I'd think, 'This is her,' but that doesn't mean that I was working from the outside in. The core of what you're doing is something completely different. If anybody thinks it's dressing up, they've got another thing coming. It's nothing to do with that at all. That's only a very small part of what we do."

"We've all seen people that are just purely technical," said Kevin, "really boring actors, and you say: 'All right, I heard you, your diction was great, but who cares about you?' There's nothing going on *inside.* They're hollow. On the other hand, I've seen a lot of people who purport to be *feeling* everything, and doing what they imagine Brando did, which is absolutely not true. If you look at Brando's performances they are highly theatrical.

"I think most good actors work pretty much the same way, which is a mix. I think anybody would respect the work of Stanislavski. However, Stanislavski wrote a couple of different books. He didn't just write *An Actor Prepares.* He wrote *Building a Character, My Life in Art,* and various others. If you look at pictures of Stanislavski playing something, he lays on some of the makeup and the wigs—it's pretty outside-in. And yet Stanislavski's the one we think of as inside-out all the time.

"I think there's a misinterpretation of what Stanislavski was saying about the art of acting. Some actors get too 'Hey, I'm de king of France,' " (Kevin began to move around in his chair with a swagger) " 'dat's de way I feel like playing de king of France, because I feel like, uhhh, I want tuhhh.' To them they're being truthful. Their nose itched so they did it this way. But that's just as phony and just as worthless as the opposite way."

"And just as mannered," added Claire.

A few weeks earlier a well-known actress was fired from a New York play before it opened. The producer and the director said her devotion to the Method was sabotaging the production. The producer said, "Lee Strasberg will have a lot to answer for on the Day of Judgment." Does too much emotion on the stage get in the way of good acting?

"I can't see that it could if you know how to control it and produce it," said Claire.

Kevin recalled, "Sometimes when I have been fairly deep in a character, who was kind of a wild and crazy guy, something would happen. There have been times when I've lost it. There have been people in the audience who have gotten on my case for various reasons. But I don't think that's the right thing to do, but it has happened. I wouldn't say it's too much emotion. As Claire said, the more emotion, the better—providing it's controlled and channeled into the work and not just something that comes out of the dark place."

Does an actor have to feel the emotion in order for the audience to feel it?

"You damn well hope you can feel it," said Claire. "But not every night. If you're unfortunate enough to be in a successful play, I don't believe it's possible *to feel* on the same level eight times a week. It isn't that you ration yourself and say, 'Well, tonight I won't' or 'Tonight I will.' You are only a human being.

"I played *A Streetcar Named Desire* in London for eight months. I would say that in that particular play, it almost always took you along with it, but the net result was that for a year after it, I was not very well, and I'm not so sure that this is a sensible way to do it. That play is notorious for doing that to the actress who plays Blanche.

"The horrible evenings for me are when you actually *don't* feel, and you feel that you're somehow fooling the audience in some cheap way. The fact is that after those performances, people will rush around and say you were never better, at which point you tear your hair out. It isn't the magic of the theater, but there is something intangible. You can't grasp it. You can't teach it. You can only do it."

Can an actor objectively judge her performance?

"You obviously can't," said Claire. "All I can say is the only way I can judge it is to say that I myself was not satisfied. But I cannot judge the effect on an audience. I think I can, but then something like that happens and people say, 'That's the best performance you've ever given,' and you yourself felt extremely hollow. I can't give any reason for it. I simply don't know why it should be."

Claire has had a long and successful association with Shakespeare's women. Her Juliet with the Old Vic was so successful it saved the theater from bankruptcy in its early days. At the time of our session, Claire had been performing a reading that was a portrait of some of Shakespeare's female characters. What relevance do Viola, Juliet, Desdemona, and Portia, Brutus's wife, have for us today?

"They are great women," said Claire. "There's a great story to be told. They speak to us. As far as I am concerned they speak to me as if they were written today. I think many people who hear them feel the same way. That's the only way to approach the parts, as though they were written about us, about people we know or about yourself. I don't know about *relevance.* That's when one starts to talk about political things or moral things, which are not my bailiwick."

Those particular women have their strength in common. For example, Viola is shipwrecked but in the end it's her strong will that rescues her. Juliet is a difficult child because she is so obstinate. Desdemona is independent enough to marry against the will of her father. And Portia says to her husband, "I am the equal of you. I am your wife, the daughter of a great man. Do you think I am not strong with such a husband and such a father?" Then she stabs herself in the leg to demonstrate her strength. Were these women chosen because of their strong-willed nature?

"I chose them for no other reason than that they appeal to me," said Claire. "I was drawn to those particular characters. Not to prove a point, but simply because their spirit and energy and guts attract me. But I also find poor Ophelia just as equally touching and moving. You can't perform her in a one-woman show because there isn't enough there. She's far from strong, poor girl. She goes under. Yes, the parts seem to me to form a kind of cohesive group. I wasn't trying to make a statement, but from a performer's point of view, they are gutsy, strong, vibrant women."

When Claire performs her evening of Shakespeare's women she is alone on the stage. I asked her how she dealt with the absence of other actors.

"They are all there," said Claire with a dark and penetrating gaze. "I imagine them. One thing we haven't mentioned is that to be an actor you have to have a very strong imagination. Most of us have probably had that since we were children, and we've channeled it into this let's-pretend-world, which we then take as completely real. So they're there for me. Probably in an extremely childish side of me, I've kept that alive. I'm acting with people who are not there but who *are* there."

Is a solo performance the same for an actor as ensemble work?

"It's a different affair," said Claire. "I do enjoy it when there's a terrific audience that you can actually play with. Most of the time it's been that. But it's different. It's something else. I wanted something in my pocket that I could do by myself because I find that the actor's life, waiting for the phone to ring, is just infantilizing in the end. Some of us feel we have to take our lives into our own hands because the waiting is too damn passive, and if you're not a passive person, it's very destructive."

"You have to generate your own work these days," said Kevin.

How does an actor survive financially in the theater?

"I don't know," Kevin said. "I'm a jewel thief on the side, so I have something to fall back on! There's obviously too many actors for the number of jobs that exist, but I think if you spread it around, some commercials, something that's related to performing, but isn't strictly speaking performing, you can survive.

"The problem in this country is that the industry is split between two coasts and you have to make a decision at a certain point in your career whether you want to stay in New York and try to become a stage actor. By stay in New York I mean do some regional theater, but basically aim toward Broadway and become a working actor in the theater instead of going for films and television. If you want to do television, you really have to live in California. And television has *the most* work for actors, but really the pay scale isn't that great. I don't know how anybody makes a living just doing guest shots on television these days. Unless you become a celebrity or a leading actor where you can command a good salary for the work you do, it's very hard to survive. I don't recommend it."

Many of England's best-known actors have made their reputations playing kings and queens and lords and ladies in Shakespeare's plays. Then they, in turn, have been knighted. In the film *Richard III,* Claire worked with five theatrical knights: Sir Laurence Olivier, Sir John Gielgud, Sir Ralph Richardson, Sir Cedric Hardwicke, and Sir William Walton, the composer. She has also worked with many others in a number of productions. When there is a royalty created among actors does that create a rift with colleagues?

"No," said Claire. "It's a bit of a lark, that's all."

Could it be compared to winning an award in this country?

"I don't think that means much either," said Claire. "It *is* like winning an award, or being the honored artist of the Soviet Republic, or whatever they hand out in each country."

"A lot of it has to do with longevity," said Kevin. "Awards here are totally meaningless. It's nice to get them, but they don't really have much value."

In addition to his acting career, Kevin had embarked on a career as a director. At the time of our sessions he was about to direct himself in a production of *Other People's Money.* An actor who directs himself in a film can watch the dailies. I asked Kevin if he thought it would be difficult to direct himself in a play.

"We'll see," said Kevin. "I wouldn't try it with any other play except this one, for the simple reason that I've directed the play before. I directed the Chicago run without me in it. I've been involved with it as an actor and as a director and now I'm just combining the two. I've been with this particular show almost too long, so I want to see what it's like to do a completely new production and try to direct myself away from some of the things that I got used to when I was doing it as an actor."

Why was *Other People's Money* never moved to Broadway?

"Donald Trump offered to," said Kevin. "Who knew? Donald Trump offered to pick the show up and bring it right to Broadway. The producers decided that they [would be] selling out. They already had standing room only, eight performances a week, albeit a small theater. They didn't want to risk it that, if we moved to a bigger theater, suddenly the audience would disappear. The ticket prices wouldn't have gone up that much. But they still would have gone up maybe another twelve dollars. So they decided [to stay]. I wanted to go to Broadway. I didn't want to stay down in the Village. I get a nosebleed south of Thirty-fourth Street. But I deferred to their wishes and we stayed there and it's still running. So they must have done something right."

Theater is a collaborative affair. The playwright writes the script, and then the actors and the director become part of the creative team. How does an actor make his contribution to the conception of a role?

"That's what rehearsals are for," said Claire. "That's what those wonderful four weeks are. That's why most actors enjoy them more than they enjoy performing. That's when you do it."

"The director has to create an atmosphere that's creative," added Kevin. "What I can't stand is directors who come and have *no* opinion. They just sit there and say banal kinds of things. They should have an opinion about how the play should go, and then let the actors have their head so they can explore. Eventually they have to make decisions and say, 'Well, it was a nice try, but I don't like that choice. I like the other choice better.' "

"Basically one relies on them for first-rate criticism," said Claire. "In my case, because I have done so much classic stuff (for lack of a better word), you can't just keep grinding out the same old play. One hopes that the director will have some new and fresh conception of the play, which you agree with *before* you agree to work with this director. It may well be that he'll tell you *Hamlet* takes place in the subway, and you'll say, 'Well, get another fella.' But basically you want him or her to have an overall interesting conception of the play, to discuss it with you, to discuss it with the other actors, and then to come with an open acceptance of what each actor will bring.

"The wonderful thing that one prays for [is] someone sitting there who you know is a first-rate critical mind, so that if she says, 'I don't like your choice,' you say, 'Okay,' instead of thinking, 'Oh, she doesn't know.' Then you're left in this amorphous state of not knowing who's in control or who to rely on."

"The first priority of the director is the play," said Kevin. "The director has to have a concept of the play, an idea of the set, and then [he has to] make sure that the actors are fulfilling a particular vision. The director has to have a clear idea of the *entire* play. Then each actor's individual contribution will hopefully meld together into a realization of that overall concept, which the actors will feel very comfortable doing."

"The truth is that one prays for that kind of director," said Claire, "but rarely finds it. At least, that's my experience."

"I've directed a little and I enjoy it," said Kevin, "but I don't consider myself a director, because I can only direct things that I'm madly in love with. I could never do it for a living. If somebody said, 'Hey, Tony Danza requested that you fly out and do an episode of "Who's the Boss?" ' it's not in my genes to do that. But if I found a piece of material that I really liked, then I get crazy.

"I'm not really that good a director because I get very involved personally with the cast. I don't mean intimate, but personal in the sense that it becomes like four weeks of intense getting to know each other. I learned by watching other directors.

"The director I enjoyed working with the most was Alan Schneider. Alan and I did four plays together. A lot of actors didn't get along with Alan because he was very tough and all he cared about was the play. His major assumption was that if he hired you, you knew what to do. You knew *how* to act. He didn't want to teach you how to act. So I find myself, without even knowing it, behaving as a director the way Alan used to, which is to sit there and give notes and get up there. Alan used to go right in your face. It was kind of disconcerting. He'd lean like nose to nose with you, and give you the note, and then as soon as he gave you the note, he'd rip off the page and throw it over his shoulder and he'd move on. We used to have a guy who'd follow him with a wastebasket and Alan would throw his notes and the guy would catch them as they went flying."

"He was a damn good director," said Claire. "I'd loved to have worked with him. And that kind of passionate involvement is what one wants. It's wonderful when it happens."

Does an actor have the opportunity to come up with more of his own choices in Shakespeare because of the lack of stage directions?

"I've only done one Shakespearean play in my whole life," said Kevin, "which I guess tells you something about me and the American theater."

"More about the American theater," said Claire.

"It was just one of those things," explained Kevin. "I started working and I went from here to television to film to stage to film and then finally, a couple of years ago, Joe Papp gave me a chance to do *King John.* It turned out pretty good. I didn't pay much attention to the stage directions, whatever they were. I didn't pay much attention to the verse either. Once I got it emotionally right, the verse seemed to take care of itself. I feel kind of silly saying this with Claire here."

"I'm sure it's perfectly true," said Claire.

Kevin continued, "I didn't realize *the kick, the joy* you get. Instead of saying," (he coarsely poked the air) " 'Now *take* off! Get outta here and take the message and come on back!'

"Instead of saying that, he says (I hope I don't butcher it), 'Set wings to thy heels.' " Kevin's voice took on a lyric power, deliberate and yet filled with urgency. " 'Be Mercury, set feathers to thy heels and fly like thought from them to me again.' When you start dealing with that, there really isn't any other way. You get into it. That's what Shakespeare's all about, isn't it? It was just such a fantastic experience to do that, and I think it's great that there aren't all those stage directions because that's what's kept it so fresh."

"Also, does one really take a lot of notice of stage directions?" asked Claire. "Ibsen, for example, is very clear and precise. If you're in trouble in an Ibsen play, and you go back and read the stage directions, you think, 'Oh, *that's* what the old boy meant!' But there are very few writers whose stage directions you would follow as an actor."

Should an actor concern himself only with normal acting problems in Shakespeare and let the language come automatically?

"It doesn't mean not to pay attention to the language," said Kevin. "I said I didn't concentrate on the verse and the meter when I was working on the character at first. When you finally get into running it and knowing the lines and playing it, the meter very often does take care of itself. There is no other way to say some of the things because Shakespeare has constructed it that way. There were certain times when I took a pause that was not indicated in there, but I basically did it the way that worked best for me and that was clearest to the audience emotionally."

"What's marvelous about Shakespeare is you have a score to sing," said Claire. "It's there for you. I don't mean you should sing it. It's there so that anyone with half a brain can actually pick up this very simple rhythm very, very easily. If you have a problem with a line and it doesn't make sense, sometimes if you bash it out" (she began drumming on the table with her knuckles) "you'll think, 'Oh yes, of course, that's where I must accentuate the word,' and it's actually there for you. That's one of the marvelous things about Shakespeare.

"When I was a young actress I hadn't the faintest idea and it's only really since John Barton at the Royal Shakespeare Company that people have gone into short lines and long lines and feminine endings. He believes that these props in the score will hold the actor up and I think he's right. He's written a wonderful book called *Playing Shakespeare*. I found it extremely useful and interesting, although I've come to it very late in life because I never used any of these things myself.

"We took it for granted that for an actor worth his salt, the emotion will tell you how to speak the line. But you've got to have an ear. If you've got a tin ear you might as well go home, and if you've got a tin ear, nobody can teach you anyway. But now there are certain rules that I tell my students because they come completely blank. They don't know what they're in for. All they know is that they are frightened for some reason of this language. So one says, 'Well, these are the rules which you can really learn in half an hour.' No singer would attempt to sing a part before they'd learnt music and before they could read the score. These kids have to be given keys to this and when they have them, they find it very easy. It's the same as any other acting. You're playing a role. You have to make it personal or key it or tie it to something that you know, so that it's a *living* person that you're playing. And speak as naturally as you can. The verse is there underneath you to hold you up."

Do actors know from an early age that acting is their chosen profession?

"I had no intention of being an actor when I was growing

up," said Kevin. "I was the guy in high school who would slam the kids who were in drama class into the lockers, because I had an anti-intellectual thing. After I was in the service for two years, I went to work for IBM and that's what I thought I was going to do. Through a long, convoluted story, which I would have to be drunk to tell you, I wound up going to acting school just as a joke. I didn't want to go. It was almost a dare. I wound up in acting school and I still didn't buy it. I studied there for a year. There were a lot of attractive women there. It was an interesting place to go after work.

"Eventually I started to get more and more interested in it because every once in a while I would see somebody do something good and it would really work in class. And then I was very fortunate to get a teacher named Ellen Green (not the actress Ellen Greene), and she was a former dancer and when she got to an age where she couldn't dance anymore with Martha Graham, she became a teacher. That's all she wanted to do. I guess I was a little in love with her and it was like *Good Morning, Miss Dove.* She could have had me jumping through hoops of fire. Finally she was the one that said, 'Let's make a decision here. Let's start doing some work if you're going to come here.'

"So I started to do some very good work in that class and I began to feel a wonderful sense of power that comes with controlling a scene or a performance and getting the information across. And then she kicked me out because her theory was that I had gone so far with the internal work—and she didn't teach theater, she only taught acting. So I went from there to Uta Hagen and I studied with Uta for almost three years. Uta also worked that way, but she also cared as well about actually getting employed. So she prepared you for how to get into a theater and how to hit the back wall. A lot of actors give great performances that can't be heard. She helped me with things like that, the more technical stuff. And she helped me with my confidence. So I was very lucky. I had two really terrific teachers and they had a big influence on me."

Is it more difficult to act on the stage or in the movies?

"It depends," said Kevin. "My thing has been the grass is always greener. When I'm doing a film, and I'm sitting around waiting and waiting and I realize that the scene I'm doing today is the scene after some major event has happened to my character that we haven't shot yet, and I wonder how I'm going to do it, because you shoot out of sequence, then I long for the continuity and the discipline of the theater.

"But when you get into a long run and you go in for that Sunday matinee after playing the show for six months, you long for the kind of glamour and measured-out-in-teaspoons kind of work that you do in film and television. Not so much television. Television to me is low man on the totem pole, because they just work too fast for me. But certain movies are really a joy to work on. You can actually do some pretty good work. I admire actors who can work in film who have that kind of technique. It's just incredible how [they] keep it all in their head so that by the end there's something to put together that makes a performance.

"Physically it's harder to work in the theater. Emotionally, especially if you're an impatient sort, it's harder to work in film, because you just have *no* control over anything that's going on. You could do your absolutely most brilliant take and somebody somewhere messed up, or the sound wasn't good or *something,* and you gotta do it over. And then you have no control over which take they use! At least in the theater you make a choice and you get out there and you play it and you go, 'Ooh, I like this. I'm going to do it again tomorrow.' But in film you do a few takes, and then six months later the director decides which he or she likes. I've had some pretty grim experiences seeing films that I've been in. Six months later, you sit there and you go, 'How did that happen! Why did he use that?' "

"They both have drawbacks," said Claire. "The thing about the theater is that if you could do only a limited run of three months, I think there's no question that for the actor, that's the great pleasure. The sweep of the play you can't compare to anything else. The repetition in the commercial theater is deadly for an actor, and I myself have withdrawn from it.

"I like the meticulousness of filming exactly as Kevin says—you do a scene the day before yesterday that takes place in three months and [another scene] the day after tomorrow that takes place three months before, so that you have to have this plan and you have to try to build very carefully something that is fragmented and put it together in some kind of a shape. I find that very exciting. The difference between Kevin and I is that my television has mainly been done in England. And

I enjoy television more than anything because, in a funny way, you get the pleasure of both. It *does* go much quicker. Generally more in order. And somehow you get the intimacy of film but you do feel in a way that you get almost the sweep of the theater. I've enjoyed television more than anything else that I've done."

I asked Claire if she were to end our evening with a soliloquy, which one she'd choose.

"Well, I would try to think of one to suitably close such a lovely occasion," she said. Then with hands clasped, and in a beautifully modulated voice, she recited:

"Our revels now are ended. These our actors,
As I foretold you, were all spirits and
Are melted into air, into thin air;
And, like the baseless fabric of this vision,
The cloud-capp'd towers, the gorgeous palaces,
The solemn temples, the great globe itself,
Yea, all which it inherit, shall dissolve
And, like this insubstantial pageant faded,
Leave not a rack behind. We are such stuff
As dreams are made on, and our little life
Is rounded with a sleep."

C H A P T E R S E V E N T E E N

LIV ULLMANN

"If the biggest, warmest feelings I have had, had been on the stage, I would be tremendously unhappy with my life."

Liv Ullmann in "I Remember Mama"

Liv Ullmann was born in Norway and lost her father at an early age. Lonely and self-conscious as a teenager, she turned to religion and reading, and discovered she could get attention with recitations. Though she failed to pass her audition for Oslo's National Theatre School, she persuaded her mother to let her study dramatics in London. On her return she was again refused at the school, so she joined a small repertory company and made her stage debut in the title role of *The Diary of Anne Frank.* After three successful years with the company, Liv was welcomed into the National Theatre and the Norwegian Theatre in Oslo, where she played Juliet, Ophelia, Saint Joan, Nora in *A Doll's House,* and other major roles. Liv met Swedish filmmaker Ingmar Bergman while working on her first Swedish film. For Bergman, she starred in *Persona, Hour of the Wolf, Shame, The Passion of Anna, Cries and Whispers, Scenes from a Marriage,* and *Autumn Sonata.* She also worked with other directors abroad and in Hollywood, starring in such films as *The Emigrants, The New Land,* and *The Abdication.* For her performances in *Hour of the Wolf* and *Shame,* Liv was named best actress of the year by The National Society of Film Critics in America, and for her work in *Cries and Whispers* she received the New York Film Critics Circle Award. Liv won a Golden Globe and was nominated for an Oscar for *The Emigrants.* She made her New York stage debut as Nora in *A Doll's House,* and has also appeared on Broadway in *Anna Christie,* the musical *I Remember Mama,* and *Ghosts.*

I got to know Liv Ullmann by corresponding with her. In her letters, as in her books, there was a charming simplicity of language, and a vibrant interest in life beyond the world of theater. When I invited her to be in our series, she was traveling around the world as the official goodwill ambassador for UNICEF and the vice-president of the International Rescue Committee, but she agreed to make time to join us. That night there was a luster about Liv. In her polka-dot blouse and dark pant-suit, she was taller than I had expected her to be. Her soft hair flowed casually to her shoulders and her bright, animated eyes often seemed to be searching for an answer from some faraway place. Her voice was a lilting reminder of her Norwegian roots and it conveyed emotion with every word.

In Liv's book *Choices*, she wrote that, as an actress, it wasn't *her own* emotions she was portraying on the stage; it was, rather, *the emotions of the characters* who lived through her. Several of my guests had said they lived their lives more fully onstage, when it came to expressing emotion. I asked Liv if she thought these actors were confusing themselves with the characters they played.

"They might be confusing themselves with their characters," said Liv, "but what's more important is that they are commenting on a kind of poor life. If the biggest, warmest feelings I have had, had been on the stage, I would be tremendously unhappy with my life. Where I felt the most fulfilled has been always in encounters with people, sometimes in rehearsals for a play, but never, never did I feel that this is life, that this is the closest I am coming to life.

"I believe we should express our feelings in life. Today

people are so poor because they are so scared of showing emotion, so scared of touching each other, so scared of showing their own vulnerability. We are flying to the moon, but we don't know how to contact the person at our side. We are sitting by the TV and we are becoming very passive people. I believe life only has opportunities the moment you really recognize or are recognized by another human being. This also includes sitting in an audience and recognizing something about yourself with a person on the stage, a character, words of a writer."

Does this mean that the emotional life of the actor should equal the emotional life of the character she portrays?

"Yes," said Liv. "If you are to show parts of life, how can you do that if you never really touch life yourself? You can do a pretty good copy in a film, but you can never, never really move somebody on the stage if you don't come from a well of experience and understanding yourself.

"It's so sad. Sometimes in Norway, where I am from, you meet some of these very old stage actors, and their life was always only theater. And you sit and you talk with them, and all they want to talk about is this part, and this premiere, and this review, and this line. I think it is sad. If I die and if I met God and He asked me, 'What did you do?' I would hate to have to say I was an actress. I want to say I was an actress, but I loved, and I did mistakes, and I traveled, and I did this and that, and I want to do it all again. But I'd like to tell Him a long story."

In the eighteenth century the French philosopher Denis Diderot said, "Actors do not have sensibility in real life. If they did, how could they show it night after night on the stage?" Diderot also claimed that actors lacked a certain humanity because their profession prevents them from devoting time to their mothers and fathers, wives, children, brothers, sisters, and mistresses. He said actors can only be other characters if they have none themselves.

"It's very dogmatic," said Liv. "Actors who are working hard obviously have less time, in terms of hours and minutes, to give to those they love, than if they had a boring job to which they didn't give so many hours. But I think that the shorter time they are spending with those they love is time given by a fulfilled person. So it's quality time.

"I think Diderot has a point in saying [that] to always show emotions is dangerous for a character. Don't you kind of deflate yourself? Yes, you would, if you were always using real emotions. If I really had to cry and suffer, myself, to be able to make my character cry, in the end I would use up my emotions on the stage instead of in life. As long as an actor is learning his or her craft, and learns to *imitate* but not go through the emotion, then you are not deflating yourself. So it is a choice you have to make as an actor."

There seems to be a similarity between Diderot's words and what Liv wrote in *Choices:* "What I do cannot be based on my feelings alone. Then I might be fantastic one evening, but because it was all my emotion, I wouldn't know what made me laugh or what made me cry. Then how could I produce it at the next performance?"

"The interesting thing," said Liv, "is to learn your craft in a way that you know how to produce it at the moment you are supposed to produce it. Not by whipping yourself into a lot of emotional things. But knowing how the hand will shiver in a moment of anxiety. Knowing how the skin will blush in a moment of great feeling. Know how to produce it without necessarily feeling it yourself. That's the fun of it.

"If you are in a film studio, just before they say, 'Camera,' you are relaxed and you are Liv. And they say, 'Camera go!' and because Liv has prepared herself, she knows her lines, she has studied the character, she has made an understanding of what this character is about. The instrument that is Liv is prepared and allows the emotions of the character to come out and the blush to happen, because she believes in the character. By some magic, which is knowledge, which is preparation, which is this strange thing, acting, it happens. You don't even know you blush, but you do. It's the character who blushes through Liv."

Does this also apply to the theater?

"Absolutely," she said with great emphasis. "In the theater, you have this wonderful thing which you don't have in film. You have rehearsals where, together with the director and the other actors, you interact, you explore. It's like being detectives in human behavior, in human thoughts. You explore together, and one day during rehearsals, your character starts to walk by itself. You are getting a limp, which you didn't even know your character was going to have, but it all added up."

I told Liv I had been using some questions from William Archer's one-hundred-year-old questionnaire, which was entitled *To Feel or Not to Feel?* For him, the question of emotion in acting came up in relation to the plays of Ibsen, which were being produced for the first time. Archer was Ibsen's translator and staunch defender.

"He's a good translator," said Liv. "But since I'm Norwegian I can control him in a way that American actors, of course, cannot. I know because I've done two Ibsen plays in Norway. I know that [Archer] missed certain magical points. I can give you an example. In *A Doll's House,* Nora, she is saying all the time, in Norwegian she says, 'I believe that *the wonderful* will happen.' That is a very childish way of expressing oneself, and Ibsen wrote it like that. Archer was probably trying to help either Nora or Ibsen, for he makes her believe that *the magical* will happen. Now that is something different. Because magical is something that might come from heaven or something that suddenly just happens. But for *the wonderful* to happen, that is not magic. That is if you use your fantasy of childhood—the wonderful will happen. That is something beautiful. Nora says it so many times that you know in the end when she has said this laughingly and laughingly and laughingly, this woman is not a happy doll. This woman is really a child who is longing to break out and be a woman. She is a womanchild waiting for the wonderful and feeling the wonderful might never happen. You miss that in Archer's translation because she is waiting for magic, for a magician."

Archer may have made another mistake as well. Archer asked actors whether they felt they had a greater effect on the audience when they were feeling emotion or imitating it. But if it's *the character* feeling the emotions *through* the actor, then it's not up to the actor.

"But you see, it's me too," said Liv. "It's my understanding of this emotion. It's my experience of it, or having seen it in you or somebody else. It's my understanding of it and how I would like to project it and say, 'Do you recognize this? This is how I see it.' "

Liv leaned forward in her chair. "You know, acting in a way is really something like when lovers meet. When it is the best is when the two of them look each other in the eye, and they see something in the eye that they also recognize about themselves. And they see in the other's eyes that that person is recognizing the same in them. That is what happens.

"It happens from the stage. The actor is so aware of what is happening in the audience, the silence, or the coughing or whatever. The actor knows when the audience is part of the whole thing. It's a give-and-take. The feelings that are part of it are feelings of recognition, but [they are] not feelings of personal trauma. It's like when you see a wonderful film. It's not that you go into personal trauma, it is just a kind of elation, whether the film is wonderfully sad, or wonderfully happy. It is elation that right now something happened that I understand, that is part of who I am and why I am.

"I can say it another way with an old Zen story. An old lady is walking on the street, and behind her walks a young man. And the lady sees that this young man is kind of following her, and she turns and she says to the young man, 'Young man, why are you following me?' And the young man says, 'I'm a Noh player and one day I may be asked to play an old lady, and I am following you to look at your gestures and the way that you move, to see how I would act an old lady.' And she says, 'If you want to act an old lady, you cannot do it by *following* me and copying my gestures. You have to look *at* me and understand me, and then find the truth of me in your own heart.'

"That's what it's all about. It's what the audience is asked to do when the audience is most happy. Find the truth in your own heart of what you have just seen. And it is what the actor is supposed to do, not feel their own thing, but find the truth and plant it in somebody else's heart."

Ordinarily, we think of an audience as identifying with the character on the stage. But audiences also share the experience with each other. We laugh more when we are with other people.

"Like love," said Liv, smiling. "And it's more fun to share than to identify. It's more fun to look at the play and *not* think all the time, 'This is happening right now. This is real.' It's more fun to watch it, and to know this is theater. And at the same time recognize it as a piece of life, a piece of life that you belong to. It's not something that you are apart from. You are the audience. You go into fantasy land and forget where you are. What it really is, is a piece of life that you recognize is happening now, that you share, but not necessarily believe is a reality."

Even if the audience knows it's watching a play, it has to suspend time and place in order to become involved. In that sense, it *is* like love, which has been called a divine madness.

"Sure," said Liv, "if crazy can be fantasy and wonder and recognition and all that. When we were small and we were painting trees, and you would paint a tree, and it would be black and have red dots and look strange, and you would have a wonderful grandmother who would say to you, 'What a beautiful tree!' and recognize it immediately. And then some other stupid grown-up would come and say, 'No, trees do not look like that. They have brown trunks and they are green.' And you never paint trees anymore with that pleasure. The wonder of acting, in its best moments, is when you are allowed to paint black trees with red dots, and you sit there and you know that's *your* tree, and actually it's *my* kind of tree, too. There are no rules, just recognition, just magic, fantasy, and wonder."

If the actor is totally absorbed and concentrating on what she is doing on the stage, how can she know what is happening in the audience?

"You're right, you do not see them," said Liv, "but *you hear them.* You hear the silence. Or you hear the unrest. You know when somebody gets up and leaves, each time that happens. And it might be for legitimate reasons. It might not have to do with what you are doing. You really die a little. Audiences should know how much they are a part of what is happening up there, because an actor is so tuned to listening, listening, listening, and they are doing it. And it is so wonderful when you have this silence or this laughter or this sharing. And it is so deadly when there are these papers of candies and the restless things. I've even experienced, during a season of baseball, the men who must have been dragged by their wives to the theater, have their radios with earphones, and when they take them out for a moment, you hear little excerpts."

I asked Liv how she came to do *Ghosts* on Broadway.

"It's my trouble with English again," said Liv, cupping her hands. "I was sitting in Norway and I got a telegram from an American Broadway producer [asking] if I would come and do Ibsen's *Ghosts* and I thought, that's fantastic. I translated it in my head and yes that must be the equivalent of *When We Dead Awaken* in Norwegian. I always wanted to do *When We Dead Awaken* and so I telegraphed back and said, 'Yes, wonderful, I'm coming.' I was very flattered I was going on Broadway. Only just before the first rehearsal I was telling a director friend of mine, 'You know I'm doing *When We Dead Awaken* on Broadway.' I said this in Norwegian. He said, 'Oh, what is that called in English?' I said, '*Ghosts.*' 'Liv,' he said, 'that's the play about Mrs. Alving and her sick son and all that!' And I didn't dare to telegraph back to the producers and say, 'You know, I think I'm too young to play fifty years old,' because I was not that yet then. But I went and I did the play and I had a wonderful time."

Liv has written about her role as Mrs. Alving: "Already within me I feel the woman I am to portray. I whisper her words and imagine her thoughts." I told her it sounded like a pregnancy, with the character coming alive in her. I asked Liv how an actor learns to do that.

"It comes with the territory," she said. "I don't think everybody can be an actor. Like in every profession in life, you have to have a talent for it. Yes, working on a part is like being pregnant, because you gather as much information as you can, and the more you gather, the heavier you are, and then one day, out comes this new creation and it's fun. But it's not magical, and it's not for everyone."

If Liv considers herself a "sieve" or the conduit for another character, it could be construed that she functions like a medium. There are certain people who maintain that actors have supernatural powers, and some of these people are actors. For example, Shirley MacLaine, a wonderful actor, says that the characters she plays are not mere playthings for our entertainment. Shirley says they are the spiritual essences of people who have lived in another time.

"I think Shirley MacLaine is a wonderful actress," agreed Liv. "But when she works, she doesn't have time to do that other stuff. She is very interested in people, and curious. In the free time we go off and do other things, and it shouldn't be confused. I am sure her way of acting is not mystical at all. She has her feet on the ground as an actress."

When we watch actors on talk shows on television, they occasionally come across as having the same personality as they do when they play different characters. How does one know if one has the talent necessary to be an actor, as opposed to the talent for being a popular personality?

"There are different kinds of actors," said Liv, "and there are some that we really look upon as great actors who were personalities, like Gary Cooper and Cary Grant. They were wonderful but they were given this kind of personality and it is that strange thing, you don't know. You meet them at a party and you don't see it, and suddenly you put them on the stage and they stand out, or you put them maybe on a talk show and they just make you want to see and hear more about them.

"And then you have the other kind of actor who puts on the disguise, who plays a different kind of character on the stage and you do not recognize who they are in private. But what it is, nobody really knows because many, many actors, they are boring, they melt into the wallpaper privately. Something happens the moment they get up on the stage. And of course, some might even be talented only for auditions and it doesn't necessarily mean that they are good actors.

"The two auditions I've done in my life for theater school, I flunked. And I know others who came into theater school that year and they have never been actors. So that's another kind of talent, that you know how to deliver cleverly right there and then."

Liv writes that her unconscious is the real character. When she was quite young, she played roles like Nora in *A Doll's House* and Shaw's *Saint Joan.* How does the actor's unconscious prepare her to play challenging roles when she is still so young?

Liv smiled with a kind of girlish glee. "I think all of us live the most and fullest as children. Even more so than children today, because there was so much to fill our fantasies at that time. I, at least in Norway, lived a childhood without television. Television had not come to Norway then. Of course, the older you are, the more experiences you have, and the more things go into your unconscious. You will know that, as an actor, when you do a part several times.

"The way I did Nora the first time is very different from when I did it the last time. During the time in-between I gathered up a lot of information, a lot of understanding, not the least was about being a woman. Women's liberation was getting stronger the last time, more than when I did it the first time. Also I had observed things. I had done one film, where the character always walked on her tiptoes, and I didn't really know why, although I had observed it once, this tiptoe walking. I used it again the last time as Nora, and there it was perfect. It was perfect because I had experienced it with another Nora we met in Italy.

"We visited with Fellini, and he is married to a very, very wonderful actress. Ingmar Bergman and I were there, and the stars of the evening were, of course, Bergman and Fellini. Somewhere were Fellini's wife and I. Fellini was going on and on, and he was wonderful and fantastic, and for a moment he went out to the kitchen, so Ingmar turned to [Fellini's] wife. He wanted to know her too, and he asked her something about one of the films, and suddenly she answers, and she is singing, and it was so beautiful and poetic, I will never forget it.

"In the middle of the song, Fellini came in again, and he looked at her and he said, 'Oh, I can't leave the room for a moment and you make a fool of yourself!' Instead of getting angry, she turned out to be a Nora, because she tiptoed out of the room. I watched her go out in the garden. She didn't say a word. She had been so deeply hurt, I'm sure, and she came back and gave Fellini and me and Ingmar flowers. All the time she was tiptoeing, as if [to say,] 'Please, I hope I am not making too much sound. I hope I don't exist too much in the shadow of this man.' And that stayed with me. I'm not even conscious that I observed it then. Then when I did Nora the last time, Nora also is tiptoeing: 'Please don't be bothered by my very existence.' Things like that stay with you.

"Another story about Nora illustrates how things change when you have done it several times. The first two times I did Nora in Norway, and the last time I did it in the United States. When I did it, women's liberation was at its strongest point, about fifteen years ago. I was doing *A Doll's House* with Sam Waterston, and we had a wonderful time together. He played Helmer.

"On the first day with an audience, a remarkable thing happened. People were applauding as soon as Nora came on the stage. The women were so for Nora. They talked to me from the audience saying, 'Oh, come on, get him!' and poor Sam Waterston, who was used to being in sympathetic roles and receiving beautiful acclaim, suddenly he is being booed. He took it personally, and he was very, very distressed.

"The next day I suggested that we should do some gymnastics together before we went onstage, just to get his mood up. So we did, and he twisted his ankle very slightly, so he had to go onstage with a stick. I tell you, the audience was much more subdued in terms of me, and, of course, nobody booed Sam. When Nora left, they still applauded, but much more subdued. The next day, and this is the honest-to-God truth, Sam came with two crutches! He played the rest of the whole engagement on crutches, and I never got applause when I left him. Today, Sam still refuses to admit why he was on crutches, and probably that was subconscious too, but on crutches he was."

Nora in *A Doll's House* walks out from her marriage in the end of the play, but she doesn't walk out to have an affair with somebody else, she walks out still in love with her husband and in hopes of finding herself. Many women today find themselves in Nora's situation. When an actor plays Nora, does it affect her personal life?

Liv paused. "I don't think a role in itself has an effect on an actor and changes his life, but I do think that all the preparation, all the reading you do, all the thoughts you have (why is she going, where is she going, and all that), has an effect on you. The more you study something, the more involved you are in the process of what makes somebody go from there to there.

"The question of choices and why we make choices, which I went deeply into, they did have an effect on me. For example, I don't believe that Nora was a Joan of Arc and banged the door and left to become president of America. I believe she was a very insecure woman leaving the house, locking the door after her, not knowing at all where she was going, and maybe even coming back the next day.

"The important thing was, for the first time in her life, Nora had made a decision to question what she had been doing in life, why she was doing it, and to start wondering, 'What do I really want with my life?' For that, she needed the action of walking out of the situation where she was not true or real to herself, not to become something else, but to become who she was, not to become whatever Helmer or society, or whoever they were, expected her to be.

"I think choices are very important parts of our lives, and I believe the way we make choices—the way we neglect to make them out of fear, out of love, or because we are scared of what other people may think of us—I think that describes us as human beings. The choices we make or the choices we don't make, they are the finished portrait of ourselves that we cannot change."

There is a parallel between Helmer and Nora in *A Doll's House,* and Johann and Marianne in the film *Scenes from a Marriage,* which had so much to say about marriage and relationships between men and women. In *Scenes from a Marriage,* Ingmar Bergman wanted Johann and Marianne to go and see *A Doll's House* in the film at one point. In Liv's book, she states that the person who is left behind is the one who grows. Marianne is the one who is left behind, but it's as if she takes on the choices of Nora.

"Yes," said Liv, "she does in a way. I think of all Ingmar Bergman's pictures, that picture is the one where he is describing a contemporary woman, and in a very true way. I don't always think the one left behind is the one who grows. But I know that the one who really has to struggle when the relationship breaks up, the one that has to go through the emotions of sorrow and hurt and questioning, *that* person has a much greater chance of surviving, and coming out on the other side maybe a more understanding or mature person than [the one] who, without thought, leaves for another love and goes right into that. It's terrible to suffer and to have deep sorrow when a relationship is over. The only positive thing about it is that it gives you a chance to reevaluate, and maybe become a richer person in the end, if you can go through all that process without coming out on the other side with a lot of bitterness and hate."

We have discussed how an actor approaches a role. With Mrs. Alving, Liv says in her book, "Her face is one I saw once while waiting for a traffic light to change. A pale, sad face behind a window. The portrait of a lost life that vanished in a passing car." Does that mean that when the actor is originally putting together a role, she models it on a physical person that she has seen?

"It's all that material that gathers up in you," said Liv. "It's part of your luggage, of living. It goes for most creative artists. It's what we see. When we need it to write something, or paint something, or act something, we open up our fantasy books, or luggage, we look for what we can use for this person, what gestures.

"Once in Cannes, at a terrible gathering, a stupid Hollywood producer was sitting there and he was so obnoxious. He took his spoon and used it as a mirror to look at himself. The whole evening became wonderful, because I couldn't wait to think what part will I be able to use this spoon in. I have never been able to use it because I only get these neurotic, sad women and they don't use spoons. But one day, I will."

Liv originally thought of herself as a comedian, and here she is playing all these tragic roles!

Exasperated, she exclaimed, "I still think of myself as a comedian, and I am amazed why I am always getting sad parts! Only once in my life did I get a comedy, and I did it, but that was wrong for me. I was thirty years old, and Norwegian, and with an even heavier accent than I have now. I came to Hollywood and at the time I was offered everything because they thought, 'Oh, maybe it's a new Greta Garbo.' " Her hand swept the air broadly as she mocked a mogul's enthusiasm. " 'You never know.'

"That year the big comedy was *Forty Carats.* I was competing with Elizabeth Taylor and Zsa Zsa Gabor, very different types, but also another age group. I was thirty, but because I was so hot, they gave me *Forty Carats,* and the whole point of this film is that the woman is *forty,* that she is a very sophisticated *New York* lady, and she is to fall in love with a twenty-year-old boy. Now they give it to me, who is thirty, and as the boy they put a twenty-year-old man, Eddie Albert. I was even less sophisticated then, with an accent." Her eyes rolled as she smiled. "It became a tragedy."

It was the search for a comic role that drove Liv into *I Remember Mama.* She thought she was going to sing and dance and be merry. Instead, she found herself caught up in a Broadway musical fraught with trials and tribulations. Liv has written that at one point during the experience she wanted to open up a pizza parlor or become an astronaut.

"That's what you dream about when you do Broadway shows that try out in other cities," Liv acknowledged. "I've heard people say the best revenge one could wish for Hitler is that he would be in a Broadway show trying out in Philadelphia. It was really a terrible experience but also wonderful because this was Richard Rodgers's last musical and, of course, I said yes. Here I am from Norway and I'm asked to do a musical that Richard Rodgers is going to write for me!

"I was hot on Broadway at this time. I had to meet Richard Rodgers and he said, 'I'd like to know what kind of scale you have, so could you just sing something for me?' I said, 'I really cannot sing.' I told the producers and they said, 'It doesn't matter, you're so charming it doesn't matter.' Here I was with Richard Rodgers, who at that time was a very old and very frail man, and he said, 'Well, you know I have heard everything. It's okay. Just sing "Happy Birthday." ' So I sang 'Happy Birthday,' and it's true, the man aged ten years in front of me.

"I had seven solos in this musical! It was incredible. It went good for a while when I just rehearsed with the piano. Then in Philadelphia we were going to open for an audience and I said, 'But I need to rehearse with the orchestra a long time before, because I don't recognize melodies in different places.' And they said, 'It's going to go fine.' "

Liv's hands tightened around the arms of her chair and she looked slightly shell-shocked. "It was dreadful, but it wasn't only me. It was many guilty people in this, and, of course, they fired everybody. Every day there was somebody fired. They couldn't fire me because I was the star. And Richard Rodgers was Richard Rodgers. But everybody else, I assure you, was fired.

"Each day after the performance, the producer would sit in somebody's dressing room and they knew when they came in, if he was sitting there, that was it. We called the door the revolving door. We had five or six cats for one part and their cat attendants. We had children (because [in the play] Mama had five children) and we had the children's mothers. And some of them got fired. It was an experience! But I wouldn't have been without it in my life, because I was on Broadway.

"When I was thirteen, my mother forced me to go to dancing school, and I really wasn't very attractive and in dancing school in Norway, the girls are on one side of the room, and the boys are on the other side of the room. And the dancing teacher would say, 'Okay boys, *engager* the lady,' and the boys would storm over, and of course four girls would always not be stormed at. And I would always be among them.

"And then a terrible psychological thing; after the next dance these four girls have to stand up because they have to be danced with too, and they were to be *engaged* first, and the teacher says, 'Okay!' and the boys would *crawl* over. Terrible! Or you would be dancing with somebody and you would hear him say, 'Shall we change?' to somebody. I promised myself then and there, when I'm grown up I am *never, never* going to dance! Talk about life experience! How good it is to go through traumas. Here I am on Broadway with seven solos, with an orchestra, *dancing,* being the star with professional Broadway dancers! And I did it. Six months of it! In Richard Rodgers's last musical."

By all reports, another difficult time for Liv was her experience with the director of *Ghosts,* who shall remain nameless.

"I've forgotten his name," said Liv.

He had Liv doing improvisations instead of working on the play.

"He hadn't prepared," explained Liv. "He was too busy with something else, so he used the rehearsals to ask us to improvise, because that way he didn't have to give us any direction. Part of his improvisation (that he had learned in England) was that we didn't play our own part but we played *somebody else's part,* and we weren't to read the lines of the play, but we were to make up other lines that kind of covered what the lines of the play were. So we were ill-equipped and not prepared for the opening."

When does improvisation have its place?

"It can be wonderful during rehearsal," said Liv, "during a part of a day's rehearsal. It can be beautiful during a film if a scene is locked and you cannot find your way out of it, and you improvise and see what happens then. Be very clear when you watch what happens during the improvisation to take what was best of that and then put it in the framework of the reality. Improvisation is just a kind of tool to be used later in the main framework."

There was a moment during this process of working on *Ghosts,* when Liv became uncomfortable and wasn't moving where she thought she ought to be. The director said, "Listen, I'm famous for my movements."

"He said a lot of strange things," Liv sighed. "And he liked to talk a lot, too. You will always find that the best directors are the ones who say very little, but they will create a framework for what you are supposed to do that kind of spurs the fantasy.

"A good director will watch you in a way and listen to you in a way that really makes you want to give everything you have. Again, like a lover, he is somebody who recognizes you, and even if you are not able to come up with what he wants, he will see what you are trying to do. He will try to coach more out of you by giving the right kind of encouragement. The bad director will be the one who says, 'In this scene you come in and you are very much in love, and your heart is going *bung bung bung bung,* and you take a pause one, two, three, and you say your line.'

"If you are sensitive, which actors are supposed to be, this will be ringing in your head, and then you will come onstage and you will be *bung bung bung bung,* and one, two, three, and you will say your line. You will become like him! It's terrible. You were never used! The good director will always use the talent he has. The bad director will always want to be used himself. He wants the actor to be a copy of what he would have done if he were an actor."

Speaking of *good* directors, Liv has said that Ingmar Bergman helped her find economy of expression and the smallness needed for film work. Is that training also helpful for the stage?

"Yes," she said, "because Bergman says that you should trust your emotions. Trust your instincts. Don't be scared that people will not recognize what you are trying to show. If you are really feeling it and understanding it within yourself, you don't have to put that extra thing in, that extra exaggeration to make them recognize it. It's the same onstage. Of course, onstage you have to project. You have to give everything a gesture, your voice has to be bigger than life, but it must still be part of life. It cannot be a caricature of life."

Does that mean a good director should never give a line reading?

Liv's expressive eyes narrowed. "The moment you are with a director who gives a line reading, rest assured he is not a good director. A good director knows you can never, never do that."

Peter Patilzsch directed Liv as Grusha in Brecht's *Caucasian Chalk Circle.* Liv credits him with giving her the idea of *the counter-emotion* (the idea that there's a grimace behind every smile). I asked Liv if directors teach acting when they direct.

"Oh sure," she said. "The best directors let you know more about acting than you did when you started working with them. It's boring to see a performance which only shows one side of a character, one side of an emotion. We all know that when you watch a Woody Allen film, you are so full of laughter from this one scene, but you know that part of what you are laughing at is something tremendously sad. Something tremendously sad that you understand, too, and that he understands. Nothing is completely black or white. If that is what you show onstage, it is boring. You must show both sides. That is what makes it interesting."

The relationship between the actor and the director often becomes complicated. There was an instance during the filming of *Autumn Sonata* . . .

"Ingrid Bergman made me proud to be a woman," said Liv. "I would sit and watch her and see her integrity and her braveness to say what she felt, to call a spade a spade, and she did. Because all of us who had worked with [Ingmar] Bergman before, we knew that you don't question him. He's the master. But she questioned him all the time and there were a lot of confrontations.

"I remember once there was a long, long scene where the daughter, who I played, is angrily going on the whole night, shouting at the mother, telling her that because she had been a pianist, traveling, giving concerts, she had been failing her daughter.

"This script was written by a man who clearly felt that a woman should stay at home and if she went out and did something on her own, she would fail her children. Obviously, both Ingrid and I disagreed with this. We said, 'Can't you change a little this concept?' And Bergman said, 'No. Absolutely not.' Then we said, 'Can we act in a way that goes a little against the characters you have written?' And he said, 'Sure, you are the actors.'

"So I did my daughter, who was forty years old, as a little whining because you cannot—at forty—still continue to blame *everything* on your mother. Some things, yes—but not everything. And Ingrid played the mother strong and with integrity, but this specific scene was written so this pig-tailed woman I was playing goes on and on, pages and pages and pages, telling the mother how terrible she had been and how she had left her, and how alone she had been.

"And it's a whole night and then comes the morning and the sun comes up and finally comes the time for the mother to speak. In the script it's written wonderfully. I would have loved to do that scene! I thought, 'Oh, I would have done it so movingly. She's not going to get it.' Because the mother just stands there and she looks at the daughter and then she says, 'Oh, please hold me. Please love me.' So I do my monologue, going on and on and on and on and so comes the time for Ingrid's scene. And she says, 'I cannot do that! I want to smack her in the face and leave the room!' And it was so wonderful and it was so true.

"But there was a big confrontation because Ingmar got furious. He wanted her to say the line. She didn't want to say the line and so they both went out in the corridor and we heard shouts and everything out there. And finally he won and she came in. But then, magic happened. When you see the film, look at Ingrid Bergman's face when she says the lines. She says, 'Please hold me. Please love me.' But she says it with the face of a woman who society has brought up to say, 'Always say you're sorry. You should be guilty because as a mother you've failed. And say it again and again. You're sorry, you're sorry.' But the face is *angry*. She's saying it through anger. A face that says I have finally had enough of saying I am sorry. The words are coming out 'I'm sorry,' but the face has had it. And it was the face of Ingrid. And it is a wonderful, wonderful scene, where the actress really contradicted the lines she was saying. I will always remember her for that specific moment, and many others."

I asked Liv how she prepared for the long, intense monologue she had just described.

"It's very well written," she said. "Once I started to learn the lines—which was the problem because it's fifteen minutes nonstop—once I had learned them, it just came out. And I have such a luggage of anger, memory, and experience that I could draw on. Anger at my mother. Anger at myself. And scenes from my own life. Somehow my preparation was already done in life and it just flowed."

How does an actor know when to stand up for her own interpretation, as Ingrid Bergman did, or when to give in and avoid confrontation with the director?

"It's very hard, I can tell you," Liv said with a sad smile. "With Bergman I don't take up the fight because he's so wonderful and I trust his judgment. But I find more and more, the older I get, that I have these confrontations and I'm not listened to. The director wants it his way and then we have a quarrel and in the end he is the director and maybe I have to give in, and I find it *deeply* frustrating because I feel that I have so much to give in terms of experience and it is so sad that maybe a younger director will not use that and listen to that. Why does he limit me to only what *he* sees and what *he* wants? Very often I find that I back down in the last moment and do it his way because that's how I am brought up, that the director has the last decision.

"But I find that the older I get, it is more and more frustrating. Also because you work with a lot of directors who are not the best, because really the good directors will allow you freedom. But there are not that many good directors around. I feel it's worth fighting for if you are brave enough. I sometimes give up for peace and I regret it after. I am thinking of the last film I did, some scenes that I know I would have liked to do differently, but in the end I couldn't be bothered to discuss it anymore so I did it his way. And I regret it. My advice to an actor would be: If what you feel, you really feel is true to your heart, just stay with it—because you are right."

In previous sessions we have talked about how the actor's creations are like statues in snow. They disappear. They are gone. But the writer's creation remains. Does writing offer a different kind of satisfaction?

Liv's eyes lit up. "When you say that, of course it does. It is strange. You are doing a part like Nora, and you love doing it. I *love* doing it, and the third time I knew this is going to be the last time and the last performance. Yes, you are like a snowman, because spring is coming, and those evenings are like saying good-bye to a loved one you know you will never see again, whereas in writing it will always be there.

"It resembles acting because you do create imagery. You do create feelings. You do create a person, and you take that person and you show it to people and you say, 'Look, do you recognize this? Does this talk to you?' And it will always be there. There is great satisfaction in that, and there is great sadness. Theater work, as contrasting with film work, is of the moment, but maybe *because* it is of the moment, it has that special magic, *because it will never happen again.* Right now, if it is alive, it is more alive than any other kind of art, surely more than film."

Liv's acting and writing have led her to one of her most important roles, as goodwill ambassador for UNICEF. She has written about the places she has visited and about the children of Bangladesh and Cambodia. I asked how her experience on the stage had led to her work with UNICEF.

"I don't know," answered Liv. "But I know that when I was doing *I Remember Mama,* ten years ago, I had just turned forty. I was standing in the wings, and I was suddenly thinking, 'Here I am again with a wig, and with costumes and in makeup, and I always used to say the most important thing for me is to be a human being.'

"But that's not how I lived because most of my forty years, since I was seventeen, I was in a film studio, I was on the stage, I was in somebody else's dress, speaking somebody else's words. So what happened to Liv? When was she doing her thing? And right around this time, when I was thinking these thoughts, I was invited to visit camps for Cambodian and Vietnamese refugees, in Thailand and in Hong Kong. It was at a time in my life when I was really wanting to do something else than acting. I wanted to be a person in life, to be part of life, to touch life, not in a costume, not with somebody else's lines, but as Liv.

"I think I can tell you what I mean, if I tell you that the woman I loved most in my life was my grandmother. She was really my best friend. She died when I was very young, but before she died we shared everything which had to do with fantasy. She would really make me believe that stones and flowers talked, and that the veins of the leaves were alive, and that they would hurt if we ripped them off the trees. We had a wonderful time together. I would sit on her lap, and she would smell so beautiful in the nape of her neck. After she died, I was always sad that she was not there to share in everything that happened to me, all the wonderful things, the successes.

"Then I went on this trip, and I came to an island called

Macao, and it was a refugee camp for boat refugees. In the middle of this refugee camp, there was an isolated camp for refugees with leprosy. I went in and I was very scared, because I had thought that you could get the disease, stupidly the way we think about AIDS now, that by touching and looking you can get AIDS. I was so uneducated.

"I was standing there, and there was an old woman lying on the mattress. She was lying in a fetal position and she was sobbing. Her face was eaten up and her fingers . . . and I just didn't dare to do anything about the sobbing. There were nuns who took care of people in this refugee camp, and one of them came by and she kind of pushed me, saying, 'How can you look at somebody sobbing like that?' So I was more or less forced to go down and hold this old lady from Vietnam. And the fantastic thing that happened was that this lady smelled like my grandmother! Obviously, *that* was to be in touch with life, and to me [it was] more important than anything that had happened in the forty years before. So, in a way, that's how my involvement started, because my grandmother was out there, and my sister and my mother, and these are words we say, but they happen also to be a reality."

Liv's concern for people is reflected in her choice of projects. She had just finished making a film called *The Rose Garden* in Germany with Maximilian Schell.

"It is based on a true story about twenty Jewish children who were murdered," explained Liv. "In the last days of the war they were hanged to hide that medical experiments had been done on them. The S.S. Obersturm Führer who was in charge, he is still a free man in Frankfurt. The movie is about a court case where one tries to put him on trial. That is fantasy because he never went on trial. He's a free man but we try to put him on trial and I play the lawyer and Maximilian plays the brother of one of the murdered children. It will open in Venice at the film festival, but whether it comes here or not I don't know.

"Unfortunately, it's very hard for European pictures to be distributed in this country because few distributors really can afford to take the risk. For the general public, it's only American pictures they want to see, so you see very few of the European pictures which are made, which is sad in a way because wonderful pictures are made there. And it would be nice for me, since I mostly do pictures in Europe. People wouldn't think I'm out of work all the time. At the airport, not long ago, a woman came over to me and said, 'Didn't you used to be Liv Ullmann?"

Certain actors like Vittorio Gassman appear in American films and don't make the same impression as when they make a film in their own country. When he appears in Italian films, Gassman explodes on the screen with a dynamic personality. I asked Liv if she felt she had a similar problem.

"Yes," said Liv. "Something happens with European actors in American films. They are sometimes miscast because they're put in films for the wrong reasons. I'm sure when he first came here, Vittorio Gassman was like me—they let him do anything. They didn't think about what was right for him. I think it also has to do with where we come from, the kind of references we have. Maybe we fit into more reality-based films. Also the language is obviously a hindrance. But I think since our references are in the culture of Europe, maybe the whole concept of being European makes us more at home [there], although I wouldn't say that everything Vittorio Gassman has done in America is bland. And neither will I admit to everything I did in American films as bland. But I do see a reason why we would be more at home in European films. It has to do with the whole environment. I wish I knew an answer for your question, because almost no European actors ever made it in American films, really, to be American film stars. I don't know why. There is a reason."

I asked Liv what she was planning for the future.

"I would like to continue acting," she said, "maybe do a play or a film, one a year. I really want to write another book. My daughter's getting married. I'll be a grandmother soon. I would like to continue working in a creative way for the United Nations. And in the next ten years maybe I could learn some more, because I have a lot of holes in my education. I would like to sit down and get some book learning, because I feel I've learned a lot in life, the university of life. But I'd like to sit down in a classroom again and go back to the books again and maybe with the understanding I have now, learn literature, philosophy, do something with my brain. I believe it's much more healthy than starting to worry about age and face-lifts and things like that."

Liv recently wrote and directed a film. I asked if she was expanding her artistic horizons.

"I wrote a short film," she said, "which was part of a feature film. Five women writers were invited to write about love. The title was *Love.* Nancy Dowe, Antonia Fraser, and several others. I was one of them and I was also invited to direct my part. I loved that experience but it was a short film of fifteen minutes. I do not know if I would like to stay with a whole feature film, the long time that it would take, but I do know that this experience was incredible. To be on the other side of the camera and to hear what they say about actors when they leave the room! And to be the one to say, 'Camera!' and the camera goes, and *nobody* stops the camera before I say, 'Cut!' and then they cut, and I say, 'Lunch,' and everybody goes to lunch." Liv became giddy as she recalled the impact of her commands. "I loved it. And what I loved the most was to have complete control.

"This was a love story and because it has to do with what we have talked about, I'll tell it to you: We see an old man who wakes up alone in a double bed. And he goes out of the bed and he has his bath, and his little head is coming up from the bathtub, and then he goes to the kitchen and he gives the cat some milk and he makes his breakfast. He's very old and he's very alone. And then, suddenly, he's starting to be a little more smiling, and he starts to prepare a basket. And he puts a checkered cloth in the basket and he presses orange juice and he makes a bouillon and everything goes in the basket. And then he goes to the bathroom and he looks in the mirror and you can see he's making himself ready for a love encounter. And then you watch the old man walking on the street and everybody's passing him, back and forth, because he's an old man. Who cares?

"And he comes to a hospital. It's a big white institution and he walks through the corridors and nobody sees him. He's just this little old man. And he opens a door and then comes the smile, because *she* is there. And she is lying in a bed and you can see that she is long since gone mentally. And he sits down at her bed and he puts the checkered cloth on her tummy and he pours the soup and he spoon-feeds [her] the soup. And then he gives her the orange juice. And then he reads from the Bible about love. And finally, he goes to the window and on the windowsill there is a flower.

"I remember when my grandmother was in the old people's home, she was not allowed to have flowers there because the nurses wouldn't have time to water them. So it was the same in this hospital too. The old man has brought water, so she's allowed to have flowers in the window, and he waters the plant. Then he goes to her again and he just strokes her so beautifully. And he leaves. And he is the guardian of their love. And again we see him on the street, and people are going back and forth, back and forth, they don't notice him. But *we* know that this man has a destiny. And the reason I love it is that I believe that that is what life is all about. It's about touch and love. And sometimes only one of us is there to love those who cannot give love back. I just love my film."

CHAPTER EIGHTEEN

COLLEEN DEWHURST AND ZOE CALDWELL

"You act because that is the thing that makes you well."

© MARTHA SWOPE

Colleen Dewhurst in "A Moon for the Misbegotten"

Zoe Caldwell in "Colette"

© MARTHA SWOPE

COLLEEN DEWHURST is of Irish-Scotch-English ancestry. Her first ambition was to be a flyer, and then at Downer College for Young Ladies, a Milwaukee finishing school, she decided to become a journalist. When she wrote and acted in a skit during her freshman year, she discovered the stage was her real vocation. Colleen enrolled in the American Academy of Dramatic Arts and also studied in a class for "working actors" with Harold Clurman. She was seen for the first time on Broadway as one of the neighbors in *Desire under the Elms.* Her "first important chance" came as Kate in the New York Shakespeare Festival's *The Taming of the Shrew.* Colleen won her first Tony for *All the Way Home* and received another for O'Neill's *A Moon for the Misbegotten,* directed by José Quintero. Her other Broadway credits include the revival of *You Can't Take It with You* with Jason Robards, *Mourning Becomes Electra, More Stately Mansions,* Edward Albee's *The Ballad of the Sad Café, All Over,* and the revival of *Who's Afraid of Virginia Woolf?* Colleen has appeared in the films *The Dead Zone, Tribute, Annie Hall,* and *When a Stranger Calls.* On television, she won Emmy awards for her performances in "Murphy Brown," *And Those She Left Behind,* and *Between Two Women.*

ZOE CALDWELL was born in a working-class district of Hawthorn, a suburb of Melbourne, Australia. Her father was a plumber who took a great interest in the theater and her mother had performed in Gilbert and Sullivan operettas. At the age of eleven Zoe played in *Peter Pan* at the Tivoli Theatre in Melbourne. Educated at the Methodist Ladies College in Melbourne, she worked as a perfume-counter saleswoman and as a bottler in a pickle factory before joining the newly founded Union Repertory Company. Zoe has played Bianca to Paul Robeson's *Othello,* and Cordelia to Charles Laughton's *King Lear* at Stratford-on-Avon. She also appeared in *All's Well That Ends Well, The Changeling, Love's Labour's Lost, Richard III, The Merry Wives of Windsor,* and as Cleopatra to Christopher Plummer's Antony. Zoe won her first Tony Award for Tennessee Williams's *Slapstick Tragedy,* her second Tony for her starring role in *The Prime of Miss Jean Brodie,* and a third Tony for *Medea.* On television, she has been seen in *The Lady's Not for Burning, The Apple Cart,* and *Lantern Hill.* She was also featured in Woody Allen's film *The Purple Rose of Cairo.* Among her honors, Zoe Caldwell was awarded the Order of the British Empire, by Queen Elizabeth II.

The moment Zoe Caldwell walked out on the stage with Colleen Dewhurst, I knew we were in for a theatrical evening. Zoe and Colleen were friends and had worked together. I could feel the electricity as they seated themselves to the audience's applause. I told them that so far in this series we had not been able to come up with a useful definition of acting. Then I asked them if there was one.

"Not that *I* know," said Zoe.

Zoe and Colleen did not speak like the rest of us. With both of these women of the theater—and most particularly Zoe—each word was a morsel to be chewed over, savored, and (when emphasis was called for) stretched to new limits. Colleen's hearty laughter often sparked her speech, which was a husky, salt-of-the-earth brogue. Zoe purred each word and cajoled the language into obeying her bidding. Words somehow seemed more alive when she spoke them.

Many of my guests had said that acting is something we all do every day. This makes it harder to find a definition for what the actor actually does on the stage.

When Zoe heard this, she straightened up like a cat arching its back, and took a deep breath. "Acting . . . if you *really* are a professional actor, a serious actor . . . you act because that is the thing that makes you well. It isn't a choice. 'Will I be an actor? Will I not be an actor?' If you have that thought in mind, you will *never* be an actor . . . You *need* to act to make yourself well. I was born with a small motor-skills disability. I only found out that I was born with a small motor-skills disability when my son was having problems in kindergarten and they suggested I take him to Katerina de Hirsch, who was *the* great guru of learning disabilities. She said, 'Yes, he has a small disability which he has from one of you.' My husband said, 'Well, it's not me, I'm perfect,' and I realized it was me.

"I am hopeless with numbers, so I choose to ignore their existence. I don't learn telephone numbers. I don't even know my own. I don't take them into my life. My son is having the same problem, but he's twenty, and it's tougher for him because, number one, he's a fella, and number two, he's born in this computer age, when it seems that numbers are everybody's thing.

"I was in my first dancing concert at two years and ten months, not because I was brilliant, but because I realized very quickly that my large motor skills, like movement and dancing, and eventually, speaking—that was my power. That was my health. I get sick as a dog sewing on a button. If you bake bread, that's your power. That's the thing that makes you really well . . . you bake beautiful bread.

"We should have a world where, if you are a great baker of bread, you bake bread. If you know how to dance, you dance. Then *everyone* would be well. If only we could take all the sick people that we see around us, walking the streets of New York, and really say, 'What is it that makes you well?' and allow them to do it, I think we wouldn't have such a sad, sad society. I'm just privileged. Colleen is privileged. We get to do what makes us well."

"Acting is as Zoe says," Colleen added. "The reason you really can't give an overall interpretation of it is that what every actor does is individual. You can stand backstage and watch ten people get ready to come on, or watch them in rehearsal, and in one sense, they're all coming from a different place. And whatever works for you, that's it."

Colleen has been associated throughout her career with the women characters of Eugene O'Neill, and she has played them with great success. What attracts an actor to O'Neill's women?

"They say there are wonderful accidents in this world," Colleen replied, "and one of the ones I have grown to accept is that Mr. O'Neill was a playwright at the time that I began to arrive on the scene. Yes, I love his women because they have great passion, and they are not constricted by an everyday fake morality. There is something they want, and something they need, and that is what drives them through the play.

"O'Neill is almost like a great exercise. He demands us to go to what I call 'the danger area.' You can't get away with just coming out, because he reads like melodrama. If you won't go with him, then that's what you are doing up there: melodrama. I know nothing, really, about Mr. O'Neill. I was just lucky that he was around.

"I used to point to José Quintero and to Jason Robards and say, 'They know everything about Eugene O'Neill. I know nothing about O'Neill. I do not read about him. I just read his women.' That's what I do. Then I do like José says, 'Cross out all the stage directions and proceed to act what he has said,' instead of looking at things like 'falling down screaming' and 'tearing off clothes.' José would say, 'I asked you to read all the stage directions at the first reading. Now cross them out. I just wanted you to know the passion of the writer and what he intends.' "

Colleen played Carlotta, Eugene O'Neill's widow, in a one-woman show called *My Gene*. The play was set in the violent ward of a hospital and Colleen was alone on the stage for two hours. I asked her how she managed transitions into madness when she had to do it by herself, without having other actors to work with.

"I know more about their marriage than I want to know," said Colleen. "I tap-danced a lot in the beginning—Zoe knows what I mean—in the first fifteen or twenty minutes I just was up there tap-dancing, going as fast as I could, giving out information like an encyclopedia. I'm not happy with *My Gene*. There were certain things I was happy about . . .

"Transitions are a talent that some actors have. I don't mean that it's a trick. Transition is just not difficult for me. Madness is not really difficult to play. You can go over the line if you go there. So, feeling that I've been close enough to madness, it is not a hard place to find. In terms of transitions, one of my problems is I can't describe what happens. (That's why I couldn't teach.) It just *happens*. Or on a lot of occasions it *doesn't* happen and you might as well give it up."

I asked Colleen if she had a favorite among the O'Neill ladies.

"Probably now," she said, "I just have a favorite in terms

of a woman I never wanted to play: Mary Tyrone in *Long Day's Journey into Night.* I never thought about playing her. I never read the play. But when I did do it . . . There are some ladies that you leave too soon, because there is a lot more to the lady than you've got, and you sense that you were cut off in midstream. I would like to try that lady one more time, just to, as José says, 'put a period to it.' But I don't really have any favorites."

"I had a very *strange* experience with my Mary Tyrone," said Zoe, rolling her *r*'s, "because Jason [Robards], who is, without any question of doubt, the definitive older brother in all the O'Neill plays," (she looked to Colleen for approval of what she was about to relate) "wouldn't you say?"

"Ummhmm," offered Colleen.

"I mean no one I think can play that *older brother*, the *loser* brother, I don't think anybody ever will play it as well as Jason. But Jason had bought the idea that he was also the great interpreter in the *directorial*" (Zoe's tongue seemed to curl around the word) "department of Eugene O'Neill. So he decided to do *Long Day's Journey into Night* . . ."

Colleen interrupted Zoe's dramatic pause with a murmured warning, "Easy."

"What?" asked Zoe.

"Easy."

"Easy, yes, snap," said Zoe, "or did you mean *take* it easy?"

Colleen laughed. "I tried to be as subtle as I could, darling."

"You're no fun to be on a panel with!" Zoe said. "Easy. What is that to say to somebody? Easy! I was going to let you in on this wonderful story! But now, since you said no, we'll move on to something else. I can't go on obviously." Then, suddenly Zoe had a change of heart and said, "Oh, I'm going to go on, because it's thrilling actually.

"So Jason's directing of *Long Day's Journey into Night* was we had Michael Moriarty playing the brother who has TB, and then we had a young Irish actor, who *committed suicide* just shortly after the production, and I was playing Mary Tyrone.

"Before we went into production, Robert, my husband (and also the producer), had said, 'Go and get the cuts from Harold Clurman. He has the best cuts.' So I went and got all the cuts and I said, 'I want to put all my cuts in,' and they said, 'That's fine, we're not putting any cuts in, but if you want to take cuts as Mary Tyrone that's fine.' So then we started to rehearse it and Jason would say, 'Aahhhhhhhhhhhhhhh. Wahhhhhhhhhhh. What a play! Waahhhhhh. Wahhhhhhhhhhh. What a play!' And that's how he directed *Long Day's Journey into Night.*

"So when we opened in Ann Arbor, Michigan, it was about seven hours long, because I was the only one taking cuts. We were all sort of derelict. I mean he had his TB and he didn't care about anybody else. He had his drinking problem and he didn't care about anybody else. He had his meanness, I had my addiction. I didn't care about anybody. We were derelict. And Robert kept saying, 'Why don't you get Harold Clurman? Get Harold. Just get Harold. Get Harold.' We *could* have got Harold, but we got José. José could give us ten quick days before he went to Sweden or Norway, or wherever Liv Ullmann hangs out to do, what's that play called, you know, the play about the girl!"

"Anna Christie," said Colleen.

"Anna Christie," nodded Zoe. "So anyway he came in and he said, 'Well, you're all derelict. It is *black Irish passion*! That's what it is. It is *black Irish passion*!! Then he said to me, 'Did you ever meet Carlotta Monterey?' And I said, 'No. I never did.' And he said, 'Oh, she was fantastic! Fantastic!' So I thought, 'Aha! I see what Mary Tyrone is.'

"So, when we opened at the Kennedy Center, everyone else was still sort of playing derelict except I was playing" (Zoe stood up and made a grand gesture to the ceiling). "Now I grew up thinking you had to keep the audience awake and in their seats. That was the responsibility of the actor. I *was* keeping them awake and in their seats . . . also in a state of shock!

"José went away and Robert said, 'Get Harold, will you! Just get Harold!' So we got Harold. And Harold Clurman came and he saw one performance and he said, 'Zoe, I want to tell you a story. There was a very great actor in the Yiddish theater named Schildkraut and he had a young son, who was just beginning in the Yiddish theater, named Joseph Schildkraut. Rudolph Schildkraut was the senior, Joseph the junior. And so Schildkraut senior went to the first performance of Joseph Schildkraut.

"And he sat at the back and on the stage came young Joseph wearing a very large, very black, obviously false beard. Eventually it became too much for Schildkraut senior, who stood and said, 'Beard, beard. Where are you running with my son?' And Harold said, 'Zoe, I love you, and I think you're a very good actress, but sometimes when I'm sitting in the audience and I see you playing, I want to stand and shout, 'Characterization. Characterization, where are you running with my actress?' And I understood. And he stood right there at the side of the stage for eight weeks in all, and made me do *nothing*. *Nothing* in front of audiences. *Nothing*. And I then knew what acting was . . . So that was good that I told that story?"

"Once you got into it," conceded Colleen.

I mentioned that Colleen once told an interviewer, "You cannot phony up O'Neill." How can an actor tell when a playwright is phony?

"Zoe and I have struggled through certain plays," said Colleen, chuckling at the memory, "where you didn't feel you had a very big base to stand on. If you can tell that the writing is phony, you're just not in the play, not unless you're starving, which can happen too, where you fool yourself that maybe you can do this. I have seen some actors bring base and work to a play and to a part that is just obviously their own greatness. I have seen some people where I'm just amazed, and only by really listening do I realize that there is almost no play there, except what they are doing."

I asked Zoe and Colleen what attracts them to the roles they choose.

"Before I married Robert," said Zoe, "whatever the next part that was offered to me, that's always the part I took. I think that's the only way you really should function as an actor. When you sit back and say, 'Is this the right part? Is this the right director? Is this the right theater?' that's not such a good thing. I think it's better if you just take the part and keep working.

"But once I married Robert and had such a *swell* life, and two *horrendous* children, I found *that* so fascinating that I now do select, and when I select, it's because I'm always attracted to something that maybe I won't succeed in. I want to try. People say, 'Oh you really should play such and such, you'd be *marvelous*!' I say, 'Yes, I know I would be and I don't intend to have a go.' What I really love playing are things that really challenge me. How about you, Colleen?"

"Watch out, David!" said Colleen about Zoe's effort at playing moderator. "There's a takeover going on!"

Zoe had directed Colleen, and they had asked to appear together. Being on the stage with these two theatrical dynamos made me feel at times like a lion-tamer.

Colleen forged ahead without answering my question: "I do have to tell you of something really great that very few people saw, because it was years ago. One night I turned on the TV and saw Zoe playing Bernhardt. It was shot in Canada. It was one of the most incredible performances I have ever seen, because she *was* Bernhardt. What she felt or saw in that woman was one of the most incredible things to watch, with that camera right on her. I could not find Zoe at all! I often wonder where that tape is. I have seen other Bernhardts [but] I have never seen anything like that." Colleen settled back in her chair. "There's no need for a comment here . . ." Then she turned to me. "Now what was it you asked me, darling?"

I repeated my question.

"I think," Colleen replied, "that in the beginning, as Zoe says, I was so eager to work, anywhere, anytime. You spent your whole time leaving the city in the summer, and you were so grateful you even got a summer stock job, and then you always lost the apartment because you couldn't afford to keep it while you were in summer stock. You had to come back and find another apartment.

"I can't remember how many years of stock I did, and auditioning and looking. It was just when off-Broadway was coming up. I would work anywhere, a loft, anywhere at all, because if you look upon the body, but particularly upon the mind and the heart, they really need that exercise, if that's what you do. And that can take the place of almost anything else in your life—in one sense, *before* I had the children, and then to get *away* from the children. To have an identity, aside from the station wagon, and the other things. It took me years before I began, because it seemed to me that that whole period was stretching and wanting to stretch, but I never really thought I was doing it because of this or because of that. I was just climbing on the stage, or the platform, anywhere it was, and acting, sometimes terribly, I'm sure.

"We were the original Method people. We were very boring because we never stopped going to class. God forbid we should go out and look for a job, and find out what it was like to do it! We just liked to talk it to death, and the great revelation was finally Harold Clurman, who had a class, and we had it at eleven-thirty at night for actors who were working. The first class, I was so excited because he had only working actors, except for one, and that was me.

"The first night with him, there was a group of people from the Actors Studio, Sandy Meisner, Joe Anthony, all of us were Method, very Method, and now God had decided to teach, and we were the chosen. I never forgot Harold getting up in a small room at 50 Central Park West, and he looked out at us and he said, 'You see this?' And he hit the stage. He said, 'It's not real.' He said, 'You see that door there? It doesn't lead anywhere. I do not wish to see the day your dog died when you get up here. I do not wish to see your little souls. I wish to see the souls of kings and queens, if that's what I ask for. I do not want to see you in the kitchen. I do not want to hear you cry, simply because you are so excited that you *can* cry, and you are so emotionally moved yourself. The house is not moved, of course, but you are terribly moved. It's like laughing through a joke, all the way through it, so that by the end of the joke, nobody's laughing.'

"It was fascinating, because we were hostile out there during the speech. It was like, wait a minute, you don't want to see my soul? You don't want to see the depressions that have entered my life? And he said, 'I want to hear you. I want to see you move well, and if I ask you to run across the stage and run up the side of the wall and across the ceiling, I want to see you attempt it. I do not want a discussion about it. I'm the director.' He said, 'Now I will give you your assignments. You will not pick your own. I will tell you what I'd like to see you do.' (This is from the gentlest human being that ever lived!) 'I will tell you what I'd like you to do and I'll tell you who I'd like you to have as your partner.'

"I never forgot because when he got to my name, I had my pencil ready and he said, 'Colleen, I'd like you to do *The Heiress.*' He said, 'I'd like you to do the scene where the lover does not arrive to take you away. Then I'd like you to do Constance in *King John.*' I put down '*King John.*' He said, 'Then I'd like you to do something from Racine's *Phèdre.*' I [wrote] that phonetically. I could do Racine because I had lived in Wisconsin. I spelled *Phèdre* F-E-D-E-R. Now this is a girl who considered herself very well educated. And I *was* fairly well educated.

"I went and found these things. I had a very nice librarian on Tenth Avenue and Fiftieth Street who looked at it all and said, 'I'll tell you what that is.' I did the others, but when I did *Phèdre*, I never forgot it because I looked at it and there was some *long* speech, and I looked at it and went, 'Uhhhso.' I said, 'Well . . .' So I was very busy. I came on and I had all kinds of little things that I did during this speech.

"It was agony to get up in that class because you felt those were the real peers out there. Harold sat there and then he said, 'I saw Edwige Feuillère do [*Phèdre*] in Paris. I remember, she came onto the stage and she stood absolutely still in the middle and she just looked out and she did that whole thing. And then she turned and she left.' And Harold looked at me and said, 'Thank you very much, Colleen.' And I learned a great lesson. A *great* lesson."

Harold Clurman's orientation was from the Group Theater and Stanislavski and yet Colleen's story made it sound as if Clurman was saying forget all that stuff. Had he changed his point of view?

"No. He had not changed at all," said Colleen. "What he felt, and quite rightly so, was that we had become so self-involved, we had begun to think that just by the fact of us *existing* and having wonderful *moments,* we'd become a clique.

"It just was always about self. The audience did not matter. There was not an interrelationship between the house and the actor. If you couldn't hear me, *your* problem. Because something is *happening* to *me.* And because something is happening to me, you are in the presence of great glory.

"We went through all kinds of things. If you used your hands down here, you were a groin actor. If you used it here you were a heart actor. If you used your hands there, you were an intellectual actor. I went through days of watching myself move and thinking—the groin? the heart? [Harold] felt he was seeing this very self-centered group of actors coming up, lauding themselves and criticizing anything else.

"We did a lot of talk about, 'Ummm. Yes, it was good but it was such a *technical* performance, don't you think?' It was just technique. You weren't really seeing real feeling. It didn't matter what your fellow actor did. You may do anything bizarre that you wished to on the stage if it came to you to do it.

"Harold really pulled us into scenes and into doing things. There was still hostility but he was so exciting up there! He could literally throw himself off the edge of the stage in the middle of speaking to you because what he was saying constantly was, 'I love you. I admire you. The profession you are in has meaning. It has meaning for the human condition. For the country. For everything. So do not believe otherwise because you're starving tonight, because you can't afford the subway even to get here. Just remember that you must have pride. If you have pride in what you do, then only one thing is important in live theater and that is that this room and this theater be all inclusive at one level. You are playing to bring them into that play with you.' Harold went back to the basics. They all disagree as to what Stanislavski *really* said, is what it comes down to."

Stanislavski was an actor as well as a teacher. He became interested in the problems of acting from his own experience on the stage. Do actors make good acting teachers?

"Zoe could teach," said Colleen. "Zoe would be a wonderful teacher because she would meld both sides. Zoe can teach for the same reason that makes her able to direct. She does, as she says, love the actor. And she is not afraid to criticize because there is great honesty in her. You sense that it isn't to hurt. It's just to correct it.

"I couldn't teach. I've done master classes where people have invited me and the whole thing is an agony for me because I either say, 'Oh that's just so, *so* . . .' I end up Miss Nice Girl: 'Now let's see. That was from *Glass Menagerie.* I recognize that. That's a nice scene and interesting that you chose it. I uh, I've uh . . . That's an interesting part of the play where that occurs. I think that you certainly are on the track.' I just want to get out of the room because I don't have the honesty to say, 'Number one, forget it!' because I may be wrong. Because actors who are at one stage one year may not be there three years later. They may have made absolute bounds taught by someone correctly.

"I have no patience. I wish I did. I've learned a little with the kids but I want it *all* to happen. I can talk to very close friends if they ask me and I go and sit during a preview. I do have a correction area that's good where I can see and smell and feel that that scene's off. I can think about that and maybe give them a response there, but to direct them, no."

Zoe's home was in Australia, where she studied and began her career. She was a member of Australia's Union Repertory Company, and then the Elizabethan Theater Trust. One of the roles she played was Bubba in *Summer of the Seventeenth Doll.* Zoe could have gone to London with that production, but she was warned if she did, she would be typed as an Australian actress. How important is it for an actor's career to avoid being typecast?

"It depends how brilliant you are," Zoe said. "If you are Carol Channing, and you are extraordinary, then people don't want to come and see Carol be anything but Carol, and they are right, because what she is, is extraordinary. There are two kinds of actors: There are personality actors, and character actors. I'm really a character actor, so I can't afford to be typecast."

Both Colleen and Zoe have performed an astonishing number and variety of roles. For Zoe the list includes Cleopatra, Ophelia, Saint Joan, Mother Courage, the Madwoman of Chaillot, Colette, Jean Brodie, and Medea. Colleen has played Camille, Portia, Cleopatra, Kate, Lady Macbeth, the O'Neill ladies, Mrs. Follet in *All the Way Home,* the mistress in Albee's *All Over,* Martha in *Who's Afraid of Virginia Woolf?,* a lunatic, a psychiatrist, a madam, the mother of Murphy Brown on television, and in a Walt Disney movie she's the only person in the world who can talk with Bigfoot. I asked Colleen and Zoe if there were any roles they *wouldn't* do.

"I wouldn't do Lady Bracknell," Zoe replied firmly, "because I know exactly what I would be like."

"I need to understand why the woman is what she is," said Colleen. "I probably have played more than my share of women who would be considered villainesses, in terms of what they do and the way they react to things. I remember when I was offered the role of the nurse in [the play] *One Flew Over the Cuckoo's Nest.* I wouldn't do the part and my agent said, 'It's with Kirk Douglas,' and I said, 'I just really hate her.' She said, 'What does that have to do with it? It's a leading role! You can't always play women you like!' I said, 'It doesn't have to do with that. I don't understand this lady at all. I don't know where she is coming from. I could give her a whole background, and I would hate to waste my time doing that kind of thinking.'

"I also turned down *J.B.* The same agent said to me, 'Why would you turn down that part?' I said, 'I just can't stand her. She's so good. She's so suffering. I would have to come out every night and say to the audience, "I don't believe in this God that we have just spoken of. Nor do I believe in this kind of a woman." ' Those are the only things that would make me turn down a role. I would hate getting inside that skin, not because it's good, bad, or indifferent. I would just hate having to get inside that lady. But I haven't turned down many roles."

One of the themes of these discussions has been the importance of actors taking risks. When Colleen played Gertrude in *Hamlet* for Joe Papp, she portrayed her as a sympathetic woman in love. Was that a dangerous choice?

"No," said Colleen. "The choice was made for me in rehearsal. I wanted to play as many Shakespeare women as I could. Joe called up and said he wanted to do *Hamlet* and would I do Gertrude, and I said, 'Who is doing Hamlet?' He told me and I said, 'I don't know, Joseph, I really don't think so.' Half an hour later he called back and said, 'If I told you Jimmy Earl Jones was going to play the king, what would you say?' I said, 'Give me half an hour, I am going to go read it again.' I read it and called him back. I found out later he had called Jimmy Earl back and said, 'What would you say if I told you Colleen Dewhurst was going to play Gertrude?'

"It became very simple within a few readings. With Jimmy right there from the beginning, there was no justification needed. I don't like to justify why women behave as they do, I only want to understand. This woman was made for this man. That was all it was about. She wasn't terribly bright. She loved her son but she was mad for this man. She could see nothing but him. So from the beginning I just played it as a woman who, from the moment she entered the stage, was hanging on him. She couldn't stand not to touch him, not to be with him, because he was so glorious and spoke so well, and he was so courageous."

"I don't think that's dangerous," said Zoe. "That's the *only* way to play Gertrude. How could you play Gertrude and *not* love Claudius?"

"Dangerous is when you take a role that you know is going to be a stretch," said Colleen, "and you say, 'I'm going to do this. I want to do this. I am not an actress if I don't go for that role, if I don't play that.' There are roles you have missed and you won't be able to go back because of age and play certain things, and that's the only thing you would dread, that you never got cast in that part. Sometimes you have to go all the way. And you know you're going to have to go *all the way*. There's never going to be a night or a matinee that you can cheat or that you can be tired. You're going to have to take her every inch to the edge of that chasm, and then over and into it. You're lucky if you get two performances a week that are completely fulfilling. That's what a professional is.

"There's nothing worse than what I call a walker who comes on and says, 'Oh, the audience stinks, what does it matter?' To see Zoe in *Medea* was to see a woman go, 'Ahhhhhhhhhhh! That's what I'm playing. I'm doing it all. I just took it all off, and you're looking at it, and this is what I am.' " There were tears in Colleen's eyes. "That makes me cry . . ."

Zoe took several risks when she played *Medea*, which paid off in her winning a third Tony award. Her husband, Robert Whitehead, directed.

"That was a risk," said Zoe.

Judith Anderson played the nurse.

"That was a *big* risk!" exclaimed Zoe. "I was the second woman of Corinth when Judith came to Australia to play Medea. She had played it for fifteen years, and this was at the end of her time of playing it. She had played it all over America and she was extraordinary and it was very much her role. My husband, Robert, produced *Medea*, and Judith and my husband fell afoul of one another and decided never to see or speak to one another again.

"Forty years later, Judith is living out in Santa Barbara, and she decides it is time for *Medea* to be done again, and that *I* am the one who should play it. *Judith* decided. And she decided that she would play the nurse. You didn't have to be very bright to know that Judith was going to play Medea again through a younger person—me.

"Judith said, 'You're going to wear my old costume, which is in the Robinson Jeffers Museum. You'll wear the castile gray gown. You will wear my wig and my sandals.' I said,

'Judith, I've had children, I'm broad in the hip. You've got marvelous hips and terrifically firm breasts and I can't get into your gray castile dress. It will never fit me.' She said, 'You can at least try it.' I tried it and it fit. So I said, 'My head is a different shape, I can't possibly wear the wig.'

"I said, 'Judith, I can't play your Medea. I can't be you reincarnated. I can play *my* Medea, which will probably never be as good as *your* Medea, but that is the only Medea I can play, and I *need* you on that stage as the nurse, and I *need* you to support me and give me all the help you can, but you cannot play it for me!'

"What Judith was doing was what bad parents do with children. She really wanted to choose the groom, and I was going to wear her gown, and have the kind of life, etcetera. It's bad parenting. Judith had never had children and didn't understand what one does as a parent. But she is an *extraordinary* woman. A *marvelously* funny, witty, bright woman. And she very, very quickly learned the joy of parenting. She allowed me my *purple* rag and my *strange* wig and my *odd* Medea, and she stood by and supported me. And always onstage, if I needed her hand," (here Zoe took my hand) "her hand was there. If I needed her near me," (Zoe put my hand on her chest) "I could have her body . . . That's *real* loving . . . That's *real* giving . . . That's *real* parenting . . . So in a funny way, Judith at the age of eighty-six learned the joy of being a mother."

In addition to the risk of having her husband direct and Judith Anderson as the nurse, Zoe also chose to play Medea differently. She emphasized what the critics called a scorned sexuality, which was intended to be Medea's motive for killing her children. Was this a new idea?

"No," said Zoe. "I think actually it was Robinson Jeffers's, and before that, Euripides'."

Colleen laughed loudly and then said, "*All right,* David . . ." as if to soften the blow of Zoe's mocking response.

Actors need to find something to like about the characters they play, even when they do terrible things. Medea kills her children. Was there something to like about Medea?

"Of course," Zoe said. "What woman or man, what person has not given all of themselves, at some stage in their life, all of yourself to another human being? And what do you end up with? Nothing. Nothing. And who are the most to be feared in this world? People who don't have themselves any longer. They are the most dangerous. We all understand that. We've all of us done that. And then you draw back from it, because your health tells you, you cannot give everything to another human being.

"She gave him her magic. She was a virgin and a priestess. She was the king's most favorite daughter. She had everything. And he came into her palace and when she first saw him, a white dove came down and pecked at her heart and caused three drops of blood, and she was his forever. Everything he demanded of her, she gave, until there was a point when there was nothing there . . . So, of course, he went up the hill to the palace, to the *young, blonde, blue-eyed* girl. Medea was older. She was the dark-skinned witch from another country.

"Often you read about it in the paper. Seriously, you do! When you have somebody from Trinidad, and they come and they fight for their man, and they give him *everything*. They work and they put him through school, and he goes off when she has given everything." Zoe took a long pause. "And she kills her kids.

"She doesn't kill her kids because she doesn't love the kids. It's almost as though she wants to be rid of anything that has to do with *him*. Because she has been brought to nothing. That's the whole point of Greek drama; the purging of some human emotion. We do it on the stage. That's the great thing. *You* can sit in the audience and say, 'Yes, I felt like doing the same thing. Oh God, I feel so much better now!' Because you don't have to do it. The actor and the playwright have done it for you. That's theater, isn't it?"

Colleen nodded. "Get it *all* out."

"If we had more really super theater, we'd have less psychoanalysis," suggested Zoe. "*Weren't* a lot of analysts in Greece . . ."

How often do actors get opportunities to alter parts and present their own conception of a role like Gertrude or Medea?

"I don't think it's a case of altering," said Colleen. "Your most dangerous area is your director. Sometimes you go in and you are very excited about the play. You're very interested in who is playing with you because there is an exchange up there, and maybe you have someone who is not going to exchange with you, who is not going to be with you every minute, who is not going to give you that energy.

"Sometimes you discover you have a director who possibly doesn't know what is going on himself, and it takes you awhile, because for a week or so you just kind of go along. You say, 'Well, that's what he does. I act, he or she directs, so they must know what they're doing.'

"It is probably the most destructive thing to find yourself in the hands of someone who really doesn't know. It's great to have that director who will say to you, 'I wonder, Colleen, what would you think if, when she came in there, that possibly instead of that, you tried such and such.' You go, 'Okay,' because a good director is trying to take you to another depth, and another view, and sometimes you try it and you go, 'Thank you. That's interesting. I'll go that way because that way explains what happens in the next thing.' Sometimes, though, if you have a good director, he'll go, 'Forget what I told you, forget it, it doesn't work. You're right. Stay where you were.'

"Eventually, it's like a wonderful orchestra. Suddenly, you find yourself onstage with a group of people in a play, and you recharge, folding into each other. You can have actors you play opposite who are bringing so much to the role. We all know actors and actresses who *do not* wish to work with the best actors. [But] the best give you energy.

"There will be nights on that stage where you may have played it for six months, but suddenly you look at each other and you know that you are moving. It's like a wonderful tide that's come in, and you're both on that tide, and you're both riding that wave together. And everything that touches you is going well, and you know it and you come off and you go, 'Whoo, what a night!'

"Sometimes people will say to you after you have finished, 'You just must be so tired doing that part.' If it goes well, you come off and you go, 'Thank you!' You've gotten rid of it. I used to say, 'I got rid of that day, I got rid of that week. Possibly a year, possibly a lifetime is now dumped. I've said it all out there.'

"The most exciting thing is that an audience will take you at their own point of consciousness that night. You get mail that is astounding, telling you the experience they had, watching that play and your performance, and what happened to them. That is why the theater, as part of the arts, has such a reason for being. Because something happens between you and that dark house out there, when they begin to breathe with you, and you know it.

"You get mail telling you that they haven't cried for twelve years, and they cried that night and they didn't know what it was, and they went and got another ticket and came back to the play again to try to find out. You'll have people analyze what you did up there, and you go, 'It's not what I was playing.' But that need, in that house, that night in that darkness, in that singleness, in that aloneness, can be one of the most wonderful experiences. I've had it out there sitting in a theater, and I've had it on the stage, where you suddenly knew that they were soaring with you, that they were demanding you to go there. They were literally saying, 'Come on, give it to us. Come on. Come on. Come on!'

"I have been directed by Zoe and I wish to be directed by Zoe again. Directing is the ability to guide you and to keep you out of harm's way, and to keep you from going down the wrong trail. You can often pick the wrong trail and start down it as fast as you can go, thinking you're doing wonderfully but you're no help to anybody else on the stage. You're just all by yourself up there and playing for yourself and to yourself. I would plead for more and more directors, true directors. I just want to see those nondestructive, creative, interesting directors come out there because I want *them* to push [me] that one step further.

"The only thing you must recognize right away in our profession is if you have destructive thoughts hidden behind what is directing you. Zoe would move faster than I to that thought. Zoe is very quick to say, 'I don't like that' or 'I won't do that.' I'm one of those people who keeps laughing for a week and then goes crazy. *Then* I scream. Instead of having stopped it all earlier, I just think, 'Well, they can't possibly be that crazy, I'm sure this will straighten itself out. No one can be paying them all that money to direct when they can't direct.' Zoe just comes on and immediately goes, 'He can't direct.' "

Zoe's directing career began when she directed Colleen in *An Almost Perfect Person.* I asked Zoe what made her want to direct.

"Well," she said. "I'd sat around so often. I never spoke to my fellow actors because that's a law in the theater. You never give an actor notes. I would sit and watch actors being bruised by directors and not helped and I thought, 'I think I could help them.' And I do adore actors and I have compassion for them. I wanted to help. And then someone said, 'Would you like to direct this play?' And I said, 'Yes,' because I thought I better do it and find out if I can. And if I can't, then shut up. So I thought I'd better have the best I can get, so I asked Colleen would she play this part. Also I know Colleen. Colleen's so feminine and funny! Colleen had played a lot of" (Zoe switched to a throaty lower register) "Mother Earth parts. And I thought, everyone should see how funny and feminine and darling she is!

"I remember Kate Hepburn rang and she said" (Zoe did a perfect imitation of Hepburn's quivering voice) " 'I hear you're directing a play.' And I said, 'Yes I am.' And she said, 'Is it a part for me?' And I said, 'No.' She said, 'Why not?' I said, 'Because the woman has to *lose,* Kate, and if you played it you'd have to win.' She said, 'Who *is* it a part for?' And I said, 'Colleen Dewhurst.' She said, 'Oh . . . Well, I won't even try. I won't even audition for it then.' Anyway, Colleen was marvelous. It was not such a swell play [but] she was so funny! And people said, 'I didn't know Colleen was funny.' She's marvelous to direct."

Anything that entertains us in theater can also enlighten us. But there is a lack of plays that deal with serious subjects directly in today's commercial theater.

"A lot of it has to do with cost," said Zoe. "The unions have made it very, very difficult, excuse me, Colleen."

"The actor is only eighteen percent of that huge top you see there," replied Colleen, assuming her president-of-Actors'-Equity hat.

"I'm not saying the actors are totally greedy," Zoe said. "They're greedy enough, but they're not totally greedy. Theater is a handmade article. And you know that everything that is handmade costs more. I'm sorry about it because we should have a great volume of plays, we've got all those musicals. But even the musicals aren't as good now because the musicals were better when they had a body of plays that they came out of. Now, how many new plays do we have in a season? It's something to do with the society we are living in. I do think we've become a very gratified society with all our things and Reagan didn't help.

"Theater always flourishes more when people are suffering. All those Eastern bloc countries had marvelous theater. Maybe now [that] they're becoming more free, their theater will suffer, who knows? During the Depression, the theater was extraordinary in this country, *extraordinary*. People have to suffer a need to go into a warm place and experience something with their other human travelers. The need is not so strong. What do you say, Colleen?"

"We lost audience," said Colleen. "And like we are in this country, we never discover anything until we start talking about it ten years after it's happened. It was beginning to happen in the late sixties, early seventies. By the eighties we began to know that we lost audience. We lost the young. The theater in its way is one of the last ramparts in this society of free speech. When I say free speech, I don't mean only politically. I mean actually reaching out and trying to talk to each other about what is happening to us and why we are what we are.

"I feel the same about great comedy. There's nothing like wonderful comedy brilliantly done. We gave up understanding that the arts belong to the people. They started with the people because there was a need. From drawing on cave walls, churches, singing, acting, painting, music, need, need, need, need. We have relegated it to a kind of elitist discussion."

"We sure have," agreed Zoe.

"People are intimidated by art," continued Colleen. "I go to a museum to see paintings. I want to go alone because I can't discuss what the *brushstroke* is. I go alone because I don't want to have an expert with me to explain it all to me. The same with music or anything. Not that I don't want to be educated in it. I do. I would like education with that to help me appreciate and move further in my likes and dislikes. But I do believe that the theater has an important part in our lives and we have given that up."

"Also, I think we have done a very, very big disservice by putting so much power into the hands of one critic," declared Zoe, "the critic of *The New York Times*. I don't mean [John] Simon. What's his name? Frank Rich. I *don't* mean Simon. I *really* don't mean Simon." Zoe went basso profundo with extravagant loathing. "You don't *know* how much I don't mean Simon! Or perhaps you do!

"Frank Rich is a perfectly nice chap. I mean he's a roly-poly nice chap who has a great sort of love for the theater and he is always looking for what I call boutique theater. Does it have this style and the pooty pu poomtee, cutting out a whole lot of other stuff. Now it has nothing to do with him. He's not a bad man!

"Clive Barnes, when he was the critic of *The New York Times,* was the critic who closed a show or made it a hit. Now Clive is there at *The New York Post* and he's going, 'It's great! It's great!' The show closes. It closes because Frank Rich doesn't like it. Now if Frank Rich went off tomorrow and Laurie Weiner took over, which she may well do if something *terrible* happens to Frank, Laurie will then have the power. *Whoever* is at *The New York Times.* I don't know how that came about but it's a very, very sick situation."

Maybe we can't do anything about the critic situation, but is there a way to encourage playwrights? Colleen once said that there are hardly any interesting plays for women over forty-five.

"You can't get a playwright to write roles for women," said Colleen. "You can complain. It's become much better in some ways and in others it has not. It's okay for someone like me, who is older and a woman, that if a role comes along and there's maybe six or seven of us who have some kind of a name, we will get that role. But beside us are thirty or forty actors who are wonderful but who never quite made it to getting a name. And now after the age of forty-five, fifty-five, sixty, they are not called on anymore.

"We have created a monster because we are the generation of women who broke through and what we're looking at in some cases is we're looking across desks at women who have exactly the same façade and the same attitude as the men that we tried to dethrone who were cardboard cutouts! It goes back to what we were talking about before in terms of theater and where we are with the arts. We are not dealing with truly what the problem is. I mean, we are not dealing with the people we are. We're not writing about us."

We spoke about an actor taking a risk when she chooses

a role that stretches her. Does an actor also face danger when she walks out on the stage?

"I think just the very act of theater is dangerous," said Zoe. "Anything that is alive . . . *Living* is dangerous, so that if you're alive and I'm alive and we're facing one another . . . It's dangerous tonight!

"This is why I hate all the technical equipment that we are surrounding our theater with. It gets in the way of communication. You know, film isn't dangerous. You can make a marvelous, sexy, saucy film but it isn't *dangerous.* The act of viewing it is not dangerous. Television isn't dangerous. You could throw *a boot* at your screen. They'll still go on talking away. Throw *a boot* at an actor on stage. He might jump down and hit you! He might throw that boot back if we had a real theater, where people said, 'BOOOO!' and 'CAN'T HEAR YOU!!!' I wish people would do that.

"It's no good being at a cocktail party the next night and saying, 'Well, she was perfectly swell, but I didn't hear a damn word she said.' It's no good! Say it *then*! Then I can do something about it. And also, what is good, is adrenaline goes through the audience, adrenaline goes through the actors, and with any luck you get a better performance. So I do beg you, if you can't hear, say, 'SPEAK UP!' And if you don't like it at the end, say, 'BOOO!' That's a healthy theater!

"We charge fifty bucks to go into a show on Broadway. You can't hear it . . . Did you see *Orpheus Descending*? Could you hear it? No! Did you shout, 'SPEAK UP, VANESSA'? It's very healthy! I've had people say to *me* in the theater, 'Speak up!'

"Once, when I was playing Medea in Australia, I [made] a great leap at [the actor playing] Jason, and a girl in the front of the audience laughed. I kissed him and she laughed. (The power must always stay on the stage. The power must never be in *your* laps. It must always be here, because that's the way you feel safe. If you suddenly run away with the power, it's no good.) [The girl in the audience] laughed, and I looked at her." Zoe spoke gravely and slowly and her luminous eyes narrowed to a drop-dead squint. "She stopped laughing. I went back into the clinch and kissed him . . . She laughed. Everybody began to laugh . . . I thought, 'We are not going to be able to play this play.' So I said, still embracing him, I said,

'SHUT UP!!!' And she laughed again . . . And I said, 'YOU ARE A RUDE PIG!!!'

"We played the hell out of the play and at the end the whole audience cheered and cheered and cheered, *because something had happened*! Something *new*, something *alive* had happened! Rock concerts are alive. I don't blame our kids for not wanting to go to the theater. Rock concerts are exciting! We have to make our theater as exciting and as dangerous as that!"

EPILOGUE

When I started "The Magic of Theater" series I wanted to gain more insight into how actors convince us they are other people. In our conversations I learned about the complicated and difficult process actors go through in order to inhabit the skin of another person. Although each actor has his or her own unique method, they all share the need to live truthfully on the stage. We in the audience also have a need: We *want* to believe.

Theater began as ritual. Its original purpose was to placate supernatural powers. Today it celebrates the magic of human beings making meaningful contact with each other.

During the writing of this book, Colleen Dewhurst passed away. Whenever I think about the need we all share in the theater, I remember Colleen's words on the night we spoke:

"Something happens between you and that dark house out there, when they begin to breathe with you, and you know it . . . That need, in that house, that night in that darkness, in that singleness, in that aloneness, can be one of the most wonderful experiences. I've had it out there sitting in a theater, and I've had it on the stage, where you suddenly knew that they were soaring with you, that they were demanding you to go there. They were literally saying, 'Come on, give it to us. Come on. Come on. Come on!' "

SELECTED READINGS

Brockett, Oscar G. *History of the Theatre.* 4th ed. Boston: Allyn and Bacon, 1982.

Chekhov, Michael. *To The Actor.* New York: Harper and Row, 1953.

Clurman, Harold. *On Directing.* New York: Collier, 1972.

Cole, Toby, and Helen Krich Chinoy, eds. *Actors on Acting.* New York: Crown, 1970.

Lewis, Robert. *Method—or Madness?* New York: Samuel French, 1958.

Meisner, Sanford. *On Acting.* New York: Vintage, 1987.

Olivier, Laurence. *On Acting.* New York: Simon and Schuster, 1986.

Stanislavski, Constantin. *An Actor Prepares.* New York: Theatre Arts Books, 1984.

Stanislavski, Constantin. *Building A Character.* New York: Theatre Arts Books, 1981.

Stanislavski, Constantin. *Creating A Role.* New York: Theatre Arts Books, 1961.

Stanislavski, Constantin. *My Life In Art.* New York: Theatre Arts Books, 1952.

Strasberg, Lee. *A Dream of Passion.* Boston: Little, Brown, 1987.

INDEX

ABOUT THE AUTHOR

David Black was born in New York City and educated at the Ethical Culture Schools. He attended Harvard College, and after graduation he pursued an operatic career in Europe. After several years on Wall Street as an award-winning salesman, he began a career as a Broadway producer. He has produced eighteen shows, winning Tony Awards and presenting some of the theater's brightest stars. In 1968 he was invited to produce the presidential inaugural gala. Mr. Black has directed in New York and London and has lectured and given master classes in theater throughout the country. His first book, *The Actor's Audition,* was published in 1990. Mr. Black complements his teaching with a career as an artist.